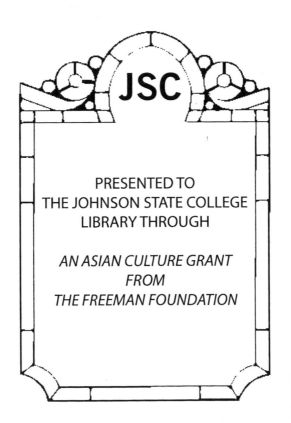

CHINA'S NEW ORDER

CHINA'S NEW ORDER | WANG HUI

Society,

Politics, and

Economy

in Transition

Edited by
Theodore
Huters

Cambridge,
Massachusetts

HARVARD UNIVERSITY PRESS
London,
England
2003

306. 0951
W184c

Library of Congress Cataloging-in-Publication Data

Wang, Hui.
   China's new order : society, politics, and economy in transition /
Wang Hui ; edited by Theodore Huters.
      p. cm.
   Includes bibliographical references and index.
   ISBN 0-674-00932-0 (alk. paper)
      1. Social movements—China. 2. China—Social policy.
   3. China—Economic policy—1976–2000. 4. China—Politics
   and government—1976– 5. Democracy—China.
   I. Huters, Theodore. II. Title.

   HN733.5.W3624 2003
   306'.0951—dc21   2003050802

CONTENTS

PREFACE

For this book to be published in English is entirely a matter of chance. Between the fall of 1999 and the summer of 2000, I accepted an invitation to be a visiting scholar in the Critical Asian Studies Program at the University of Washington, and at the same time taught a graduate course in the department of history dealing primarily with the intellectual history of the Qing dynasty. I thereby took temporary leave of the intense debates going on in Chinese intellectual circles at the time. Once "Contemporary Chinese Thought and the Question of Modernity" was first published in the journal *Tianya* (Frontiers) in 1997, I was involuntarily drawn into the extended intellectual debate that had been ongoing in China since 1989. The article was soon translated or republished in *Social Text* in the United States, *Sekai* in Japan, *Tangdae Pipyong* in South Korea, the *Hong Kong Journal of Social Sciences*, and *Taiwan: A Radical Quarterly in Social Studies*. In the fall of 1999, Professor Perry Anderson asked me to explain this debate in China in the pages of the *New Left Review*, which led me to formulate a systematic explanation of the ten years following 1989 and the ensuing split in the Chinese intellectual world. Soon thereafter *Taiwan: A Radical Quarterly in Social Studies* expressed the hope that I would write an essay in response to the critiques of my article by Chao Kang, Chien Yung-xiang, and Chu Wan-wen.

At the time my energies were focused on the study of New Text classicism in the Qing dynasty, so considerations of time and inclination alike prevented me from returning to a discussion set in motion by an essay I had written several years before. Even more important, because of deficiencies of historical analysis, intellectual debate in China could no longer proceed on the basis of a discussion of side issues, and the absence of an evaluation of the 1989 social movement in this debate was one of the reasons that there was a considerable amount of confusion surrounding the whole discourse. Consequently, I decided to undertake an understanding of this dispute among Chinese intellectuals by placing it in the context of a historical transformation that pivoted around the 1989 social movement. Hence the origin of this little volume.

More than a dozen years have now passed since 1989. For those who experienced the movement, the dramatic changes that have transpired during these years have transcended anything we could have imagined, both in China and in the world at large. Fourteen years ago no one could have predicted the extent and speed of this historical transformation. The 1989 movement marked the end of the socialist movement of the twentieth century, as well as the beginning of a global capitalism marked by distinctly new implications. It is unavoidable that any reevaluation of this movement entails a summing up of the twentieth-century socialist experiment, but it must be said that the time for this thoroughgoing assessment of the historical process has yet to come. It must also be said, however, that the very uncertainty surrounding this historical process in itself constitutes an intellectual challenge. The understanding and evaluation of this historical movement are important not just to the debates within the contemporary Chinese intelligentsia, but also to our understanding and evaluation of twentieth-century Chinese history.

In the early morning of June 4, 1989, as I departed from Tiananmen Square in the company of the last group of my classmates, I felt nothing but anger and despair. For the greater part of 1990 I lived in the depths of the Qinling Mountains of central China, and that brief experience left a lasting and indelible impression on me—I suddenly realized how far my life in Beijing was from this other world. In the months and years that have followed, I have endeavored to create a link between these two worlds, and via this link to proceed to understand the events and the changes that we have gone through. To a great extent, my critiques of certain of the discussions that have gone on in the Chinese intellectual sphere arise out of a sort of self-critique, a critique based on a sense of the need to reconstruct the historical relationship between the world of the intellectuals and the other world outside it. While this short book is in no way a comprehensive historical explanation, it does stand as an effort at understanding both history and myself gained through actual participation in the ongoing process of the contemporary world.

This book has as its core the 1989 social movement, and describes what people often refer to as a "transitional" historical period. As I describe it, "transitional" is both historical process and historical myth, but in ordinary practice, these two uses are inextricably entwined. The transition of historical process refers to the reality of the unraveling and transformation of the regime of traditional socialism, while the transition of historical myth provides evidence of a teleology to this process of unraveling and transformation—that is, it is explained as a transition from a despotic, planned, and dark past to a democratic, free, and bright future. This myth of transition is built on a concept of natural and spontaneous historical development. It is my intention through a historical analysis of the 1989 movement to expose the background power relations behind this "natural" and "spontaneous" process, as well as to highlight the inherent historical relationship between this process and the predicament in which contemporary China finds itself. In this sense, the implications of "transitional" are indefinite, or, it is perhaps better to say that "transitional" marks an indefinite historical process. It is also in this sense that this book is in fact a search for the various social forces that have been able to influence this indefinite notion of transition.

As was the case with that movement of over a decade ago, my thinking still centers around the idea of democracy. The "democracy" discussed here, however, is not just one of the multitudinous ossified concepts of democracy, nor is it based on a ready-made notion of democracy brought forward only to judge Chinese performance. Democracy, like all other great ideas, has been continuously brought into play and manipulated through all sorts of practical applications. It has also continuously revealed the predicaments it has been engulfed in by contemporary events, to the point of showing indications of ossification. That does not in any way mean, however, that we should cast aside the concept and its values. Democracy is the sort of force that has been constantly expanded by the development of history; it is something that in itself requires creativity, renewal, and advancement in broader contexts and in more concrete ways. Because of this, when I say we need a democratic practice to cope with the problems that now face us, the democracy I am referring to—even though it includes the sum, the reflection on, and the development of all historical instances of democracy—by no means refers to a ready-made pattern that can be readily copied. Rather, it should be a creative process, a broad social reality that takes into account specific political, economic, and cultural practices. It is precisely for this reason that I have attempted to see the predicament facing China and the crises afflicting the rest of the contemporary world—including the so-called democratic Western world—as different facets of an interrelated historical process.

My thinking and my writing have benefited from the assistance of countless friends, and I would like to take this opportunity to thank them. Professor Rebecca Karl exerted Herculean efforts to translate both "Contemporary Chinese Thought and the Question of Modernity" (for *Social Text*) and "The 1989 Social Movement and the Historical Origins of 'Neoliberalism'" (for *positions*). After the completion of the first draft of "The 1989 Social Movement," she gave me a number of helpful criticisms and suggestions. Friends, including Wu Yumin, Sun Ge, Chen Yangu, Chen Weigang, Shang Wei, Qian Liqun, Jin Dacheng, He Zhaotian, Wang Chaohua, Dong Yue, Zhang Xudong, Xu Baoqiang, Cui Zhiyuan, Gan Yang, Huang Ping, Wang Xiaoming, Li Tuo, Lin Chun, Ye Weili, Vivek Chiber, Viren

Murthy, and Sanjay Subrahmanyam, all read drafts at one time or another and offered suggestions; He Zhaotian even carefully checked my notes. In 1999–2001 Professors Leo Ou-fan Lee, Tani Barlow, Wen-hsin Yeh, Martin Powers, Theodore Huters, Zhou Minglang, Hu Ying, Kang-i Sun Chang, and Rudolf Wagner invited me to Harvard, Washington, Berkeley, Michigan, UCLA, Colorado, UC Irvine, Yale, and Heidelberg to talk about contemporary China and the discussions going on among Chinese intellectuals; I gained much from the discussions that followed my presentations. Finally, I should express my thanks to Harvard University Press, to the anonymous readers of my manuscript, and to my editor and translator, Ted Huters. It was Lindsay Waters's stalwart efforts that enabled this book to be published so quickly. I followed the suggestions of the anonymous readers in revising and expanding the original draft. Ted Huters is an old friend of mine, and he has supported my research for some time; his assistance is not limited to the work he did in translating the first essay in this book. Without his efforts, the publication of this volume would be unimaginable. It goes without saying that I take full responsibility for the major points set forth herein, as well as all shortcomings and infelicities.

Several years elapsed between the first draft of "The 1989 Social Movement" and its appearance in print. At this time so soon after the turn of a new century, people are constantly changing their views of the past at the behest of unexpected historical change. This book records the thinking of one person who underwent such profound changes in China. The year 1989 represented the beginning of transformation on a global scale; and I hope, along with others from different backgrounds and with different experiences, to gain an understanding of this as yet undefined transition.

Wang Hui
Beijing
January 2003

INTRODUCTION

Theodore Huters

It has long been a matter of concern among Chinese of even modest educational attainment that there is a far greater attention to and knowledge about the West among ordinary Chinese than there is awareness of China among Westerners. This relative ignorance on our part is surely one of the principal reasons that the image of China and the Chinese in the West has been subject to such extreme variation during the past century or so—from the heathen Yellow Peril invoked by Wilhelm II in the 1890s, to peaceful farmer defending against foreign and domestic abuse during the war years of the 1930s and 1940s, to blue-clad ant mindlessly obeying the orders of an Orwellian Party in the 1950s, to cheerful and honest citizen of a New China after Nixon's visit in 1972, and on to the more recent perspective of China as an economic powerhouse and future military threat to the new global order, populated by a people with a dangerous tendency to antiforeign extremism.[1] These transformations of China's image in the West have been documented and lamented by scholars,[2] but this long succession of changes does serve to underscore one apparently unalterable fact: China remains remote and alien to us, but less from anything arising out of its long and complex history than as a result of our own lack of serious attention given to it. And with China thus stubbornly cast in the role of our "Other," we have a difficult time imagining that anything that happens there can have any relevance to our own lives. As Gloria Davies has pointed out in the prefatory remarks to her valuable collection of translated essays written by Chinese scholars in the 1990s, this distancing of China has exerted itself even within the realm of Euro–American cultural studies, in spite of that discipline's self-imposed task of examining the whole of the contemporary world.[3]

As the world is brought together with increasing rapidity, however, isolation from such a significant portion of it as China must be regarded as no longer possible or desirable. To the extent that our ignorance had been justified by such notions as Francis Fukuyama's "end of history" thesis, in which the rest of the world is envisioned as moving on its own momentum toward a society modeled on ours (or, as having no choice but to do so, whichever applies in any particular case), the events of the past few years have made such complacent assumptions untenable. Leading the parade in casting doubt on safe projections of the future is increasing uncertainty that an integrated global market economy will be the panacea that it was thought to be a few short years ago. In light of the revelations of American corporate malfeasance and market manipulation in recent years, reconsideration of the unabashed enthusiasm for an economic order anchored by what had seemed an ever-rising stock market has become the norm even in the editorial sections of mainstream newspapers like *Times* of both Los Angeles and New York. This even as the Bush administration seems bent on rendering final and irrevocable the deregulatory trend launched by the Reagan administration in the early 1980s, a trend that can be plausibly argued to be at the root of the abuses. Much of the recent reconsideration has been focused on Latin America, where the limitations on government spending imposed by the harsh terms of the International Monetary Fund and World Bank have come into sharp conflict with popular demands and needs, and where the recent bankruptcy of Argentina and the Brazilian presidential election have highlighted the distance between the economic vision propagated in Western financial capitals and life in the rest of the world.

It should not come as a surprise, then, that there has been a contemporary debate on these very same issues in China, where deregulation and a rush to join the world market have characterized government policy since at least as early as 1992, and have been implemented even without the ministrations of the major international organizations charged with furthering an open global economic regime. The only surprises, perhaps, are that the debate in China began long before the demonstrations against the World Trade Organization in Seattle of November 1999, which can probably be regarded as having given the revisionary trend in this country the high visibility it now has, and the prominence that the debate has had in an intellectual community that we in the West too often regard as being disablingly limited by strict government censorship. Wang Hui has been a leading figure in the contentious discourse within China over the relationship between the changes that have taken place in post-Mao China and the force of global capitalism. He has, more than anyone else, served to prevent this discourse from becoming an exercise in abstraction by relentlessly insisting on attention to detailed analysis of the process of globalization. In the first of the two essays translated here, in fact, Wang Hui explicitly links the concerns of the Seattle demonstrations (and those in Washington, D.C., the following spring) with those expressed at Tiananmen in Beijing in 1989: they were both, he says in section 1, "directed against a comprehensive system of political provisions having to do with ordinary life, a systematic program aimed at creating and expanding a comprehensive market society."

Wang Hui's long essay on the origins and aftermath of the 1989 social movement is essentially a complex summary of the social and economic changes China has undergone over the past twenty years, along with a detailed account of the debates that have been ongoing in Chinese intellectual circles since the early 1990s concerning these social and economic transformations and the dynamics that lie behind them. Wang's argument progresses in a frankly teleological fashion, assuming that—like the Chinese economy itself, perhaps—the discussion of these issues has grown more mature and to the point in the years since 1989. As he says, "In the past twenty years social thought on the Chinese mainland has never been as intricate and complicated as it is today, something that I believe to be a reflection of the crises and rifts that characterize the mechanisms and controls working in the contemporary world." Like much contemporary Western analysis of this transformation, Wang's account focuses on what are most often taken in the West as the contradictions of the process, notably rapid economic deregulation conjoined with a still highly intrusive state.

Unlike most of the Western commentary, however, Wang Hui does not take these features to be inherently paradoxical, but rather simply as elements that are characteristic of the new global order as a whole, in which considerations of economic growth and development have trumped every other concern, particularly those of democracy and social justice. He believes that the Chinese case is particularly revealing of how the process works. The essay offers an extremely pointed critique of the economic and social policies pursued by the Chinese government in the years after 1985 and the "neoliberal" ideology that has justified them. As such, it has never been published in mainland China (although it has circulated widely within the country on the Internet), and an earlier version of the essay appeared in Taiwan in *Taiwan shehui yanjiu jikan* (Taiwan: A radical quarterly in social studies) in late 2001. An abbreviated version also appeared in French in *Le Monde Diplomatique* in April 2002.[4] The final section of the essay, "Alternative Globalizations and the Question of the Modern," with its crucial discussion of the functions of the nation-state in the contemporary world, was, however, written specifically for this book.

At its heart the essay is an impassioned plea for economic and social justice and an indictment of the corruption brought on by the explosion of "unregulated" markets, a phenomenon that had become evident in China long before it did in the United States. The core of Wang's argument is his important observation that terms like "free" and "unregulated" are largely ideological constructs masking the intervention of highly manipulative, even coercive, governmental actions on behalf of economic policies that favor a particular scheme of capitalist acquisition, something that must be clearly distinguished from truly free markets. As he says, "The creation of today's market society was not the result of a sequence of spontaneous events, but rather of state interference and violence." In other words, were there no governments to set the terms and guarantee the structure of the markets that the advocates of this system—the neoliberals—claim to be regulated only by a Smithian invisible hand, these institutions would not have come into existence in the first place, could neither sustain themselves nor function as they do. This has marked a fundamental change in the world: "the core of the neoliberal conception of globalization . . . no longer recognizes the division between politics and economic characteristic of the nineteenth century, but rather envisions the workings of the economy, markets, and capital as replacing the political and social spheres."

Wang Hui sees new openings toward social, political, and economic democracy in China as the only agencies by which the exploitative and unstable conditions brought about by this particular configuration of market society can be remedied. He thus combines an open mind toward the possibilities inhering in socialist economic mechanisms—which he is careful to define as leading to social democracy and "safety-net" social guarantees rather than as manifestations of the ideology of pre-1979 state control—with an urgent call for democratization in China, both of which he contends the reigning ideology of neoliberalism sees as anathema. The essay also contains a firm sense of how powerfully economic and social trends in the world are converging. While Wang is primarily concerned with tracing recent Chinese history and China's particular problems, as well as creating a mode of analysis not dependent on prepackaged imported ideas, his argument also speaks to issues affecting the entire global community, and offers theoretical insights that are widely applicable. While it is safe to say that Wang closely hews to his fundamental argument, the essay's density and the immense amount of detail included in it make for a challenging text. But the thicket of specifics he sets out has the real virtue of preventing the piece from becoming reductive: the very richness of the evidence presented guarantees the reader multiple perspectives on the course of developments in China over the past two decades.

For all his evident erudition in matters of political economy, Wang Hui is neither economist, historian, nor political theoretician by training, having studied modern Chinese literature, first earning an undergraduate degree from what is now Yangzhou University, followed by a Ph.D. from the Institute of Chinese Literature of the Chinese Academy of Social Sciences in Beijing, supervised by the prominent scholar of modern Chinese literature Tang Tao. Like a number of other important contemporary Chinese critical intellectuals, Wang initially developed his analytical faculties via a series of influential studies of Lu Xun (1881–1936), the enormously complex figure almost universally regarded as the founder of modern Chinese literature and the greatest writer of twentieth-century China. Wang was active in the movement at Tiananmen in the spring of 1989 that was eventually suppressed in the early hours of June Fourth. His participation led to a yearlong exile in the remote countryside in northwest China's Shaanxi Province, an area as notable for its persistent poverty as for its propensity to drought. This sojourn provided Wang the opportunity to experience the deep poverty of much of rural China as well as to develop a clear sense of how little lasting benefit to such areas were the reforms of the early 1980s once attention shifted to the reconfiguration of the urban economy. He was also deeply affected by the naive faith the local population had that a visiting dignitary from Beijing like himself could eventually return to the capital and effectively represent their plight to the ruling mandarins. Much of the passion that so evidently suffuses his writing on social and economic injustice can, in fact, be traced back to the sense of obligation he took upon himself after bearing witness to these pleas for redress.

Both before and after he was in Shaanxi, Wang spent a number of years as a research fellow in the institute from which he obtained his Ph.D., only recently moving to Beijing's Tsinghua University, where he is professor in the school of humanities and social sciences and affiliated with the department of Chinese. Wang also was coeditor of the important academic journal *Xueren* (The scholar) during its relatively brief run in the 1990s, and since May 1996 has served as coeditor (with Huang Ping) of *Dushu* (Readings)—a journal whose role in Chinese intellectual life is in many ways comparable to that of the *New York Review of Books* in the United States, although a good deal more pointed in its critiques of the status quo. *Dushu* is, at any rate, the most important organ of opinion in the "New Period" that followed the general transformation of Chinese institutions and intellectual life after the death of Mao Zedong in 1976. Wang is, however, quite candid in his lack of illusion about the latitude for critique open to any organ of opinion in China today. As he says of the journal he edits: "*Dushu* . . . [while g]enerally seen as the standard-bearer of free thinking, . . . is by no means an unofficial publication; it is published by a state publishing house and administered by the Bureau of Journalism and Publications. It therefore has no real power to resist state intervention."[5]

Wang's own focus of scholarly inquiry is Chinese intellectual history of the past three hundred years, particularly of the late nineteenth and early twentieth centuries. He has followed his pivotal work on Lu Xun by writing a series of stunningly original and well-researched articles on such pivotal transitional figures as Yan Fu (1853–1921) and Zhang Binglin (1869–1936), men who, like Wang himself, were widely conversant with and open to both the Chinese and Western intellectual traditions.[6] What all these subjects of Wang Hui's research have in common is profound engagement not just with ideas in the abstract, but with the possible means of their implementation. This is particularly true in the case of Lu Xun, who added an intense consciousness of the need for assessing one's personal responsibility when participating in or even contemplating the nature of any social movement. It is not hard to see the legacy of these great thinkers at work in the intensity of the commitment that Wang brings to his discussion of contemporary issues.

Wang Hui's entry into the long series of debates on China's political and economic future was primarily in response to a present sense of crisis at that moment, and he brings his vast erudition and sense of historical sweep to a complex of issues that he feels he has an obligation as a concerned Chinese intellectual to address. While the result is a pragmatic text addressed to a complex of urgent social issues, it is at the same time—aside from basing itself in a broad-based reconsideration of the huge question of Chinese modernity—engaged most intensely with questions concerning the distance and possible convergence between contemporary Chinese and Western critical discourse. In taking account of the multiple levels on display in the first essay in this book, it is also impossible to dismiss the relevance of Wang's historical studies to his perspective on current events and his intellectual reflection on them. As the Shanghai scholar Luo Gang has said of Wang:

> He points out that a consideration of China's experience over the past hundred years or so is an important aid in evaluating the process whereby China is presently engaging with the global economy. . . . He has formed a view that the most valuable aspect of modern Chinese thought is to be found in those approaches that reflect a skepticism about and critical reevaluation of classical modernity and which are not a simple affirmation of classical views of modernity. He has pointed out that there is an internal tension within earlier Chinese views on modernity, an appreciation of which can invigorate our own intellectual debates. By contrast, other intellectual activists and groups, for example, the "liberals," are interested in expunging these contradictions and tensions.[7]

Luo's perspicuous remarks also point out the remarkable extent to which Wang Hui's essays are devoted to tracing and critiquing the course of intellectual debate in contemporary China. Westerners, and Americans in particular, inured as we are to the notion that the word "intellectual" tends to be coterminous with "professor," may find this focus odd and somewhat abstracted from what we would take to be the main issue—the social situation itself. To assume this, however, would be to overlook the long history of intense social engagement on the part of Chinese intellectuals. To a certain extent this is based on the historical fact that for the seven or eight hundred years before 1900, a man's status (women were excluded), both intellectual and otherwise, as well as his qualification for government office, was determined by rigorous examination in the Chinese humanistic canon. The heavy emphasis in this canon on personal moral conduct thereby almost guaranteed that political discourse was carried out in a register saturated with moral concern, whatever the actual interests that might have been at stake. If anything, this association of high levels of education with an ethical imperative to influence national policy only increased in the twentieth century, when the leadership of efforts for reform (or "enlightenment") in virtually all sectors of society were led by groups of people who by then very self-consciously thought of themselves as a united body of intellectuals (*zhishifenzi*, literally, "knowledgeable elements").

The so-called May Fourth, or New Culture, movement of the late 1910s is emblematic of this augmented social role of the intellectuals. Named after a student demonstration at Beijing University in 1919 in opposition to the unfavorable terms inflicted on China by the Treaty of Versailles, this movement, originally highly iconoclastic, came to embody the aspirations of the educated to provide their nation with both moral and intellectual leadership.[8] In the years since, this predilection for political and social engagement has led to a highly complicated relationship between intellectuals and political power: at times they have stood in steadfast opposition to governmental abuse; at other times they have become deeply implicated in its works.[9] Overall, however, while prominent intellectuals had formed the core of the Communist Party at its founding in China in 1920–1921, once in power after 1949 the Party enforced various policies that sharply limited the agency of this group. In the New Era that gradually unfolded after Mao's death in 1976 the intellectuals once more sought to assert a leadership role in society by recalling their role in the Chinese "enlightenment" of the late 1910s and early 1920s. While Wang Hui is critical of the naive optimism of this line of thinking that characterized the 1980s, he is equally opposed to the post-1994 "postmodern" denunciation of the intellectuals' aspirations to play a leading role in society as an anachronistic relic of a bygone era.[10] Since the postmodern position was most often associated with and a celebration of the advent of a new society in which a commercialized and amoral popular culture held sway, Wang's opposition is perfectly consistent: in a neoliberal order marked by ubiquitous commodification, only the critical mobilization of a tradition of strong intellectual advocacy can hope to show the way toward any serious resistance.

The Historical Background

Before addressing the specifics of Wang Hui's argument in more detail, it is necessary first to sketch out, inevitably far too briefly, the historical background of China in the latter half of the twentieth century. The new government inaugurated by Mao on behalf of the Communist Party on October 1, 1949, immediately undertook comprehensive political and economic programs to address the catastrophic conditions the country had been left in after twelve years of near-constant war, against Japan between 1937 and 1945 and the civil war between the Nationalists and Communists that followed the end of World War II. In addition to having a common underlying ideology with the Soviet Union, given the U.S. involvement in supporting the Guomindang (Nationalist, or "KMT") government during the civil war of the late 1940s, the American entry into the Korean War in 1950, and General MacArthur's bellicose utterances as United Nations troops under his command approached the Chinese border with Korea, the new Communist government was drawn ever closer to its northern neighbor, in terms of both political and of economic policy. The years immediately following 1949 were devoted to consolidation of political, social, and intellectual control, to land reform, to the straightening out of the devastated fiscal system inherited from the prior regime, and to a general effort to restore an infrastructure damaged and neglected after so many years of strife. Many of these reforms were accompanied by much violence and coercion, by-products of the rapidity and often ad hoc means by which extremely far-ranging changes were put into effect.

The outlines of the repressive consequences of the political program that followed the new regime's coming to power are relatively well known in the West,[11] but the details of the economic program that form the immediate background to Wang Hui's discussion of contemporary economic issues are considerably less familiar outside China. After it proclaimed its existence, the new government, with considerable Soviet assistance in the form of loans and advisors, engaged in a Soviet-style process of rapid industrial development. The principal feature of this process was the exploitation of both urban and, particularly, rural surpluses to invest in new heavy industries, a number of which were in and around the new capital in Beijing, but more often in the interior provinces at some distance from the older industrial heartlands around Shanghai and in the northeast (that is, Manchuria). The exploitation of the rural areas was particularly acute, and had the net effect of drawing a sharp economic, demographic, and cultural line between country and city. The rural standard of living had been conspicuously lower than that found in the cities long before the Communists came to power, and the relative ratio of that difference changed little for many years after the founding of the People's Republic.[12] It should also be noted that the new social order included the vast expansion of new systems of public education, health care, and housing for urban workers of all types. While these efforts tended to be rather poorly funded, the social benefits were real enough, and in many ways substituted for any general rise in wages, which stayed quite low throughout the country right up until the 1980s.

The statistics for economic growth for the 1950s were impressive, particularly during the first Five-Year Plan, which was in force between 1953 and 1957. It was during this time that private ownership of industry was all but phased out and, in a remarkably short period during 1955, the countryside was organized into agricultural cooperatives, in which an egalitarian policy of labor contribution substituting for land contribution in determining individual incomes to co-op members. With the socialization of agriculture thus all but accomplished, Mao was close to being assured that the basic work of consolidation of the new regime had been accomplished, and he turned his attention toward increasing the pace of economic growth. As he said at the time, "The aim of the socialist revolution is to liberate the productive forces,"[13] illustrating just how closely linked the questions of economic development and the move toward socialism were in his mind. As a result, 1956 saw amplified calls for increases in production, a campaign later dubbed the "Leap Forward" *(yuejin)*.

As the Five-Year Plan neared its end, however, it became increasingly clear that agricultural growth, even under the new regime of collectivization, was not keeping up with the impressive growth being registered in the industrial sector, and it was thus, as Jonathan Spence has observed, "hard to see how more could be extracted from the peasantry to pay for the heavy industrial growth that was mandated by the Soviet model."[14] Based on the impressive speed with which rural collectivization took place in 1955–1956—far faster than even the most optimistic planners had anticipated—a series of utopian schemes that began with the original "Leap" of 1956 was launched that aimed at simultaneously bringing China closer to socialism and significantly increasing the rate of economic growth.[15] Contrary to popular understanding (both in the West and in China), not all of these moves were initiated by Mao Zedong and his close supporters. Many were, in fact, the result of local initiatives by activist regional officials, which were often resisted, at least initially, by the bureaucrats charged with Soviet-style central planning. Mao, however, generally supported most of these end-runs around the governmental structure in Beijing. The devolution of central power and authority that was a major feature of the Cultural Revolution days of the 1970s[16] and that Wang Hui sees as so significant in the 1990s can thus also be seen as a dynamic in Chinese political economy at least since the mid-1950s.

In line with this sense of accomplishment after 1955, in 1956 and the first half of 1957 Mao issued calls for a new rectification movement to accompany the drive for economic growth, in which intellectuals were called on to point out the flaws of an entrenched and stodgy bureaucracy that he saw as putting the brakes on progress.

The matter around which this movement revolved was the status of the intellectuals under the new regime: since few of them were Communists to begin with and they generally came from wealthier backgrounds (regarded with suspicion by the Party), there was a split within the government leadership on how much critical latitude they should be accorded. While there was general agreement that the expertise of the educated was indispensable in building the new order, the question remained whether they should be trusted to speak out constructively or kept under close control. Through 1956 and the first half of 1957, Mao and his allies in the leadership believed that the full mobilization of this vital group of independent thinkers required a policy built on trust, and accordingly, he made various speeches advocating a liberalizing of speech under the general rubric of "Letting a Hundred Flowers Bloom and a Hundred Schools of Thought Contend" *(bai hua qifang, bai jia zhengming)*.

After almost a year of fitful development, the movement was definitively set in motion—in a more radical form than that in which it had originally been conceived—a few months after Mao delivered his famous speech, "On the Correct Handling of Contradiction among the People," at a Supreme State Conference he had convened himself on February 27, 1957 (although it was not published until June of that year).[17] There was, needless to say, considerable resistance to Mao's appeal from within the Party apparatus, and it was not until the spring of 1957 that the media launched a full-scale promotion of the campaign and large numbers of intellectuals joined the effort in full throat. If Mao had anticipated primarily approbation and calls for what were essentially minor adjustments, the extent and sharpness of the criticisms that followed came as a real surprise—particularly the number of critiques of the Party as having constituted itself as a new class, an enduring problem that Wang Hui also deals with in the first of his essays in this book—facilitating Mao's acquiescence in demands for suppression from the majority of Party leaders and the Party apparatus that had been opposed to the movement in the first place.[18]

It is difficult to overestimate the consequences of the suppression of democratic dissent in the long-running "anti-rightist" campaign that followed after the Hundred Flowers movement itself was halted in the summer of 1957. While most China scholars agree that the Party leadership's claims at the opening of the anti-rightist movement that the Hundred Flowers initiative had merely been a gambit to get what Party propaganda labeled reactionary "hobgoblins, demons, and poisonous weeds" to reveal their true natures was merely an attempt to look as if it had been in control all along,[19] this face-saving attempt by Mao retroactively to demonstrate his command over events had long-term effects on the relationship between the Party and the intellectuals who ended up being the principal targets of the campaign. One estimate is that three hundred thousand of China's most highly educated people were branded as "rightists," "a label that effectively ruined their careers in China," brought about imprisonment and internal exile for a large number, and caused serious trauma for many more.[20]

The turn away from socialism toward liberalism that Wang Hui describes as a feature of the more relaxed atmosphere in China in the 1980s must be seen against this sense of the betrayal by the Party of the intellectuals more than twenty years previously. One prominent scholar even confided to me his opinion that the nature of internal Party discourse changed for good after 1957: with those who sincerely believed in the prospects for a democratic socialism effectively removed from the scene at this time, a level of cynicism and wariness about the expression of true feelings thereafter became the norm in the relationship between Party and its members from the educated stratum.

The end of the Hundred Flowers movement if anything only stimulated efforts to achieve more rapid and comprehensive economic growth, culminating in 1958 in the "Great Leap Forward" (*da yuejin*) in industry and agriculture, a frenetic drive to catch up as soon as possible with the advanced industrial powers. The result of this campaign was a proliferation of radical policies implemented both at the behest of the central government and of overly enthusiastic local officials. More often than not, these policies, which were generally based on popular mobilization, were implemented in a haphazard fashion that took little account of local conditions and that hardly had any very clear vision of what either increased agricultural yields or industrialization actually demanded. The amalgamation of the rural population into gigantic People's Communes was one result, as was the widespread scavenging of a large percentage of the country's metal tools to meet the demand for increased production of iron and steel, the latter a policy that Mao himself acknowledged to have been a "catastrophe."[21] The ill-conceived policies that resulted coincided with a string of several years of disastrous weather and the sudden withdrawal of all Soviet assistance in the summer of 1960 to bring about severe economic depression and widespread famine in the poorer agricultural regions of the country during the "three hard years" between 1959 and 1961.[22]

Against this background of political and economic tumult, troubles between China and the Soviet Union, its socialist mentor, had begun as early as Khrushchev's February 1956 denunciation of Stalin. The two powers began to diverge sharply on policy matters: China, feeling itself surrounded and threatened by the United States, its allies, and its client states was profoundly suspicious of Khrushchev's openings to the West, his doctrine of "peaceful coexistence," and the Soviet Union's failure to support China in its 1958 struggles in the Taiwan Straight and with India in 1959. For its part, the Soviet Union's leadership was aghast at the radical economic policies put into practice in the People's Communes, not hesitating to criticize these policies quite openly. A downward spiral of ill will and recrimination followed that led eventually to the Soviet's sudden withdrawal of some fourteen hundred experts and advisers from China in the summer of 1960, and to the cancellation of all projects involving technical assistance, with the experts apparently taking the blueprints for these projects home with them. The Chinese were left with their debts for earlier Soviet loans and numerous uncompleted projects. With the country already foundering as a result of the disastrous planning failures of the Great Leap and serious floods and drought, this fissure could not have come at a worse time.

The structural similarity and temporal continuity between the Great Leap and the anti-rightist movement that had begun slightly earlier was to bring about in later years a broad sense that all the disasters of the post-1957 period were the result of ultra-leftist policies dictated by Mao and his circle.[23] When Deng Xiaoping began to consolidate his power after 1978, one of his principal rallying devices was to encourage critiques of the ultra-leftism held to have begun in 1957 and amplified in the period after 1966. These critiques focused on those who surrounded Mao—the late leader himself was exempt from direct public attack; but the implication of the critique was clear enough.[24] As the intellectuals were among the prime beneficiaries of Deng's post-1978 policies, the critique of leftism that helped in their initial justification has remained highly popular in learned circles in China, and provides a crucial backdrop to the 1990s debates.

The misery of the years between 1959 and 1962 led other elements in the Communist Party leadership to scale back Mao's power, and for a relatively brief period in the early 1960s the extremist momentum of the previous years was reversed. Beginning as early as 1964, however, the campaigns to push China more speedily toward socialism began again in earnest, culminating in the so-called Great Proletarian Cultural Revolution *(Wuchanjieji wenhua da geming),* a movement of unprecedented scale and ferocity that began in the spring of 1966. Stemming from a complex of factors, including Mao's efforts to return to power and his ability to mobilize a number of social elements that had been disappointed by the bureaucratization of the People's Republic, the movement was particularly notable for its attacks on the structure of the government, on the educational system, and on the organization of the Party itself. As had been the case with so many other movements in the People's Republic, the intellectuals were both the tools and the targets of this vast mobilization, with university and secondary students serving as its motive force—as "Red Guards"—and their teachers often being the primary victims of the resulting campaigns and personal attacks.

The nationwide disruptions that followed eventually became so severe that by 1969 Mao and his group felt obliged to call a halt to Red Guard activities, with most of these ex-students thereby demobilized sent to rural communes and industrial plants, for the most part leaving their educational careers incomplete. The university system returned to operation only very slowly, but without its traditional recruitment device of competitive examinations. Replacing these was a process of nomination by work unit, which aimed at recruiting more students from politically desirable "worker–peasant-soldier" (*gong nong bing*) backgrounds, who were officially regarded as having been placed at a disadvantage by the old system of rigorous academic examination. The number of students recruited by this new system was considerably smaller than the numbers in the pre-1966 universities, and there was a notably greater emphasis on the political underpinning of the ideas that were taught.

Following Mao's death in September 1976 and the prompt discrediting the very next month of those regarded as being most closely tied to his radical policies—including his wife, Jiang Qing—there were rapid policy turnarounds in all sectors of Chinese society. These were led by Deng Xiaoping, who soon emerged from the disgrace to which the Maoists had consigned him after April 1976. A skilled manipulator of the Party apparatus and 1950s *wunderkind* of the Party organization (while born in 1904, Deng was still considerably younger than those of equal power in the Party apparatus in that first decade of the People's Republic), Deng had long been anathema to the leftists surrounding Mao in the early 1970s. Wang Hui's essay on the 1989 social movement includes as background a precise, if overly brief, account of the changes in economic policy that came about after Deng's ascension to power,[25] but the concurrent restoration of the educational sector should also be noted, which early in 1977 witnessed a return to the traditional system of competitive examinations at both the secondary and tertiary levels.

In 1977 there followed in quick succession two national exams for admission to the universities; taking part were vast numbers of former students from that whole generation that had been sent off to work after 1969, often in extremely remote rural areas. The two university classes that were formed as a result, set to graduate in 1981 and 1982, respectively, were characterized by those who returned to their educations with considerable vigor and seriousness. Most of the students were older than the eighteen- and nineteen-year-old middle-school graduates that had in the past filled the ranks of entering freshmen, and the fact that many of them had spent years on the farm or in the factory left them with a renewed sense of destiny and of their own missions, both personal and national. One of the things most of them shared was a sense of the errors of the policies of the period after 1966, and even after 1956, and a powerful inclination toward liberalism and democracy, if only as the best devices to ensure that earlier abuses were not repeated. For a brief period in 1978–1979, the ascending Dengist regime even fostered these aspirations as part of a plan to legitimate its efforts radically to reform the system it had inherited at the end of the Mao era. With its consolidation of power, however, the regime soon sealed off most of these new avenues, creating thereby a new group of dissident intellectuals.

The New Era and Its Discontents

As Wang Hui outlines in his essay on the 1989 social movement, the economic reforms of the early post-Mao years before 1985 were concentrated in the countryside—where the vast preponderance of the Chinese population lives—and resulted in impressive gains both in agricultural output and in the rural standard of living.[26] Wang stresses that adjusting to market demand was only one of the factors involved in these reforms, which were the result of deliberate government policy measures that were successfully premised on maintaining social stability. In the period after 1985, however, with the attention of economic policymakers once again turned toward the creation of urban wealth, the discrepancy between urban and rural living standards began to widen once again, arguably reaching the pre-1978 level by the mid-1990s.[27] Wang points out that here, too, government policy was key, even though these policies consisted primarily of the devolution of political and economic authority from the center to the localities. This time, however, the refocus of economic activity to urban regions had the net result of bringing about considerable disruption to the countryside and thus to China as a whole. To give but one example, the new economic imbalance created a "floating population" *(liudong renkou)* of tens of millions of people who abandoned an unremunerative life on the farm to seek work in the booming urban economy, much of which was based on speculative building construction enabled by the devolution of economic authority to the localities.

As Wang Hui demonstrates, the initial response of the Chinese intellectuals to the reforms undertaken in the 1980s was overwhelmingly positive, as the new policies seemed at first to offer the antidote to the governmental malfeasance and economic stagnation of the last two decades of Mao's rule. This optimism expressed itself by the agreement on the part of intellectuals to call this time a period of "New Enlightenment," to distinguish the 1980s from the dark preceding years. Section 1 of Wang's essay on the 1989 movement comprises a detailed account of the social developments of that decade, with its focus on the increasing frustration among various elements of the population as the decade passed and as the corruptions and abuses of the reform process he outlines gradually revealed themselves. Rapid growth also led to increasing polarization and income inequality among urban dwellers. The combination of these sources of frustration eventually led to a national explosion of discontent in the spring of 1989 and the consequent repression, encapsulated in Chinese by the expression *liu si* ("6/4")—for June 4, the day the suppression took place. Maurice Meisner, in an adept account of the process leading up to the crucial events of 1989, has provided a pithy summary of the process that Wang has outlined in such rich detail:

[T]he dominant strains in the Democracy Movement [that is, what Wang Hui calls the "social movement"] among students and workers alike, were an egalitarian reaction against bureaucratic corruption and privilege, a liberating cultural radicalism, and a demand for political democracy. These features of the popular movement were entirely incongruous with the imperatives of the bureaucratic capitalist system that the post-Mao reforms had created and in hostile opposition to the mentality of those who presided over and profited from that system. Any serious process of democratization posed a mortal threat to the new order, and this was universally recognized by the leaders of the regime.[28]

Whatever their political orientation prior to June 1989, Chinese intellectuals were united in mute horror at the ferocity of the repression that ensued, the pain being all the sharper for its inability to be expressed openly, as the hard-won openings in the public media in the late 1980s were immediate casualties of the crackdown. Writing more than ten years after the event, Wang Hui registers the general sense among educated Chinese of the uniquely momentous consequences of June 4—among other things as having sounded a premature end to the twentieth century, as well as having "triggered the disintegration of the Soviet Union and Eastern Europe and inaugurated the political and economic structure by which neoliberalism came to dominate the globe." Immediately after the events themselves, however, there was little sense among the participants or those affected as to how to grasp what had happened, of what the international consequences would be, and even less of how things would eventually sort themselves out. Intellectual life, however, gradually rekindled itself in the years that followed, even as economic growth recommenced, reaching an exceedingly rapid pace in the three years after Deng Xiaoping's celebrated Southern Progress *(nanxun)* in early 1992.[29]

In general, Wang Hui's portrayal of intellectual life in China between mid-1989 and mid-1997 as tentative and unable to come to grips with rapidly transpiring events is shared by many who lived through and later commented on those years.[30] He divides those eight years into two periods separated by the watershed year of 1993, the year the post-1992 economic boom began to register in intellectual discourse. He describes the period between 1989 and 1993 as a period of rethinking, marked by efforts to characterize the failures of 1989 through critiques of intellectual radicalism in modern Chinese history. Scholars also produced numerous studies and compilations of research materials as part of a general reconsideration of modern Chinese history and the intellectual traditions that had constituted this body of knowledge. Wang notes that these materials and studies were to prove very useful some years later, when more theoretical inquiries into Chinese intellectual traditions were undertaken based on these groundbreaking studies.

After 1993, with the stepped-up pace of marketization combined with extraordinary economic growth, there followed numerous intellectual efforts to attain an understanding of the possibilities, as well as the pitfalls, inhering in this transformation. Wang notes in section 2 of his first essay that one of the main trends of these years was to see the growth of markets as the prelude to the eventual democratization of society, but he judges this whole trend of thought to be marred by a failure of specificity, that is, the failure "to analyze in any detail the mechanisms by which Chinese markets, Chinese civil society, and the middle class they hoped for were to be established." There were also important discussions of the nature of institutions and the capacities of the state, discussions that gained theoretical importance only in retrospect, when the restructuring of enterprises and the withdrawal of support for the social welfare system became areas of serious contention. The third major area of intellectual discourse in those years was a discussion that lamented the loss of a humanistic spirit in contemporary China, which Wang sees as an "instinctive reaction against the movement to expand markets," in spite of the general support these humanists expressed toward the ongoing transformation in China.[31] This discussion also elicited a response from a newly constituted group of postmodernists who embraced the populism of the new consumerism and dismissed the concerns of the humanists as part of the attempt to maintain their position as the cultural elite. Wang is scathing in his account of this postmodernist attack, seeing its advocates as essentially continuing the naive celebrations of the New Era that had marked the 1980s. In this period also began the contention over the proper place of imported Western theory, something engaged in by all sides of any scholarly debate in China ever since.

Wang marks the beginning of the second period with the Asian economic crisis of 1997, a time that also witnessed a slowdown in Chinese economic growth and an increased awareness among urban intellectuals of the problems that for some time had beset the Chinese rural sector. Many scholars, however, mark the start of this new period with the publication of a crucial article, "Contemporary Chinese Thought and the Question of Modernity" by Wang Hui himself, in a late 1997 issue of *Tianya* (Frontiers), a journal published in the remote southern province of Hainan, where official scrutiny has been less intense than in most other places.[32] The article, in a translation by Rebecca Karl, is included in this book as the second essay by Wang, and was in many ways a prototype of his essay on the 1989 social movement. In the words of Geremie Barmé, the earlier essay provides a "magisterial appraisal" of Chinese intellectual life after 1989. It is also a painful deconstruction of this life, in which Wang accuses virtually all intellectual factions of still being fundamentally rooted in the New Enlightenment values of the 1980s and thus unable to understand the new situation of a globalized Chinese market economy. In having failed to understand the nature and extent of the changes that had overtaken the Chinese economy and society, most intellectuals were equally unable to launch any effective critique of what had happened.

Wang's 1997 essay is laced throughout with statements like "China's modernization (or the process by which capitalist markets were created) has enlightenment as its underlying ideology and cultural harbinger. Because of this, the abstract concept of human subjectivity and the concept of human freedom and liberation, which played significant roles in the critique of Mao's socialist experiment, lack vigor in the face of the social crises encountered in the process of capitalist marketization and modernization." It is in this context that Wang called for a rethinking of the old paradigm of modernization— the avenue envisioned throughout the twentieth century as the way to catch up with the advanced West. In Wang's view, with the advent of the new global order, the devoutly wished consummation of modernity had arrived, and his anatomy of it was pointed: "The decline of the New Enlightenment movement marks the end of the most recent phase of Chinese thought. Yet, we can also say that this represents the historical victory of the ideology of modernization shared by socialism and the New Enlightenment movement." Given the magnitude of the change that Wang understands to have, as it were, caught the Chinese intelligentsia sleeping, the only real task now facing intellectuals—huge as it is—is how to offer a critique capable of setting out the particulars of this transformation to modernity and advancing remedies for the dire consequences of unfairness and inequality that it had brought to China.[33]

It would have been impossible for anyone to predict the uproar that followed the publication of this article. The strife and recrimination that resulted was astonishing, particularly to Wang himself, who had no idea that his writing would cause such tumult. Perhaps the primary cause of this outcry was the damage the article inflicted on the *amour propre* of the liberal intellectuals, who had always throughout the period since the 1980s thought of themselves as being in the vanguard of reform and resistance to state despotism. By accusing mainstream discourse as being at best ineffectual and, at worst, somehow in complicity with the sorry state of affairs attending the successful integration of China into the world market, Wang clearly touched a nerve. The most immediate result was that Wang and his few allies were branded with the label of "New Left," an appellation that, given the understandably negative attitude that the educated population in China bears toward the leftist excesses of the Maoist period, was meant to be the kiss of death, as the term "Left" has in China since the 1980s become little more than a term of abuse (rather like "liberal" to Republicans in the United States). Wang, in being similarly candid about the divisions in the ranks of the intelligentsia, also punctured another closely held notion of self-identification, namely, the romantic idea that modern intellectuals have in effect been defined by the common front of resistance they have presented to the monolithic state. This cherished idea dates back to the heroic demonstrations of May 1919, and was very much reinforced by the events of June Fourth. It is also a vision that the Party, through its fervent identification with the 1919 movement, has been anxious to support, at least when the political weather is calm.

To appreciate the full force of Wang's critique as it appears in the two essays included in this book, it is necessary to understand one of his core assumptions about the transition in Chinese society over the past twenty-five years. That is, as he bluntly put it in 1997, "in China, as in other Third World countries, those who control domestic capital are in fact the same as those who control political power." In other words, Party leaders at all levels of society have become indistinguishable from the new "capitalists" in China—it is not that they have merely abetted the process of marketization or stood idly by while this social transformation has taken place. As Wang says in expanding on his basic thesis: "members of the political elite or their families directly participate in economic activity and have become agents for large corporations and industries. Can we call them representatives of civil society? In China, political and economic elites have been completely conflated, and they participate in international economic activity." His indictment of this group is remarkable in its severity and candor. As he writes in section 3 of "The 1989 Social Movement":

> Those in charge of implementing the last will and testament of the revolution [that is, the Party leadership] carry out their dual responsibilities in an absurd fashion: on the one hand they clownishly bury all of

the reasonable aspects of the revolution and of socialism, while on the other they employ state violence and monopolization to guarantee the smooth transition of a Chinese economy in crisis to one based on market mechanisms, in the process wrecking all of the equitable features of the social guarantees contained within the old system.

In light of this, Wang draws attention to the fact that Jiang Zemin's recent call to allow capitalists into the party is thus not so much to allow a new group in, but merely to legitimate the status of those Party members who have enriched themselves in the post-Mao era. As the critic Wang Xiaoming has written in his account of the unspoken origins of the much-publicized "men of success" *(chenggong renshi)* in the 1990s, the deliberate failure on the part of the official press to mention the details of their social ascent in effect masks their bureaucratic origins.[34]

As the polemic between the New Left, which eventually resigned itself to being so labeled, and its attackers developed, Wang Hui sharpened his definition of his opposition. In the essay tracing the 1989 social movement, he uses the term "neoliberal" *(xin ziyouzhuyi)* to describe those Chinese heirs of the New Enlightenment heritage who continue to insist on the primacy of the growth of domestic and international markets over every other consideration. To distinguish this group from earlier liberals concerned mostly with resisting the leviathan state, Wang's sense of "neoliberal" draws attention to the particularly conservative nature of the latter group, with its genealogy rooted in Friedrich von Hayek's stress on the dangers of any state interference in the workings of the economy. As embodied in the policies of Margaret Thatcher and, to a lesser extent, those of Ronald Reagan, Wang's neoliberals are ideologically akin to the "neoconservatives" in the United States. In other words, as Wang uses the term, Chinese neoliberalism includes a willingness to accommodate commercial dominance and complete state withdrawal from a system of social guarantees that, in principle, New Enlightenment "liberalism" would not allow for.[35] Underlying this argument, however, is Wang's fundamental assumption that any theory that sees the economy as functioning beyond governmental intervention is simply illusory. As he continues his critique of neoliberalism in section 1 of "The 1989 Social Movement":

> The most one can say about the conflict between the Chinese version of neoliberalism and the ultraconservative state ideological apparatus is that it reflects an internal contradiction in the functioning of the state. While neoliberalism takes every opportunity to cast itself in the image of "resister," this does not prove that this ideology of the market is in actual opposition to the practical operations of the state: on the contrary, the state and neoliberalism exist in a complex relationship of codependence.

Even more controversially, Wang Hui places the neoliberals in the same camp as the "neo-authoritarians"—those who proclaimed in the early 1990s the need for strict governmental political controls to ensure the success of the economic reforms against any democratic protests at its injustices.[36] In light of neo-authoritarian reliance on governmental initiative to guarantee their social vision, this is an equation that the neoliberals would themselves most vehemently reject, but Wang is careful to specify that the underlying similarity lies in a common view of how the economy should develop: "The legitimization crisis that threatened this market extremism was expressed as 'neo-authoritarianism' and neoconservatism [that is, the use of state authority and elites to further the radical expansion of the market], which also appeared as neoliberalism from the perspective of the movement for a transnational market" (section 1; see also section 2 for similar comments). Wang Hui is not alone in this association. The scholar Gan Yang, for instance, puts it in historical context by showing how the Chinese neoliberals identify with a Burkean rejection of the French Revolution, thus distinguishing them from the mainstream of liberal scholarship in the West and placing them in alignment with neoconservatives.[37]

This post-1997 contention has often generated more heat than light, as when opponents have accused Wang and his allies of being in league with government policy,[38] but it has remained the most important debate within academic circles in China, the source of much creative thinking along with the unfortunate vituperation. It should be kept in mind, however, that the government is not comfortable with either side of the current debate, and has unofficially announced its intention to monitor it closely, evidently afraid of the extent to which candid discussion concerning the fundamentals of political economy will rock the boat of the fragile social assent it has gathered for its economist policies.

Perhaps the outstanding feature of Wang Hui's work in general, and of the first essay translated here in particular, is his insistence on stressing the political aspect of political economy and on how the political basis of economic policy must be factored into any consideration of why the policy was adopted and how it is meant to work. This attention to politics has caused discomfort on the part of those intellectuals who, having more often than not been the designated targets of one or more of the mass movements characterizing modern China, have developed an instinctive distrust of popular movements and regard calls for greater democratization as calls for rekindled social movements. Wang Hui repeatedly stresses the essentially political nature of their faith in the impersonal mechanisms of the market, which he demonstrates to be not so impersonal after all. Throughout the essay Wang points to instances in which the neoliberal response to serious policy issues is as highly ideological as anything emanating from the New Left. This reminder of the ideological basis of much neoliberal economic thinking is, needless to say, not just something that applies only in China. The Bush administration's tax-cutting fetish aside, the Asian economic crisis of 1997–1998 provided an even more apposite example, as Wang Hui has noted elsewhere. When the newly installed government of the Hong Kong Special Administrative Region intervened in its local bourse to prevent a stock market meltdown in 1998, the international financial press sounded an alarm out of all proportion to the act itself, which was after all a gambit that in the end caused no harm and may have prevented a far greater economic disaster. This violation of neoliberal shibboleth was attacked unmercifully in the business press, only to be conveniently set aside when none of the anticipated horrors came to pass.

Another of the distinctive features of the essay on the 1989 social movement is its clear call for Chinese intellectual independence and for the construction of a Chinese public sphere not dominated by the Western, particularly the American, media. Wang also implicitly and explicitly condemns Chinese intellectuals for having been too eager to jump on someone else's bandwagon, at least after the cataclysm of the Cultural Revolution ended with Mao Zedong's death in 1976. Wang has little patience for those who have scrambled after fashionable Western theory—particularly for the self-styled "post-modernists" and the conservative apologists for the world as it has come to be in the years since the termination of the Cold War. He is particularly critical of Fukuyama's "end of history" thesis, which he sees as an unspoken supposition underlying many of the assumptions of neoliberalism, a supposition based on the notion that one social system has proven itself so superior that any consideration of alternatives has become superfluous. For Wang, this amounts to an expression of belief in "the final victory of the Western social system," which preempts any considerations of alternatives. He conveys the reasons for his opposition to it eloquently in section 1: "As far as I am concerned, once this single understanding becomes the world's predominant narrative, once it becomes ironclad proof of the superiority of the present system, once protest becomes merely praise for that system, then its true meaning, its critical potential, and its historical significance will all be lost."

Wang Hui is at his most eloquent in describing the gradually flowering intellectual work in the 1990s that began to question the Eurocentrism that Chinese intellectuals had consciously or unconsciously adopted after the 1970s. He has, however, been equally intent on not indulging in any celebration of Chinese tradition, determined as he is to break up the various binaries (like China/West and traditional/modern) that he understands as inimical to clear thinking, precisely because they have been so widely assumed to be fundamental truths. Given the intense nationalism that has been in the background of virtually all intellectual trends in China over the past century, however, this call for intellectual independence has been an exceedingly sensitive issue and probably accounts for a good deal of the intense animus directed at Wang Hui over the past four or five years by his intellectual opponents. Given what Wang sees as their immersion in the China/West binary, they can only see any expression of difference from received Western authority as stemming from the same Chinese chauvinism that was on display during the most extreme of the Maoist years.

Part of Wang's effort to establish intellectual autonomy can be discerned in his attitude toward China's socialist heritage of the first thirty years after 1949. On the whole, Wang is rather vague about this, calling for a serious historical reexamination rather than casual dismissal, but he is notably nonspecific in his references to the period. On the one hand, however, he is brilliantly clear in showing how certain things have been misinterpreted in the post-1979 rush to condemn Mao's policies as a totality. He asserts, for instance, that the neoliberal determination to brand the Maoist period as having been overwhelmingly egalitarian is simply wrong, even though there certainly were calls for radical egalitarianism at various times prior to 1979. Wang's point is that any egalitarianism that prevailed in the Maoist period pales in significance when set against the hierarchical elements that dominated the social scene: the rigid distinctions maintained almost throughout between country and city, something David Zweig has called "[t]he 'great wall' erected by Maoism between urban and rural China,"[39] the vast social separation of the Party leadership from the overwhelming majority of the population, and the emphasis in the Cultural Revolution period on proper family origin as the only way to determine political virtue. Wang is unequivocal in his condemnation of these policies, and of the despotic and anti-democratic structures they both signified and helped to bring into being. As he sums up his case, in section 2:

> There are many profound cautionary tales to be learned from Chinese socialism, but these lessons have nothing to do with the realization of egalitarianism. Quite on the contrary, they stemmed from the failure of its egalitarian objectives ever to be really implemented. In other words, what deserves criticism is not the victories won by the socialist movement in the realm of equality, but the new hierarchy and notions of social status that were created in the process.

On the other hand, Wang makes clear his admiration for the ideology of socialism, with its stress on social equality and justice, pointing out how this ideology had always been firmly imbedded in modern Chinese social and political discourse and was always available as a means of passing judgment on governmental unfairness and the installation of new social inequalities. One of the leitmotifs of the essay, in fact, is how often the official socialist ideology has been at odds with state practice, both before and after 1979, and how it provided leverage for criticism of lapses from official ideals, as in some of the attacks on the Party as a "new class" as early as the Hundred Flowers period in the spring of 1957, and as a spur to efforts to work toward direct democracy now. Wang is also vexed by the persistent denunciation of "populism" and "nationalism" in China, in which the advocates for the neoliberal order accuse anyone arguing for economic, political, and social justice as simply trying to drag China back to the dark days of the Cultural Revolution. The reason for this, he says, is that "the ideology of neoliberalism and its legitimization were built on the total repudiation and moral condemnation of [the socialist] legacy," with the neoliberals thereby being able to disguise the anti-democratic thrust of their own agenda.

Wang's determination to keep his focus on China's position in the world reflects another distinctive feature of his argument, namely, his determination to hold on to the nation-state as the basic unit of political and economic policy. This notion is in sharp contrast to the suspicions of the nation-state evinced by a number of other dissenters against the neoliberal world order. For instance, there is a notable contrast between Wang Hui's approbation of the fact that, as he says in section 3, "all critical social movements since the nineteenth century have taken the nation-state as the only effective arena of political struggle, even as they have linked this struggle to their inclinations toward internationalism," and the opinion of Michael Hardt and Antonio Negri in *Empire* that "As soon as the nation begins to form as a sovereign state, its progressive functions all but vanish. . . . With national 'liberation' and the construction of the nation-state, all of the oppressive functions of modern sovereignty inevitably blossom in full force," and "The concept of nation and the practices of nationalism are from the beginning set down on the road not to the republic but to the 're-total,' the total thing, that is, the totalitarian overcoding of social life."[40]

Wang Hui is well aware of the malignant potential of the state (as a matter of both theory and personal experience), which explains why he takes such pains to explain his defense of what he sees as its necessary functions. At its core, his defense is pragmatic, based on the notion that there really is no other agency that can be mobilized for popular purposes. As he says in section 3, for instance, in regard to labor rights: "The logic of transnational capitalism demands the globalization of labor movements, but the reality we are facing is this: a global labor movement has yet to take shape, while the evidence of cooperation and collusion between transnational capital and the nation-state is visible everywhere." He thus views the state as the only entity that could exercise any popular leverage, one that could be worked with as long as it is understood that the definition of the state is not something "in collusion with monopolistic, coercive, and unequal systems, but is instead [something] taking up [its] social responsibilities . . . ; this is the principal task of all social movements that have as their goal domestic and international democracy."

Perhaps the key to this difference of perspective lies in the different historical experiences of Europe and China. As Hardt and Negri argue, the nation-state in Europe developed out of "the patrimonial body of the monarchic state and reinvented it in a new form,"[41] as a device for securing parochial advantage for a specifically defined set of populations, or rather for the commercial, industrial, and financial elites in the territories so defined. As China was continuously dispossessed of its sovereignty in the nineteenth and early twentieth centuries by a series of wars and other coercive demands foisted upon it by the powerful nation-states of the North Atlantic region (later joined by Japan), the Chinese lack of the characteristic mechanisms of these newly powerful entities worked to the severe detriment of its own autonomy, whether defined in terms of state, popular or cultural sovereignty. The mainstream of political thought in the late-nineteenth- and early-twentieth-century China, then, revolved around questions having to do with how to construct a powerful nation-state rather than critiques of its abuses.[42] Even the oft-maligned Qing imperial government in the years between 1860 and 1911, deficient as it frequently showed itself to be, proved more often than not to be the protector of last resort against the depredations of European imperialism. Modern Chinese political thought has, then, never been as quick to point out the theoretical deficiencies of the modern state as have leftist thinkers in Europe and America. Wang Hui is no exception here, phrasing his defense of the state and its capacity as a necessary device for protection against the full force of an unnatural multinational capital.

Wang does seem more than a bit nostalgic about the pre-1979 days when China played a prominent position as a leader of the Third World, and he sounds a note of bitter irony when observing in section 1 of his essay on the 1989 social movement that by the time of the American bombing of the Chinese embassy in Belgrade in 1999, none of China's erstwhile allies, acquired so painstakingly over more than two decades following the Bandung conference of nonaligned nations in 1955, rallied to China's cause. While it would be easy enough to write this nostalgia off as yet another lament about lost Chinese glory, or as simply another offshoot of the nationalism that has been a major current on the contemporary Chinese intellectual scene,[43] I do not think that is what motivates Wang here. Rather, his concern is part of his general effort to overthrow the hegemony of the idea of "the end of history," which he sees as reducing the world to an unjust, relentless, and sterile uniformity. It is an expression of regret for the diminution of political alternatives represented by the collapse of the nonaligned movement, which—weak as it most often was—was committed theoretically to working out modes of existence that diverged from the unitary model for the future provided by the rich and powerful capitalist nations clustered around the shores of the North Atlantic.

There is in Wang Hui's essay a consistent undertone of implied critique of the United States and its basic policy thrust of recent years, as when he says in section 2 that "[t]hose who monopolize the strength of the whole world in the name of globalism are actually the biggest nationalists." His criticism is not any simple denunciation of general American hegemony, but rather a specific judgment against "an American-led neoliberalism," which he interprets as "a sort of hypernationalism masquerading as globalism" (see section 3). To the extent, then, that such ideas as "the end of history" are little more than thinly disguised expressions of American triumphalism, Wang announces his opposition to them.

If nothing else, I hope that readers of Wang Hui's "The 1989 Social Movement" will come away with a sense of the diversity and richness of intellectual debate that has developed in China in recent years. The essay represents the best summary of probably the most contentious and best known of the many discussions that have been joined after 1989, albeit necessarily partial and told from an unabashedly partisan perspective.[44] It is clear from even a cursory reading that our old vision of China as a monolithic governmental entity opposed by an almost equally simplistic—if heroic—intellectual resistance to it has been obsolete for at least the past decade. To give only one example of the consequences of the rethinking of Chinese history that has gone on in recent years, there have been a number of voices speaking out against May Fourth, that intellectual and political movement that began in the late 1910s and was in good part characterized by a widespread advocacy of following Western ways. Some of these revisionary voices in opposition have spoken in a notably conservative register deploring that iconoclastic movement's well-known denunciations of traditional Chinese thought. For their part, the liberals who are also opponents of the Party despotism have defended May Fourth out of an instinctive sense of the need for openness to the world. So far, the sides are clear enough. Once one throws the Communist Party into the mix, however, the putative clarity of affiliation vanishes, as the Party counts May Fourth as being at the very fount of its own history and thus spares no verbiage in extolling the merits of its inevitability. Are we to suppose, then, that the liberals and the Party view history from the same perspective? Clearly this is not the case, at least in any straightforward fashion, but what we very evidently have here is a highly nuanced situation in which it is impossible to create hard and fast, inclusive or exclusive narratives of the course of modern Chinese history.

It must be said that Wang Hui is hardly alone in demonstrating the problems that surround the definitions and popular understandings of the various social processes that have been at work in China since 1992.[45] This difficulty has afflicted scholars and observers outside China, who have only been able to offer partial explanations of a complex situation. In the *Wall Street Journal* in February of 2002, for instance, the conservative commentator Michael Ledeen postulated that what was emerging in China was neofascism, or actually "a maturing fascist regime," something he was quick to admit "is hard to recognize."[46] Aside from alerting us to possible political trends throughout the neoliberal world order, this analysis does have the merit of demonstrating how problematic it has become to adequately characterize the system of bureaucratic capitalism that has been emerging in China. However, not only does Ledeen overestimate the extent of Chinese corporatism in the construction of the new economy, he also rather neatly sidesteps the issue of charismatic leadership, something that has been in conspicuous shortage over the past decade in China, but equally something the Italian and German examples he cites as precedents completely depended on for their popular legitimacy.

The difficulty of achieving clear definition has also afflicted the sinological community. For example, in an otherwise well-documented and clearly argued book published in 2001, the perceptive China scholar and observer of the contemporary Chinese intellectual scene Joseph Fewsmith lumped all critics of the neoliberal consensus together as "postmodernists,"[47] a conflation of what Wang Hui's essay shows to be a number of quite distinct categories. It is in its ability to avoid the temptation to reductionism that Wang's thick description of recent events and intellectual positions shows itself to greatest advantage. These examples of careless pigeonholing also serve as case studies that help explain why Wang is so concerned that Chinese intellectuals construct their own vision of the world and escape being defined by others.

It would be easy for Western critics who have taken the "linguistic turn" to dismiss the intellectual scene in contemporary China, so desperately concerned as it is to deal pragmatically with a set of crises so clearly in view, as derivative and theoretically naive.[48] Before we are even tempted to do this, however, we must also keep in mind the stakes involved in these various attempts to define the historical pathways and future possibilities open to China. To get some idea of them, we need only recall the ferocity of the "culture war" debates that took place in the United States during the 1990s concerning the interpretation of American history, into which, it must be said, politicians and intellectuals with extremely close political connections were not shy about intervening. And these American debates were not even over fundamental issues of national economic and social structure as the disputes have been in China. To the extent that these debates are concerned with the future of the national polity in China, they continue the dispute over the narrative of national history that has been at issue for the past century and more. Given the political and ideological instability in China over that long period, it should be no surprise how fraught with tension and moment the debate has been, and will continue to be. And given the speed and extent to which Chinese society is being transformed, and to which China's impact on the world is increasing, it is hard to overestimate the debate's significance.

Finally, in the essay on the 1989 social movement there would seem to be an apparent contradiction between, on the one hand, Wang Hui's powerful condemnation of the basic thrust of Chinese reform since 1985 as having moved the country toward being thoroughly embedded in the new globalized order and, on the other, his rejection of even the most remote possibility of the realization of the liberal dream that China is proceeding gradually and inexorably toward becoming more like the advanced capitalist countries, of which the United States is the preeminent example, and that this progression will solve most of its problems. One might ask, if circumstances will not allow China to end up blindly falling into a foreign mold, has not China already, then, de facto taken its fate into its own hands? What Wang Hui is actually saying, however, is this: the notion that China is heading toward an American—or "posthistorical"—future is precisely what has justified a series of moves creating social destabilization and injustice in Chinese society, and that some notion can only continue to do so. The neoliberal end that justifies these unhappy means is, strictly speaking, utopian, in that it can never be brought into existence. This, then, is the fundamental difference between Wang Hui and the neoliberals. While his critics might accuse Wang of utopianism in his holding out against a posthistorical conclusion that they regard as guaranteed by the historical record of the rest of the world (or, at least, the wealthier parts of it), the accusation of utopianism can be even more powerfully made against the neoliberal vision. Its implementation—deferred indefinitely behind what Wang refers to as "the myth of transition" at the beginning of section 1—

is no more certain than his own admitted inability to foresee the future, but to simply subscribe to a ready-made idea of economic progress demonstrates a paucity of imagination in the face of unprecedented challenge. Such failure of imagination can only open the way to even greater restrictions on envisioning creative solutions to China's myriad problems.

THE 1989 SOCIAL
MOVEMENT AND THE
HISTORICAL ROOTS
OF CHINA'S
NEOLIBERALISM

Translated by

Theodore Huters

It seems as if the twentieth century ended a bit early, in 1989, although history has continued to move on ever since. The events in Beijing of that year triggered the disintegration of the Soviet Union and Eastern Europe and inaugurated the political and economic structure by which neoliberalism came to dominate the globe. Chinese society did not undergo the same disintegration as the Soviet Union and Eastern Europe, and the social transformation in China was therefore characterized by a certain continuity. Were we to sum up this process in a simple and thus incomplete fashion, we could say that under the continuation of the system of state political power, Chinese society has pushed forward a process of market extremism, and under the guidance of state policy has become an active participant in the world economic system. The dual nature of this combination of continuity and discontinuity has defined the nature of Chinese neoliberalism. Neoliberalism depends on the force of national and supranational policy and economic power; it has also relied on a theoretical discourse centered on formalist economics in order to establish its discursive hegemony. Its apolitical or even antipolitical features (or its antihistorical method and antagonism to traditional socialist ideology) cannot in the slightest obscure the fact of its solid connection with state economic policy. Without these policy and political premises, neoliberalism would have no way to conceal the reality of unemployment, the disappearance of social security, the increase in the number of the poor, and other such features of social division behind the myth of "transition."

"Transition" is the crucial unspoken premise of the contemporary discourse on Chinese society—it presupposes a necessary connection between the process of current inequality and an ultimate ideal. Because of this, to use the existence of state interference as a way to avoid recognizing the hegemony of neoliberalism is completely beside the point. The hegemonic status of Chinese neoliberalism took shape as part of the process by which the state used economic liberalization to overcome its crisis of legitimacy. On the theoretical level, such discursive narratives as "neo-Authoritarianism," "neoconservatism," "classical liberalism," market extremism, national modernization, and historical narratives such as the various sorts of accounts of nationalism that most closely approximate the narrative of modernization all had close relationships of one sort or another with the constitution of neoliberalism. The successive displacement of these terms for one another (or even the contradictions among them) demonstrates the shifts in the structure of power in both contemporary China and the contemporary world at large.

Neoliberalism is a dominating discursive formation and ideology that has no capacity to describe actual social and economic relations, but neither is it unconnected to actual social and economic relations. As an ideology imbricated with national policy, the practical thought of the intellectuals, as well as the values of the media, it uses concepts concerned with "transition" and "development" to patch up its internal contradictions. Therefore, the most effective way to reveal the internal contradictions within neoliberalism is to establish the historical connections between its theoretical discourse (such as the free market, development, globalization, common prosperity, private property rights, and the like) and actual social developments. This will explain the complicated relationship between its pronouncements and its actual practice. It is clear that in different parts of the contemporary world, such as North America, Western Europe, Russia, and China, neoliberalism has its own historical roots and social patterns. These differences in historical circumstance have determined that there is no way to adduce convincing conclusions by merely summing up the character of neoliberalism at an abstract level.

One of the goals of this essay is to reveal though historical analysis the particular indigenous and international factors, the national policy implications, the ideological situation, and the atmosphere of both local and world public opinion that enabled neoliberalism to attain its distinctive discursive hegemony. It will also analyze the various forms of Chinese liberalism and their internal contradictions, as well as the theoretical explorations and practical critiques that have unfolded from issues surrounding neoliberalism. The practical critiques and social movements aimed at neoliberalism have included a number of key elements that are mutually contradictory—some radical, some moderate, and some conservative. In my opinion, the principal task of the progressive forces in contemporary China is to prevent these critiques from developing in a conservative direction (which would include attempts to move back to the old system), and also to push strongly to urge the transformation of these elements into a driving force seeking broader democracy and freedom in both China and the world. What needs to be explained is how the economic reforms that took place between 1978 and 1989 represented a transformation on a very broad scale—to describe them as "revolutionary" would not overstate the case. This short essay will not be able to capture the full extent of the achievements and the accompanying internal crisis of this period, nor will it be able to describe in detail the progress of the 1989 social movement—in fact, each detail touched on here would require the testimony of experts and meticulous factual investigation. What I propose to do here is only to reconstruct and comprehend the historical horizon of the issues facing China via a preliminary examination of the bases of the 1989 social movement, something I need to announce before I begin.

The Historical Conditions of the 1989 Social Movement and the Antihistorical Explanation of "Neoliberalism"

1

The 1989 social movement had a profound influence not just on China but on the whole world. No matter whether in China or abroad, in official propaganda or in analysis and accounts written for a foreign audience, by far the greater part of the discussion of this event has focused either on the student movement and the deliberations of the intellectuals or has centered on the process of deciding policy at the highest political level. Even analysis of the so-called civil society has concentrated mainly on economic entities like the Stone Company or on the part played by "groupings"[1] of Beijing intellectuals during the course of the movement. The 1989 movement, however, was an instance of large-scale social mobilization; its spontaneity and ubiquity indicate that the movement had social origins vastly more powerful than any direct organization would have been capable of. The 1980s movement for intellectual liberation and enlightenment in reality had a powerful effect on the dissolution of the old ideology and on providing the intellectual raw material for rebellion.

Taken as a group, however, the intellectuals not only lacked the capacity to provide practical social goals, but they also never understood the full extent of the social mobilization that had taken place. This was partly because, as an intellectual movement critical of the practices of state socialism, the social thought of the 1980s could neither perceive nor comprehend the social contradictions peculiar to the times. Neither could it understand the socialist tendencies inhering within the grassroots social movement nor transcend the intellectual blinders imposed by Cold War ideology. It is necessary to distinguish between two conceptions of socialism: one is the "socialism" of the old state ideology, characterized by a system of state monopoly; the other is the movement for social security that developed out of that system of state monopoly and the expansion of the market system, characterized by its opposition to monopoly and its demands for social democracy.[2] In a post–Cold War international context and in an atmosphere of reflection on "socialist" practice, this movement toward preserving social security that was so deeply embedded within the contradictions of society, opposed to monopoly and seeking democracy, has not been fully comprehended. My understanding of the 1989 social movement is based on the following three points of departure:

First, between the mid-1980s and 1989 many student movements took place in mainland China (including the movement at the end of 1986 that brought about the departure from office of Hu Yaobang).[3] All of these movements, however, were small in scale and did not lead to broad social mobilization. Given this background, why did the student movement sparked by the death of Hu Yaobang [on April 15, 1989] bring about such broad participation and mobilization at all levels of society and on a national scale? Why, also, starting in the beginning of May did national news organizations such as Central Television, *The People's Daily*, the New China News Agency, *Guangming Daily*, and the like proceed to engage in large-scale reporting of the movement? This reached the point that there came to be a "period of freedom of the press" within the organs of state propaganda that was rare in modern Chinese history, which in turn played a major role in providing the motive power for this mobilization of the whole nation and society.

Second, what was the nature of the relationship between the appeals of the student movement and those from other sectors of society? I raise this issue because the 1989 movement was not exclusively a student movement, but instead a broad social movement—

participants included workers, individual entrepreneurs, state cadres, teachers, and other social groups. Even officials from the Central Party apparatus, from the various ministries and committees that form the State Council, the National People's Congress, and from the various organs of the National People's Consultative Committee (including such "mouthpieces" as *The People's Daily*, the New China News Agency, and *Guangming Daily*) took part. In general, then, it is possible to say that, aside from the agricultural classes, which did not participate directly, all other levels of society—especially people from the large and medium-sized cities—became involved in this movement. It is not difficult to understand why the intellectuals, the workers, and other social groups took part, but why did there transpire at the same time a struggle of the state against the state, or, more accurately, internal contradictions within the functioning of the state (that is to say, contradictions between the state apparatus as a whole and some of its constituent parts that arose out of power relations, conflicts of interest, and differences in values)?

Third, why were there critiques of the process of reform itself even as the various levels of society generally supported reform? Who, or what sort of social condition, was the object of the critiques? What factors constituted the ideology of the social mobilization?

In order to be able to respond clearly to the above questions, it is first necessary to review briefly the progress of reform in China after 1978. The social reforms that took place between 1978 and 1989 can be broken into two main stages: the agricultural reforms of the period between 1978 and 1984, and the urban reforms that have taken place thereafter. The achievements of the reforms between 1978 and 1984 or 1985 were concentrated on rural problems, the core of which lay in a partial transformation of the dual social structure, in which there is an "urban–rural divide" and the social position of urban residents is generally higher than that of those who live in rural areas.[4] These reforms had two principal effects: (1) the dispersal of the People's Communes via a state-sponsored equal redistribution of their land and the implementation of the household contract responsibility system;[5] and (2) raising the price of agricultural commodities via adjustments to state policies, and encouraging a diversified rural economy through the development of rural enterprises and the relaxation of the institutionally imposed difference between city and country that had been a feature of the Maoist period's policies of urban industrialization. Because of these, the income differential between city and country gradually diminished between 1978 and 1985.

The achievements of the two reforms mentioned above accompanied the gradual relaxation of smaller market relations, but from a fundamental perspective, they were based on the experience of traditional Chinese land distribution and the principle of equality. We can sum these up as the negation of the state monopoly that characterized the commune system in favor of the forms of "small farmer socialism." The resulting increase in the initiative of the rural population lay in a new flexibility in production and the reduction of the urban–rural income gap rather than stemming purely from the liberation of markets. Through the adjustment of the prices of agricultural commodities, the state was able to provide security in small local markets (that is, the transparent markets that Ferdinand Braudel has discussed as being distinct from "market economics") and to diminish the inequality between city and country. And because urban market reform had yet to begin, for the moment small rural markets were not incorporated into an urban-based system of market relations. In an environment of low productivity, a limited surplus of products, and an undeveloped urban commodity economy, and in a process of rural reform where a relatively small discrepancy between rich and poor was based on the premise of a trend toward equality between city and country, the result was little rural bankruptcy or sharp social upheaval.[6] The market was merely one of the key factors in the rural reform of the 1980s, and at the time there was an economist who used the phrase "developing agriculture largely depends on government policy" to summarize the situation with respect to agricultural reform, something largely in accord with the ways things actually were.[7]

The process of rural reform described above allows us to understand the basic background to the urban reforms begun in 1984 even as it provides the historical circumstances behind urban economic development and its predicament. Urban reform has been myriad in scope, but most people take its core to have been the introduction of market mechanisms. From the perspective of its actual social implications, however, the core is really "the devolution of political and economic power" *(fangquan rangli)* a process by which relations of social advantage were reorganized under state direction by the transfer and apportionment of resources that had previously been directly controlled and distributed by the state itself.[8] According to research findings, in the twenty-six years between 1953 and 1978, state revenue as a percentage of national income averaged 34.2 percent (it was 37.2 percent in 1978). It decreased annually beginning in 1979, reaching a low of only 19.3 percent in 1988. With state revenue shrinking and extrabudgetal funds increasing substantially, local governments gained the benefits of increased autonomy and more control over allocation of funds.[9] The theft of tax receipts, tax evasion, the proliferation of compulsory exactions, local governmental control of bank loans, and even the growth of large-scale smuggling were by-products of the process described above.[10]

The focal point of urban reform was the reform of state-owned enterprises, which led from increasing the autonomy of large enterprises (that is, the state devolved a portion of its rights to the enterprise itself) to the closure, temporary stoppage, consolidation, or transfer and finally to changes in management rights and the transformation of the relations of production themselves. Under the pressures presented by layoffs and unemployment, the state had no choice but to adopt—at least temporarily—policies that favored consolidation and transfer over those of stoppage and closure, but the basic policy thrust did not change. Urban reform is evidently more complex than rural reform, for two principal reasons. First, estimating the value of land and other rural production factors is vastly less difficult than estimating the value of industrial resources. The redistribution of industrial resources has extremely complicated technical and structural implications that touch on various differences having to do with professional standing, division of labor, and region (and the inequalities that stem from these). Even more importantly, the redistribution of rural land was premised on the family responsibility production system, which, nominally at least, left land ownership in the hands of the state, whereas the process of the redistribution of industrial resources brought about genuine privatization.

This leads to the second reason, that the systems of ownership on which rural and urban industrial reform were based are completely different. In the original industrial system, the state based its allocation of resources on a plan, but the ownership of the resources, economic benefits, and collective or individual income had no connection with one another (for instance, large-scale state-owned factories had the advantage of a monopoly of resources, but the differences in income between employees in these units was more or less the same as the differences in income of employees of other, collectively run small factories). When the state began to forgo the right to absolute control in the industrial and commercial realms, however, what had originally been an unequal distribution of industrial resources was immediately transformed into income inequality. In this sense, the implications of the reform of urban industry are not limited to the question of ownership of the enterprises, but extend to the entirety of the national economic system. Under these complicated circumstances, the lack of appropriate democratic supervision and elaborate technical cooperation as well as the failure to cultivate a corresponding economic system caused the redistribution of resources and property to lead inevitably to serious social inequalities. These various factors explain why the urban reforms did not bring about the same equality in principle as the early rural reforms. This process resulted in various threats to the status and benefits accruing to workers and even to state employees. According to sociological research, these threats manifested themselves in the form of decline in economic status, stratification within organizations, the regression of benefits to labor, and the failure to maintain social insurance for the old, the young, the sick, the disabled, and the pregnant.[11]

Between 1985 and 1989 Chinese economists carried on a series of debates over what they referred to as "reform" (the relatively rapid reform of property rights) and "adjustment" (the adjustment of the structure of the economy under the auspices of the national government). They also debated the question of whether these reforms should be led by price reform (that is, to reform the old system of planned pricing by introducing market relations) or by the reform of the system of national ownership (that is, to carry out the large scale privatization of state-owned enterprises).[12] One of the reasons for these debates was that, from 1985 on, the Chinese economy witnessed persistent inflation and economic disruption, and if there had not been appropriate price adjustments and the cultivation of suitable market conditions, the reform of the system of state ownership would have led to large-scale social instability. The upshot of these debates was that the advocates of constructing market mechanisms through the introduction of price reform and the simultaneous implementation of enterprise reform (primarily through the contract system) gained the upper hand. This path to reform was generally successful because the functioning of price adjustment served to suppress the monopolistic quality of the traditional system, activated market mechanisms and limited the course of so-called spontaneous privatization. Comparisons to the scheme of "privatization" that took place in Russia put the Chinese process in a very favorable light.

There was, however, an internal crisis inhering in this process, which gave rise to continuing social problems. From the perspective of the market environment, this reform created a "two-track system" of pricing as a condition of the transition (that is, prices fixed by the national plan and market pricing existed at the same time, with the former pricing mechanisms concentrated in the means of production—including the means of production left over after quotas in the national plan had been fulfilled—and the latter concentrated in the pricing of consumer goods). The simultaneous existence of planned pricing and market pricing provided perfect conditions for corruption and official peculation (that is, for officials or official organizations manipulating the pricing system for speculation and price gouging). From the perspective of enterprise reform, this restructuring was meant to be led by instituting the contract system and separating politics from the enterprises themselves, but the latter was extremely difficult to implement in the absence of the transformation of the political system. What actually happened was that, under the slogan of separating politics and enterprise, what became separated were not the links between politics and economics, but those between ownership and management. In this confused process of the transition of power, a significant amount of national property "legally" and illegally was transferred to the personal economic advantage of a small minority.

Many economists refer to 1988 as "the year of the contract," because the contract system was extended from contracts for individual enterprises to contracts for foreign investment, contracts for government departments, financial contracts, and the like. Enterprises, localities, and [central] government departments used their positions under the old system to gain even greater individual advantage. This process exacerbated the contradictions brought about by two-track pricing: localities and interest groups used their power and various other means to maneuver products out of the planned system (that is, into the market), which brought about inflation and severe disproportion in social allocation.[13] Under the contract system, some of the most frequently observed forms of corruption included tax theft and tax evasion, kickbacks, misuse of public funds, and the exchange of money for official favor (such as accepting bribes for the allocation of contracts). Since the reforms began, the purchasing power of enterprises has continued to rise and the increase in the total amount of cash bonuses has continued without interruption, bringing about imbalance between aggregate demand and supply, a situation the central government has lacked sufficient fiscal resources to control. In June of 1988 the government with great fanfare announced it would cut the Gordian knot on pricing by gradually phasing out planned prices and moving toward market pricing, but the result was a flurry of panic buying and social instability. In the period that followed, the government had no choice but to move toward a policy of greater government control, which had, in any case, begun before this. The upshot, however, brought about contradictions between the state and its own creations—local and Beijing-based governmental interest groups.[14]

At the same time that the reforms of this phase were achieving some success, they also brought about certain changes that from an alternative perspective reflected new conditions of social inequality. These changes were the catalyst for the 1989 social mobilization. First, the "dual tracking" and marketization of power created inequalities of distribution and "rent-seeking" behavior that resulted from the sudden wealth brought about by the manipulation of the differences between the two price tracks. Through the exchange of power for money, public property in its entirety was thus placed in the pockets of the "rent seekers."[15] In 1988 alone, the differences between the two levels of prices in the two systems (that is, "rent") reached almost ¥357 billion, amounting to almost 30 percent of the national income that year.[16] This provided the basis for the formation of local and Beijing-based governmental interest groups, and was also the major source of systemic corruption in the 1990s. As part of this process, the conflicts of interest between the central and local governments sharpened considerably.

Second, the income levels of the various strata of the urban population began to polarize quite dramatically, something particularly apparent in the decline in income of the working class and the advent of the crisis of layoffs and unemployment; discussions about the "iron rice bowl" [that is, lifetime job tenure] system began to appear frequently in the newspapers. Third, owing to the adjustments to the taxation system and the marketization of power, the structure of the business stratum began to change, with the economic benefits accruing to the original individual entrepreneurs (the so-called individual households, *geti hu*) diminishing—this was the basis for the support given by this group to the 1989 student movement. Fourth, reforms in social benefits like housing, medical care, and wages were not implemented on a large scale, while inflation and a general sense of social insecurity created discontent not only among the wage- and salary-earning strata, but also influenced the daily lives of many public employees (that is, officials). (This was especially true in the case of the disparity between the incomes of ordinary public employees and other groups, and even more so in the extreme polarization between those public employees who had entered into market activities and those who had not).[17] It is worth noting that the 1989 social movement was essentially urban based, and it was intrinsically linked with the history of the market expansion that constituted the phase of what was called the "urban reform" that began in 1984.

We should not, however, overlook another background condition of this movement: the advance of urban reform and the hobbling of reform in the countryside (expressed most acutely in such matters as the pricing system, the household registration system, the system of employment insurance, ecological issues, and in matters of basic social organization) drove the differentiation of city and country to even higher levels. Between 1985 and 1989 rural incomes had already begun to decline, but rural society had not yet become enmeshed in the market process and the predicaments associated with it, and the "floating population"[18] in the cities had yet to reach the scale it has today. This stratum did not participate in the social movement of the period.

Social stability in the 1980s was built on the effective control of the state over society, although this power to control cannot be simplistically understood as only a matter of state coercion. In this period, with the state implementing economic reform and the intellectuals directly participating in it, as well as supplying its intellectual rationale, there was a grassroots sense (particularly among the rural population) of having benefited from the reform; the interaction of these three factors provided the 1980s reform with its legitimacy. A new situation had, however, come into existence by 1989. First, conflicts of interest had appeared among various government departments, social strata, and power centers and between the center and the localities. Second, internal differentiation within the country produced differentiation among the intellectuals: the intellectuals who participated directly in the process of formulating reform policy and its ideological propagation had, in fact, been part of the state system all along and were thus extremely sensitive to differentiation within it.[19] On the other hand, the internal differentiation of the nation included the transformation of state functions and alterations in the social division of labor such that there have been major changes in employment choice and social attitudes.

Third, the urban population has been directly affected by the possible loss of social benefits via the process of reform, and they thus no longer believe naively in the myth of reform (even though they still regard it in a basically affirmative light). Fourth, because of the extension of urban reform and further change in urban–rural relations, a new crisis began to evince itself in rural society. The elements mentioned above combined to produce a serious crisis of legitimacy: not only a legitimacy crisis in regard to the state that continued to maintain a number of features of economic planning, but a legitimacy crisis in regard to the state that was in transition to a market society. Rather than say that these doubts were the result of the aftereffects of a planned economy,[20] it would be more accurate to say that they were directed at the legitimacy of the allocation of benefits carried out in the name of reform (asking whose benefit the state represented in this), the legitimacy of the order of the allocation process (asking on what basis and in what order would it be administered and supervised, and whether or not it would be done legally), and the like.

All of these constituted the basic social conditions underlying the 1989 social movement and mobilization. The essential demands of the student movement and of the intellectuals were the implementation of political democracy, media freedom, and freedom of speech and association, as well as the establishment the rule of law (as opposed to the "rule of man," *renzhi*) and other such constitutional rights, in addition to the demand that the state recognize the legitimacy of the movement itself (that is, as a patriotic student movement). People from all areas of society supported these demands, but invested them with even more specific social content: that is opposition to official corruption and peculation, opposition to the "princely party" (that is, those scions of the elite with special privileges), demand for price stability and the "return of Yangpu" (a place on the southern island province of Hainan that had been leased at extraordinarily low cost to foreign interests), demands for social security and fairness, as well as a general request for democratic means to supervise the fairness of the reform process and the reorganization of social benefits. The issue that must be faced squarely is this: the 1989 social mobilization was criticizing the traditional system, but what it encountered was not the old state, but rather a state that was promoting reform, or a state that was moving gradually toward a market society, along with the results of this policy. I make this distinction (that is, between the old state and the state promoting reform) not to deny the connections between the two, but rather to point out how social conditions and the functions of the state had been transformed.

The actual situation was thus: the state promoting market reform and social transformation still relied for its rule on the political legacy and ideological forms of the past. The discord between the promotion of market reform and the old ideology created a crisis of state legitimacy from two different directions: on the one hand, people could rely on the nature of state economic policy to criticize the legitimacy of the state ideology and its method or rule, while on the other they could use the ideology of socialism to take issue with the legitimacy of the new state economic policy. The socialist state put priority on equality in ideology and in the distribution of benefits, but through coercion and planning it maintained structural inequality between city and country, between different economic systems, and between different regions. Under conditions of reform, however, this structural inequality quickly transformed itself into disparities in income among different classes, social strata, and regions, leading rapidly to social polarization. In the end, actual differences between two distinct kinds of state could not efface their very real historical connections.

As a movement for social self-protection, the 1989 social movement embodied a spontaneous resistance to inequalities springing from the growth of markets, but as a movement of social protest, it continued the 1980s critique of the leviathan state and its means of rule.[21] Just as the differentiation between the state types described above does not imply the existence of two distinct states, so was the social protest movement a complex social phenomenon. In this context, there are complexities worthy of particular note: participating in the 1989 social movement were a number of interest groups that had benefited greatly from a reform process characterized by the devolution of political and economic power. Because of their dissatisfaction with the adjustment policies then coming into effect, these interest groups sought to incorporate into the movement their own demands for even more radical privatization. These groups were not just the products of the reform era, but were also the direct expression of the relationships of exchange between the marketplace and political power that characterized the reform period. As a result, their demands unfolded in the space between the upper reaches of the government and the social movement itself. By pouring in funds, remonstrating with the higher levels of the government, and passing on information between the government and the movement they succeeded in using the social movement to push the state power structure in directions that would advance their personal or group interests. (There is no harm here in considering the effects the Kanghua and Sitong companies had on the movement.)[22]

The same phenomenon occurred among certain intellectuals who had close relationships with government authorities: they sought to use the movement, particularly the student movement, to influence power relationships within the government.[23] In 1989, divisions within the state had a close relationship with the proliferation of interest groups within the state itself. Within the Chinese discursive context, the ideology of what is now referred to as "neoliberalism" had already begun to germinate, with its core content being the intensification of reforms calling for greater devolution of political and economic power and the contract system, the furtherance of a comprehensive course of spontaneous privatization under the guiding premise of a lack of democratic guarantees, and the legitimization through legislative means of the polarization of classes and interests created by these individual efforts.

Because of this, the principal embodiment of neoliberalism (also called "neoconservatism") lay in the benefits accruing to social groups through the process of the creation of interest groups within the state structure. A number of its tenets had become official reform policy via the mediation of intertwined administrative and economic power. The legitimization crisis that threatened this market extremism was expressed as "neo-authoritarianism" and neoconservatism [that is, the use of state authority and elites to further the radical expansion of the market], which also appeared as neoliberalism from the perspective of the movement for a transnational market. There was, in fact, a certain transition involved here, or, perhaps more accurately, a shift of power and authority: given that the state has a role to play in offering protection, keeping things in check, and making adjustments during the course of the ongoing rush of globalization and expansion of internal markets, a certain number of groups no longer naively placed their faith in the government alone to provide impetus for market expansion, instead thinking that the power of both transnational and indigenous capital could be used to restructure China's markets and its society.

This, then, is the hidden background behind the mutual entanglement between neoliberalism and neo-authoritarianism. In this sense, certain of the contradictions between neoliberalism and the state were entirely different from the relationships between the state and liberalism in the nineteenth and early twentieth centuries, neoliberalism being the product of new relations of interest. Under severe social pressure, conflicts over the path of reform and over matters of interest among the central government, local governments, and interest groups representing various government departments were quite common—these conflicts were reflected in the continuing policy debates over reform and readjustment. Add to this the complicated and conflictual relations between nation, locality, and interest groups in an environment of globalization, and neoliberalism had often to take recourse to notions of "popular," "society," and "markets," both to be able to influence national reform policy as well as to play up its opposition to "a planned economy," "communism," or the "autocratic" state in the foreign media—particularly the Hong Kong, Taiwan, and American media. The most one can say about the conflict between the Chinese version of neoliberalism and the ultraconservative state ideological apparatus is that it reflects an internal contradiction in the functioning of the state. While neoliberalism takes every opportunity to cast itself in the image of "resister," this does not prove that this ideology of the market is in actual opposition to the practical operations of the state: on the contrary, the state and neoliberalism exist in a complex relationship of codependence. Thus the ambiguity and duality within the Chinese discourse of neoliberalism, which has by now become the hegemonic ideology globally. In this sense, the repudiation of the self-characterization of neoliberalism should not be understood as the repudiation of the "popular," "society," or "markets," but understood rather as the repudiation of monopolization, whether of markets, society, or of the populace. The purpose of this reflection on neoliberalism is to provide a theoretical basis for the practical possibility of a democratic system of markets and a self-regulating society, as well as the fostering of popular strength.[24]

As set out above, the crisis of the traditional planned economy is changing into a crisis of newly monopolized market relations. The social contradictions of 1989 should not be understood as the state promoting reform and various elements of society opposing it, but rather as people demanding even greater reform, given the decline of the old system. The crux of the problem lay in specifying the shape that reform would take. Regardless of whether we are talking about students, intellectuals, or any others who participated in the movement in support of reform (political or economic) and demands for democracy, their hopes for and understanding of reform were extraordinarily diverse. When looked at from a broader or synthetic perspective, however, the reforms the greater part of the populace hoped for and their ideals of democracy and rule by law were for the purpose of guaranteeing social justice and the democratization of economic life through the restructuring of politics and the legal system. They did not wish for a set of political procedures and legal stipulations that were intended merely to demonstrate the legitimacy of carving up social assets as they existed at the time.

There was a fundamental conflict between these popular demands and the demands by interest groups for radical privatization that were just then beginning to be formulated and extended, even though this conflict was not fully understood at the time. The latter immediately condemned the demand for social equality as a call for absolute equality or as moral idealism and, under the pretext of denouncing these as residues of the Cultural Revolution and of socialism, they took away the justification for social protest. The complicated circumstances described above should partially explain why some of the various groups that had benefited from the reform process took part in the social movement and why even many state officials and members of state organizations marched out onto Chang'an Boulevard and participated in some of the demonstrations and protests. From this perspective, it can be seen how difficult it would be to explain the nature of the 1989 social movement as being simply a matter of pro- and antireform.

From the analysis set out above, we can see that, in general, the mobilizing ideological elements of the 1989 movement included the values of democracy and freedom, as well as a notion of the equality of everyday life; in this particular period the ideology of traditional socialism was transformed into a force for the mobilization of social critique. In regard to the widespread participation of various segments of society, this final factor becomes extremely important, if extremely easy to overlook—it penetrates to the core of our daily existence. Because of this, I see a multiplicity of significance in the 1989 social movement: it was a farewell to the old era and at the same time a protest against the inherent social contradictions of the new; it was (for students and intellectuals) an appeal for democracy and freedom, even as it was (for the workers and other urban dwellers) a demand for social equality and justice. These demands for democracy that took the form of a multifaceted movement provide a broad-based explanation of the situation that existed at the time.

However, because of Cold War ideology, because of state violence and the legitimation crisis it brought about, because the student and intellectual movements lacked a thorough understanding of the historical developments described above, and because of the collusive links between the most conservative wing of the movement (namely, the interest groups created through reliance on the transfer of power during the course of privatization) and the world forces of neoliberalism, the interpretation of the 1989 social movement in the world at large has developed in a direction advantageous to those interest groups advocating radical privatization. This group has used its status as real "radical reformers" to mask its complicated relations with state power and various interest groups, to mask the true interests at stake in this process, and to present itself to the world as a progressive force moving toward the world market and democracy.

The Tiananmen incident that took place on June 4, 1989, shook the world, and in its wake initiated the collapse of Eastern Europe and the Soviet Union. With the end of the cold war came "the end of history." The upheaval of 1989 revealed the signs of social disintegration, and, with this as backdrop, the state took stability as the premise of its own legitimacy. Because the state apparatus of violence came to be regarded as the sole force for maintaining stability, it eventually obscured the crisis of state legitimacy that had gradually come into being since the onset of the reforms. The basic historical fact (or par-

adox) was that while governmental economic policy had brought
about social upheaval, the need for stability following the upheaval
became the justification for state power to expand into society. As a
result, neoliberalism's notion of "self-regulation" (and its concomitant rejection of state interference) ultimately turned into a require-
ment for control and interference. After the violence of 1989, people's concern for the social movement focused on the events of June
Fourth, the dissolution of the Soviet Union and Eastern Europe, and
the conclusion of the Cold War. The historical conditions and basic
demands that brought the movement into existence were set to one
side, and the historical possibilities implicit in the movement vanished
along with the movement itself. As was made clear above, the 1989
social movement originated out of general protest against the unequal devolution of political and economic power, out of dissatisfaction of local and Beijing-based interest groups with the central government's policies of adjustment, out of internal splits within the
state, and out of the conflictual relations between the state apparatus
and various social groups.

Taking the 1989 media as an example, it is telling to ask why the
social mobilization and its democratic demands were able to seep into
the state-controlled media. I believe there were three key factors.
First, power conflicts among political cliques, the inherent contradiction between state economic policy and the state ideology, and the
dispersal of central and local government interests rendered it impossible for the media to develop a unified perspective on the movement
as it developed.[25] Second, once the media had widely disseminated
the news, social mobilization reached an unprecedented breadth, resulting in the state's inability to exercise its traditional methods of
controlling the press. Third, there was a subtle overlap between the
movement's demands for democracy and equality and state ideology
(were this not the case, it would be difficult to understand why the
student movement established as a condition that the state recognize
it as a "patriotic movement"), which conferred on it a certain legitimacy. These three factors created a kind of instability to the interac-

tion between the social movement and the state. In other words, the brief period of press freedom and open discussion that came into being in May of 1989 was premised on power interactions among the state, interest groups, and various social strata, and its collapse was correspondingly based on the collapse of the balance of social power among those entities. The direct cause of the movement's failure was violent suppression by the state. However, the indirect cause lay in the movement's own inability to bridge the gap between its demands for political democracy and the demands for social equality that had been its mobilizing force. It was thus unable to create secure social power and to move toward institutionalizing the weak interacting social forces described above.

If we examine the 1989 social movement from the perspective of the expanding system of internal and international markets, then the demands of the movement in many respects have internal links to the protests against the WTO and the International Monetary Fund (IMF) that took place in Seattle in November 1999 and Washington, D.C. in April and May of 2000, since they all were directed against a comprehensive system of political provisions having to do with ordinary life, a systematic program aimed at creating and expanding a comprehensive market society. The content of this type of movement is highly diverse, encompassing a number of divergent goals (including a number of right-wing conservative components), but it would be a mistake to look only at the various components and conclude that these movements were opposed to freedom of communication and reform, since they embodied a yearning for equality, democratic reform, and freedom of communication. These movements, in fact, exemplify a close unity between the values of democracy and freedom and a movement to protect social security. Lacking this social pressure, there would be no motivation to rebuild the system of social guarantees, nor would there be any conception of creating a democratic market system (that is, social markets).

The discourse of "the end of history" that followed upon 1989, however, provided a clear-cut explanation of the events of that year:

namely, that it represented the final victory of the Western social system, with China as merely an isolated and incomplete historical instance. The dual significance of the 1989 social movement has been understood as being merely unidirectional. As far as I am concerned, once this single understanding becomes the world's predominant narrative, once it becomes ironclad proof of the superiority of the present system, once protest becomes merely praise for that system, then its true meaning, its critical potential, and its historical significance will all be lost. Some say this is inevitable in a period of transition, but this explanation of inevitability not only fails to get to the heart of the contradictions embedded in our daily lives, but it also confers a moral rationalization on what was a tragic development. Along with the guns of June Fourth, social protest and the social movement moved in new directions, and people have become more willing to examine and understand this movement in light of the new state of affairs. From the countless conclusions drawn by the media about the movement to the new ways in which it has been carried on [by Chinese] abroad, all have given expression to a powerful single tendency: they have all understood the 1989 social movement that took place in China as an exception to the process of "the end of history." None have realized that the huge global transformation that took place in 1989 also implies a new set of historical relationships as well as new protests and critiques of monopolization and coercion.

In regard to the ahistorical understandings of neoliberalism, I here can only point out, if occasionally with derision, a few bitter facts.

1. The creation of today's market society was not the result of a sequence of spontaneous events, but rather of state interference and violence. After 1989, the state continued with its economic revisions and reforms, but because of the threat of violence, society's discontent with the crisis described above was compressed into a tiny arena. The price reforms that had been called to a halt in the second half of 1988 just happened to begin to be fully implemented in September of 1989, three months after June Fourth, with the adjustments concentrated in the areas of price, exchange, and interest rates. We can

summarize the three-year administrative reorganization that took place between 1988 and 1991—and particularly the economic changes that came after 1989—as follows: monetary policy became a prime means of control; there was a significant readjustment in the foreign currency exchange rate, moving toward a unified rate; exports were increased and foreign trade came to be managed by mechanisms of competition and the assumption of responsibility for profits or losses; the "dual-track" pricing system was reduced in scope; the Shanghai Pudong development zone was fully opened and the various regional development zones were all put on track.

The creation of a system of market pricing and the relative perfection of markets in general were the upshot of a series of reform measures put into effect before this time. But we should still ask how it came to pass that two market reforms that had failed to be implemented in the late 1980s just happened to have been completed in the post-1989 environment? The answer is that the violence of 1989 served to check the social upheaval brought about by this process, and the new pricing system finally took shape. In other words, the new market system and the pricing mechanisms that lay at its heart were the result of political interference or arrangement, and the relationship of exchange between political power and the market could not help becoming an integral part of the new economic system. For example, as part of this process, at every level of society differences in income among regions and populations grew, with a concomitant rapid increase in the number of people in poverty.[26]

This historical transformation put the state's old ideology—a socialist ideology with equality as its goal—and its actual practice in an exceedingly contradictory situation, such that there was no way it could exercise its ideological function. The failure of the 1989 social movement simultaneously marked the failure of state ideology, and the "rigid on both fronts [political and economic]" policy put into effect after that time became, in fact a combination of dictatorial methods—relative to prior ideological mechanisms—and economic reform, demonstrating the basic loss of efficacy of the old state ideology. It was precisely under such conditions that neoliberalism could replace it as the new hegemonic ideology and provide direction and a rationale for national policy, international relations and a value-orientation for the media. It provided the systemic and ideological basis for a new group of liberals to play a dual role in the domestic and international media (that is, as advocates of state policy and as so-called public intellectuals).

2. As a set of political arrangements, the formation of a market society not only failed to ameliorate the historical conditions that had been the focus of the 1989 social movement, it actually deepened and legitimated them. After 1989 most deliberations on the movement on the part of intellectuals were caught up in the "end of history" tide described above (of course, unfortunately "history" had yet to come to a conclusion in mainland China); few people bothered to analyze the historical circumstances and fundamental demands of the 1989 movement itself. When Deng Xiaoping took his "Southern Progress" *(nan xun)* in 1992 and subsequently renewed his push for market reform, it received the general approval of local interest groups, the intellectuals, and public opinion abroad. After three years of economic weakness and political oppression, this response is completely understandable. It is worth noting, however, that the basic factors that had provided the mobilizing force in 1989 had not been resolved in any substantial way. Because of this, the principal social crises of the 1990s are closely related to social conditions prior to 1989. All we need do is observe the corruption, the smuggling, the unfair distribution, the influence of interest groups on public policy, the overdevelopment (as with real estate in Shanghai, Hainan, and other places), and the resulting financial crises, problems with the social welfare system, environmental concerns, and the like. We can instantly see the relationship here, except that now the scale is much larger, and because of the influence of "globalization," the effects are much more widespread. For example, systemic corruption has not completely severed its close relationship to "dual-track" pricing; capital flight and organized smuggling are related to the contracts under-

taken by governmental bureaus and the system of foreign trade; the crisis in the financial system is related to speculation on the property market and consequent overbuilding; the worsening situation among state enterprises is related to the worsening (rather than the perfection) of the market conditions described above.

Systemic corruption and the omnipresence of the sale of official position and honors closely resembles the sale of office in the period of European absolutism. On the one hand, it gives expression to the fact that the commercial class is still in a subsidiary position in the social structure, especially in its relationship to state authority. On the other hand, it also shows the subtle transition of the mechanisms of state authority under market conditions—the authority of the commercial class is being expanded precisely through the mechanisms of power employed in this transitional period. The problems brought about by the new round of financial reform and its accessory measures also closely resemble the problems of the days of "dual-track" pricing, although, of course, the specific content and scope of involvement are not exactly the same. Matters concerned with unemployment, poverty, social injustice, deflation, layoffs, agricultural labor, rural resources, and the like have been looked at by a number of scholars, and I am not able to repeat their findings individually. I raise these questions here to explain the historical relationship between the main issues facing the China mainland in the 1990s and the reform policies of the 1980s. It is also to explain how the expansion of unequal markets furthered social polarization and shattered the basis for social stability, thereby providing the conditions and rationale for political control and economic monopolization. It is from this perspective that the various conflicts between the state and this process of privatization can cover up neither the implications of this process for the consolidation of political power nor its profound contradictions with democracy.

3. The 1989 movement was an urban one, and it thus revealed both the inherent contradictions within urban economic reform as

well as new social problems created during the process of market expansion. Most studies take rural and urban reform as independent stages and rarely look into the relationships between the two, just as participants in the 1989 movement never considered the circumstances of rural dwellers, who make up the vast majority of the population. There would seem to be no direct link between rural poverty, urban expansion, and world trade. Whether in 1989 or today, however, these links are the necessary precondition for understanding the growth of uneven markets in China. Urban reform commenced in 1984, and urban–rural inequality began to grow in 1985; from 1989 to 1991 rural incomes essentially remained stagnant, and the income inequality between city and country returned to what it had been before 1978.[27] During the latter half of the 1980s, the population exodus from the countryside grew both in speed and scale. There has been a long-standing problem in China over the size of the population and the amount of land available, but why did this vast migration of the rural population suddenly take place only in the 1990s?

There are several reasons. First, the ongoing development of urban reform promoted the expansion of the basic infrastructure in the cities, and the policies of opening up the economy attracted substantial foreign investment, both of which combined to create a significant need for labor. Second, during the course of urban reform, rural reform did not keep in step; in fact, it lagged behind so that the gap between country and city actually widened, which had the effect of increasing the speed and scale of the migration of the rural population. Third, the opening up of the economy and the creation of special economic zones was concentrated in the coastal regions, and the disparity between the coastal regions and the interior increased even more. Further, because of the devolution of economic and political power and adjustments to the tax-collection system, there was a major change in the mechanisms for managing certain regions and economic relationships that the state had once taken responsibility for. Fourth, the loosening of the household-registration system promoted the commodification of rural labor, but at the same time failed to create any new regulations or appropriate measures for the protection of labor in this time of rapid historical change.

As a result, in the period of economic recession and deflation that followed, local urban governments, in an effort to protect their own localities, put large numbers of restrictions on outsiders who moved to their cities, thereby creating once again discriminatory policies based on status. The national response to the increased need for wage labor in the urban marketplace was the motivating factor behind the loosening of the household-registration system. At the same time, however, the complete abandonment of this system would have led to a huge rise in urban unemployment, so cities used their favorable position to develop any number of policies designed for local protection—which took the shape of various urban subsidies, educational regulations, housing, and the like—thereby resurrecting in urban settings discriminatory policies directed at immigrating outsiders. In such circumstances what results can we expect other than further disintegration of rural society, continued uneven development, and a spiraling increase in the crime rate? The fundamental effect of this uneven development in China today is the ambiguity it imposes on the rural population about their own freedom, something that ensures the labor supply even as it limits the pressure of population migration on the urban social structure.

The instance described below is a modal case explaining the structural conditions of the shape of urban–rural relations: in 1993, because, among other factors, the state had once again raised the price of grain and also because of increases in both rural enterprises and outmigration, there was a general increase in rural income. Between 1996 and 1999 (and particularly after the financial crisis of 1997), however, there was simultaneously a decrease in the productivity of rural enterprises and a large surplus in the urban labor force, giving rise to the phenomenon of a return of migrant workers and those employed in rural industry to the countryside. In many areas, however, because of a too-rapid pace of development and outmigration, it was very difficult to restore the original composition of rural locales. This created a paradoxical dilemma. On the one hand, in a situation where arable land was decreasing, the rural population had increased by some 78 million people. On the other hand, because of a lack of labor guarantees and the strictures of the household-registration system, rural labor had no choice but to regularly migrate back and forth in accordance with rises and falls in the urban economy. Of late, 10 percent of Mainland China's massive population is circulating beyond provincial lines, and if the intraprovince floating population is added to that, this number becomes even larger.[28] The divergent tendencies in urban and rural reform are concentrated on this matter of inequality. In the words of a specialist on rural problems, the crux of China's current rural crisis is the "different systems of urban and rural governance: one country with two policies."[29] This systematic inequality is premised on the expansion of urban-centered economic growth based on a market system; it has already had a huge and incalculable influence on the transformation of the structure of the urban–rural social relationship, and will continue to do so in the future.

Rural problems were not the direct cause of the 1989 social crisis.[30] The contemporary rural crisis, however, deepened in the post-1989 milieu—that is to say, under conditions of expanding urban markets. This market expansion transformed the rural population and the land it lived on into semi-commodities, thereby causing the disintegration of the social order of the countryside and of its ability to snap back. The real cause of the increases both in poverty and local taxes in today's China is the vast increase in hidden unemployment. The expansion of foreign trade and urban markets led to increases in jobs, but both foreign trade and urban markets are marked by constant fluctuation, so that even during periods when the fluctuations are not particularly obvious, the number of unemployed still rises. If we unearth the numbers of rural dwellers among the overall figures of the hidden unemployed, the limitless capacity to create poverty on the part of the process of development brought into being by so-called globalization and neoliberal market strategies stands revealed.

Amartya Sen's theoretical framework in his *Development as Freedom* pointed out two important facets of development: first, that labor needs to be released from all restraints and enter into an open labor market; and second, that this process not exclude programs of social support, public regulation of the process, or policies of governmental intervention.

In an era in which both production and consumption are transnational, this account needs to be expanded, amplified, and rethought. First, agricultural labor and the mechanisms that protect it are the keys to understanding the relationship between the market system and free labor contracts; the question of the freedom of labor contracts (of which we can take freedom of movement as an instance) is one of the principal measures of whether market arrangements in the contemporary world are truly free. Because of this, free labor contracts need to be instituted not just within the nation-state, but in economic relations around the globe. Second, one of the crucial motive forces for the expansion of capitalist markets is the simultaneous existence of free and unfree labor, and the relationship between these states of freedom/lack of freedom and social development thus needs to be studied. The free movement of labor is not something that is a result of *laissez-faire,* but is rather something brought about by a broad general plan, and is thus premised on the need to conscientiously root out structures of inequality, something not limited to the household-registration system. Third, the extension of the market system implies that the values and activities of exchange enter into all aspects of life, something that destroys all preexisting social structures (such as communities and their values) and denigrates the lifestyles of all other social groupings (such as national minorities). In this sense, to discuss the question of economic development solely from the standpoint of the significance of the freedom of labor contracts without considering the relationship between development and other social conditions runs the risk of ushering in social disintegration.

The free movement of labor, public regulation, *and* policies of governmental interference are all conditions for a market system, and a vital task for those studying the question of development today is how to limit the destruction to nature, to tradition, to customs, to manners, and to all aspects of life and values brought about by the expansion of this system. This is also a necessary step in liberating the value of "freedom" from the understandings imposed on it—particularly that of looking at it only as an economic matter—and placing it in a broader perspective. Because of this, it is necessary to make clear the definite relationship among structural social equality, respect for diversity, and the various issues implicit in economic development as one goes about defending the freedom of the labor contract. In the context of present-day China, the most important matter is to focus on the problem of the relationship between country and city. From a more radical perspective, the historical progress represented by the institution of the free labor contract (that is, relations of exchange taking the form of individual labor contracts), by which the effective surplus value squeezed out of personal creativity replaced a system of identity based on political dependence or coercion, cannot obviate the necessity to rethink the relationships established by market contracts (just think about the slave labor conditions that have arisen in China's coastal regions in the form of contracts).

4. Reform in contemporary China echoes the transformation in the historical conditions of international society, and is even more directly the result of the state's vigorous adjustments in foreign policy; reform and opening up are two sides of the same coin. It is worth noting that the concept of opening up has perhaps given rise to a serious misunderstanding, namely, the idea that the Chinese mainland prior to this time was a completely closed, autarkic society. On this point, it is necessary to give a brief account of the connection between the Cold War and Chinese foreign policy. First, the antagonism in this period between China and the West, and with America in particular, was directly related to the circumstances that brought the Chinese Communist Party to power in the first place— the cold and hot wars that came into being after the World War II formed the vital background to the foreign policy of mainland China. The Korean

War of the 1950s, the American Seventh Fleet's blockade of Taiwan, American support for the Indonesian military coup of the 1960s and the subsequent waves of Chinese expulsions from that country, the American-instigated Vietnamese and Indo-Chinese Wars, and so on all had the effect of carving up the Asian region into two completely distinct worlds. As a result of ideology and geopolitical consider-ations, China turned toward the Soviet Union, Eastern Europe, and other Asian nations in search of allies.

Second, up until the point in the late 1950s when the Sino–Soviet split occurred, there were alliances of various degrees between China and the Soviet Union and Eastern Europe; after China and the Soviet Union split, China continued to carry out the foreign policy that had taken shape after the [1955] Bandung conference, which was to fo-cus on developing broad political, economic, and cultural ties with Third World nations and the nonaligned movement. In 1972, the mainland Chinese government returned to the United Nations as China's representative, a result brought about under the impetus of the vast majority of Third World nations, thereby demonstrating the great success in the international arena of mainland China's post-Bandung foreign policy; it was also something widely approved of by people in China. The policy of opening the country up began during the period of the Cultural Revolution, which was also the period when mainland China established relations with the vast majority of world nations. The primary motivation of the opening to the West that also took place at this time was to adjust the strategic position of China vis-à-vis East–West relations, and to ally with the United States in order to check the threat of Soviet invasion.

After 1978 the Chinese government gradually came to abandon its policy thrust of uniting with the Third World and the nonaligned movement and made relations with the United States, Japan, and other advanced capitalist countries its principal focus. During this pe-riod, the Chinese policy of opening up made great strides, particu-larly in the economic and political spheres, creating ever more inti-mate and mutually dependent trade relations with the developed countries of the West. These relations, however, were not unconditional. In February and March of 1979 the war in which China invaded Vietnam broke out. This was a war completely different from any that China had been engaged in after 1949—whether resisting America by assisting Korea, resisting America by assisting Vietnam, or the wars with India or with the Soviet Union. The direct causes of this military action were complex, and included the buildup in Vietnamese military strength after the 1975 unification; the signing of the November 1978 "Vietnamese–Soviet Friendship Treaty of Alliance and Mutual Assistance," which had a military alliance quality to it; the strategic threat posed by the combination of the Soviet Union in the north and Vietnam in the south; and the December 25, 1978 "blitzkrieg" invasion of Cambodia by Vietnam.

There was, however, an even more crucial factor: at this juncture Sino–American relations underwent a profound change, revealing an alliance-like relationship built on antagonism toward the Soviet Union and its allies. On the eve of the Chinese government's declaration of war against Vietnam, China and the United States publicly proclaimed their intention to establish relations. The war itself was the true beginning of China's amalgamation into the American-led economic order, and from another perspective it revealed the historical links between marketization and violence, as well as between the national opening up and the global power structure. From this moment on, the prior internationalist policy orientation of the socialist state began to recede from the historical stage, and China's policy of opening up turned from one unidirectional focus to another, that is toward the West—including Japan and other developed areas. Nothing explains this matter better than the international response to the bombing on May 8, 1999, of the Chinese embassy in Yugoslavia by NATO (American) airplanes: at the emergency meeting to discuss the bombing held at the United Nations, not only did the Western alliance stand to one side, but China's traditional Third World allies were not willing to express even basic support.

The 1980s opening up policies functioned to cast off the restrictions of the past and to mark a separation from the aftereffects of the Cultural Revolution. It was thus generally welcomed by all sectors of society, particularly the intellectuals. Like many intellectuals, I welcomed the policies of openness and reform and continue to have a generally positive evaluation of them. Any critical perspective on the problems of contemporary China should not cover up the amazing achievements brought about through this process of reform. In undertaking a historical analysis, however, we cannot ignore the profound and complicated consequences and historical imprints left by this process, because it reveals the bias of the worldview created by the state ideology. For the generation that has grown up after the Cultural Revolution, their knowledge of the world is predominantly about the West, and the United States in particular (just as, in the past, there was another biased knowledge base, in that case about the Soviet bloc). Societies and cultures that we once knew so well—Asia, Africa, Latin America, as well as eastern and southern Europe—are now almost completely beyond the ken of popular knowledge. The intellectual reflection and literature on the war with Vietnam that took place during the 1980s was dominated almost exclusively not by pondering the war and its relationship with the new era of international relations, but rather by reflection on the "Great Cultural Revolution." In fact, denunciation of the Cultural Revolution became the sole foundation of the moral rationale behind this rethinking. This is a clear demonstration how repudiating the Cultural Revolution has become the guardian of the dominant ideology as well as of state policy, and this mode of thinking has flourished ever since: any criticism directed against the present can be cast as regression to the Cultural Revolution, and thus as being wholly irrational.

From the 1980s to the beginning of the 1990s, even though there had passed a whole decade of opening up and reform, the discursive space of the Chinese intellectuals was still restricted within the frame of the modernization of the nation-state. It lacked even the most basic international perspective and, as a consequence, such matters as nationalism, the national question, and globalization could not be conceptualized in the context of the discussion on the question of democracy. This intellectual impasse clearly explains why, after the failure of the 1989 movement, no one could find any critical material with which to rethink the movement's origins and reasons for failure. It explains why people set out to understand globalization and the experience of the market only from the historical examples of the United States, Western Europe, Japan, and the "Four Dragons of East Asia" (that is, Hong Kong, Singapore, South Korea, and Taiwan—regions marked by capitalist development) and never looked at this from any other point of view—such as through the predicaments of India, the Middle East, and Latin America. And it also explains why when the 1989 movement hailed Gorbachev's glasnost, the democratic movement in the Philippines, and the Korean student movement, it lacked the ability to understand the different social circumstances and specific goals underlying each of these movements.

It was against this background that the research and discussion in the 1990s that took reflection on modernity as its subject of departure opened up a new historical perspective, and thereby enjoyed widespread influence even as it played a liberating role. It is from this point that I wish to begin the discussion in the second section of this essay.

The Three Stages of
Thought in the 1990s and
Their Major Problems

2

1989–1993: The Reflection on "Radicalism"

If we link up the 1989 social movement with the historical circumstances that allowed it to take place, we will be able to observe quite clearly why the movement's demands for democratic freedoms were closely paired with demands for social equality; we will also be able to see plainly the sharp critique of contemporary life embodied in the movement's broad understanding of democracy. In looking back from this perspective at the numerous discussions among Chinese intellectuals in the 1990s, and their understanding of the events of 1989 in particular, I cannot help feeling that the explanations of the movement that have been advanced are vastly less substantial and profound than what the movement itself supplied. For the sake of analysis, I shall provisionally divide the discussions that have taken place between 1989 and now into three interdependent stages. I say this division is merely provisional because it is neither absolute nor teleological, and also because there are close connections as well as overlaps among the stages.

The first stage took place between 1989 and 1993, and was principally concerned with summing up the various aspects of the 1989 movement; it resulted in a consensus that was critical of radicalism. The failure of the 1989 movement caused a massive psychological shock to Chinese society, and the intellectuals had no choice but to face this grim historical situation and reflect on the reasons for this failure. During the course of this rethinking, splits between the intellectuals and the student movement gradually revealed themselves: a number of intellectuals felt that the failure of the movement stemmed from the radical nature of the student movement and its superficial understanding of democracy. This thinking about "radicalism" bore a close relationship to the trends of thought of the "intellectuals" in the 1980s as well as to the role they played in society. From the latter perspective, the intellectuals in the 1980s comprised a number of strata, with those at the highest level playing key roles in the process of reform—they not only participated directly in the molding of the ideology of reform, but also directly in the formulation of various strands of state reform planning, to the point of having extremely close relations with a number of state political and other interest groups. During the course of an extended period of working in these organizations, these intellectuals came to believe that if only the reform party were to gain power within the state apparatus, then all problems would dissolve. Because of this, they not only staked their futures on the advance of those elements in the state imbroglio moving toward reform, they also were concerned that the radicalization of the student movement would break up the gradualist nature of state reform, and thereby bring about the return of conservative forces to the stage. From this latter perspective, many intellectuals brought the neo-enlightenment reflections on modern Chinese history that had already begun in the 1980s into their thinking about 1989, thereupon establishing a relationship between the modern revolutionary movement they had long since begun to question and the new social movements to which they had once offered moral support.

As a result, this critique of radicalism quickly developed into a comprehensive reflection on the roles of revolution and reform within the entire course of modern Chinese history: radicalism came to be seen as the defining feature of the modern socialist movement, of the political revolution as well as of the cultural revolution. As one famous scholar argued, China had embarked on the radical road at the time of the 1911 revolution, and [only] the 1898 constitutional reforms and the New Policies of the last decade of the Qing dynasty were worthy of affirmation; another young intellectual criticized the general approbation accorded science and democracy since the May Fourth movement of the late 1910s, lamenting the fact that the more basic questions of freedom and order had been neglected.[31] If one takes these essays and thoughts concerning Chinese history as reflecting a rethinking of the political strategy of the 1989 social movement, and also takes them as inquiries into basic theories of democracy itself, I think they lead to important conclusions that are still valid today. Their analysis, however, was built on an ahistorical perspective, since it failed to take into account the historical factors behind the movement and the motivations for its radicalism. It went so far as to conflate analysis of movement strategy with the study of history, thereby establishing the premise on which was constructed neoconservatism's (that is, neoliberalism's) historical narrative. In a situation of extreme social polarization, "rethinking radicalism" became the most important, indeed, the decisive thesis of a portion of the intellectuals in the early 1990s.

By 1998, this way of thinking had for some people already become a highly systematic explanation of Chinese history since 1898 and a theoretical underpinning for thinking about democratic theory in the present. At its core was the understanding that beginning with the constitutional reform of 1898, Kang Youwei and Liang Qichao had mistakenly chosen the radical path, and it was only reforms advocated by ranking local officials that were both gradual and successful.[32] In the name of rejecting "direct democracy," the basic premise was opposition to political participation at the grassroots level and support for building political democracy by indirect (that is, elite) means.[33] Beginning in the late 1990s, the neoliberals revised the radical political reform program of the 1980s into a "movement for constitutional revision" that focused on establishing the right to private property. In effect, it sought to legitimate the irrational distribution of property through a legislative process, including the legitimization of illegal expropriation of public property. From this historical standpoint, the denial of social equality and democratic affiliations became inevitable.

"Rethinking radicalism" was not, however, a unified intellectual trend. For instance, discussion of the history of academic thought in the early 1990s was primarily concerned with the academic style of the 1980s, and was not predicated on any comprehensive conservative theory. Thus, criticism of this academic style did not prevent the critics from moving in a conservative direction in their political philosophies. The ideology of so-called neoliberalism was essentially a combination of notions of market extremism, neoconservatism, and neo-authoritarianism. It sought to radicalize the devolution of economic and political power in a stable manner, to employ authority to guarantee the process of marketization in turbulent times, and to seek the complete withdrawal of the state in the midst of the tide of globalization—these are the basic characteristics of China's neoliberalism. When Samuel Huntington's *Political Order in Changing Societies* was translated into Chinese in 1989, political conservatism and the rethinking of radicalism among the intellectuals flourished together, with neo-authoritarianism seizing the moment as well. Against this background, even though there was a general psychological and ideological acceptance of Francis Fukuyama's "end of history" thesis, because the new historical narrative placed the blame for the problems of the 1989 movement on the radicalism of modern revolution and reform, there arose, in fact, a general critique of the more radical and Westernized of the patterns of reform and thought that had characterized the intellectual enlightenment of the 1980s. The core of the discussion of "liberalism" in this period was a discourse that advocated liberalism in name but in fact centered itself in a resolute conservatism (and which among certain people manifested itself directly as neo-authoritarianism).

After 1989, the Chinese version of Scottish liberalism or "classical liberalism" was nothing other than a Chinese version of neoconservatism. Its attack on the tactics, timing, and moral character of the student movement was intent on deconstructing the radicalism of the

Chinese revolution and critiquing the radicalism of the movement itself without any hint of deep reflection on the social conditions and underlying causes that had given rise to the events of 1989. Under the influence of the modernizing theories of conservatism and rethinking radicalism, the neoliberal ideology was able to forgive such systemic phenomena as corruption and also to forgo opportunities for the advance of progress toward democracy through the conjoined efforts of the social movement, the establishment of democracy, and structural reform. It was thereby fundamentally incapable of making any contribution toward either Chinese democracy or democracy in the world at large.

Precisely because of this, when, after a three-year period of economic adjustment, Deng Xiaoping made his Southern Progress of 1992 and rekindled economic reform, the intellectuals were incapable of making any constructive critique other than welcoming the new trend. Local and Beijing-based interest groups welcomed the new initiative because new reforms signaled further devolution, which meant resolution of the contradictions that had arisen in the period of adjustment between central control and local interests. The intellectuals welcomed the new initiative because they believed that as long as reforms were implemented and a market economy was created, then progress toward democracy in China would eventually take place. Foreign public opinion welcomed this initiative because it meant that China was once again moving toward the fixed objective of "the end of history." The fundamental questions raised by the 1989 movement were set aside. In 1992–1993, because the problems arising from commodity pricing had been solved both by the three-year readjustment and by state violence, and because of the advance of township and nonstate enterprises in southeast China, the market environment had been relatively perfected and economic growth was rapid. A good number of structural problems, however, had yet to be solved, such as the economic burdens of state-owned enterprises, the problem of growth in the agricultural sector, and the problems related to consumerism and unemployment that followed in their wake.

Actually, after 1992 positive factors such as the growth of market mechanisms and the strengthening of local autonomy were not matched by the creation of any corresponding mechanisms of democratic supervision, nor were there any real innovations introduced in the course of the restructuring of state enterprises. As a result, this process became a hotbed of structural corruption, massive smuggling, a deteriorating financial situation, and the creation of poverty. The direct result of the Southern Progress was the appearance of many "development zones" as well as the opening of three large markets in commodity futures, stocks and securities, and real estate, factors that created the policy basis and market conditions enabling the emergence in China of a class of the newly rich. It also generated the historical circumstances by which various levels of political and economic elites could be combined into one. This was thus a process under which uneven conditions created anew social and class polarization, and which contained within it the seeds of a long-term social crisis.[34] Between 1989 and 1992, however, there was no way that the discourse of the intellectuals on related topics could broach these questions, because, at the end of three years of repression, people finally saw a bit of hope in this process of market creation. These rays of hope were so precious that even after having discussed radicalism for three years, no one was able to say whether this process itself did not bring up the question of radicalism, or whether the social conditions that had given rise to the 1989 movement were not, in fact, being exacerbated by the process of marketization. What I wish to point out is that it was precisely this sort of discussion that comprised the historical legitimization of and narrative basis for the neoliberalism of the late 1990s.

I am not completely negative about the rethinking of radicalism that took place in the early 1990s. Neither the 1989 student movement nor the intellectuals as a group were able to produce a realistic plan of action, nor were they able to deliver a self-conscious theoretical critique or a political solution to the complicated historical process described above. This cultural situation explains why the 1989 movement's internal connection between the demands for equality on the one hand and for democracy on the other remained confined strictly to the realm of spontaneous action throughout the course of the movement. It also explains why the political demands of the students and the broad-based social mobilization of the movement were never linked up theoretically in intellectual discussion either at the time or later. The biggest issue embedded here is that concepts of radicalism and conservatism both serve to conceal the actual nature of and the social conditions underlying the 1989 movement.

In the historical circumstances established by the failure of the movement, a large number of young intellectuals launched into reconsiderations of modern Chinese history, and their compilations and research on the modern Chinese academic and intellectual traditions provided significant resources for the practical task of the study of the question of rethinking modernity that followed shortly thereafter.[35] This process of reflection included serious reconsideration of modern history, conscientious rethinking of attempts to carry out radical reform on the basis of Western models, close investigation of the Chinese historical legacy and its contemporary significance, and necessary critiques of certain of the consequences of radical political action. The deliberations over the path of reform and the reflections on modernity that both took place in the 1990s were closely related to this intellectual trend. Owing, however, to the immense influence of the logic of the thought pattern described above, these explorations were unable to make a broad and comprehensive analysis of the internal contradictions of contemporary Chinese society. It seems to me that the splits that gradually developed in the intellectual community after 1994 were the result of the self-reflections of those intellectuals directly engaged in this social process.[36]

1993–1997: The Ideology of the Market, the Program of Privatization, and Its Critique

The second stage of thought took place primarily between 1993 and 1997; its starting point was Deng Xiaoping's Southern Progress of

1992 and it terminated in what is referred to as the Asian financial panic and economic crisis that took place in 1997. A substantial number of intellectual discussions took place during this period, but it would be difficult to say that they arrived at any clear consensus. The splits in the intellectual community sharpened. To better understand the intellectual climate of these times, it will help to provide a brief explanation of a few important events and the related discussions that took place between 1993 and 1997.

First, after Deng Xiaoping's Southern Progress, economic development and the pace of opening up to the outside increased and urban commercial culture (particularly consumer culture) grew by leaps and bounds. Led by Beijing and Central Television, as well as by some regional stations, a large number of commercial television series were produced one after the other. The well-known "Wang Shuo phenomenon"[37] as well as other intellectual and artistic products furthered the development of a popular culture. Second, following this surge of commercialization, a number of intellectuals and scholars turned toward the market, a phenomenon described as "jumping into the sea" (or "taking the plunge," *xiahai*); the income differential between those employed within the state sector and those employed outside it grew exponentially, leading to a crisis for the status of intellectuals in Chinese society. Third, the growth of rural enterprises, the crisis of the state-owned enterprises and the problem in the collection of state revenue existed simultaneously, which, along with the widespread attention paid to the pattern of East Asian economic systems, stimulated interest from a variety of perspectives on alternative possibilities along the path of Chinese social and economic development. Fourth, in 1993 a number of important incidents in the international arena had a subtle influence on Chinese social psychology, particularly on the psychology of the intellectuals. It was in that year that the Chinese government extricated itself from the straightened circumstances it had been in internationally since 1989, with the Beijing city government taking upon itself the task of applying to host the Olympic Games in 2000. Because of the corruption involved in its earlier hosting of the Asian Games, a majority of intellectuals adopted a critical posture toward this effort. However, when the American and a number of other governments interfered politically in the application process, thereby costing China the chance to host the Games, there was a strong psychological reaction on the part of China nationwide.

It was also in October of 1993 that the Russian president Boris Yeltsin ordered armed units to attack and suppress the legally elected parliament. This violent and unconstitutional action taken in the name of opposition to formerly communist elements in the government not only revealed the crisis inherent in the Russian reforms—particularly the "spontaneous process of privatization" undertaken with the support of the United States and other Western countries—but also reflected the long-standing contradictions of American policy in regard to human rights and democracy, as well as the reality of the extreme self-interest and antidemocratic spirit underlying them. There was thus a contrast between American support of Yeltsin's violence and its condemnation of the 1989 violence in China that gave the events of October 1993 in Russia a powerful and long-lasting significance for those who harbored an idealistic view of Western society, for those who believed that history had already concluded, and for those who considered the Cold War to be long past. At almost the same time, Samuel Huntington—a man of considerable influence in China after 1989—published his long essay "The Clash of Civilizations?" in the American foreign policy journal *Foreign Affairs,* which was translated into Chinese and published almost immediately in the Hong Kong journal *Twenty-First Century* as well as Beijing's *Reference News* (Cankao xiaoxi); it elicited widespread attention and much discussion among the intellectuals.[38] Together, these international incidents added up to a profound series of intellectual shocks to those scholars who had been in the midst of explaining the course of Chinese globalization from the perspective of the Confucian-based ideal of "Great Union" *(datong),*[39] the enlightenment-based notion of "permanent peace," or the notion that the world had been "moving in the same direction over the past three hundred years."

Against this background, a series of discussions was launched in the Chinese intellectual arena, among which the most important were the following:

1. Discussion ensued on markets and civil society.[40] This discussion very clearly followed upon the reflections on radicalism of the earlier period and consisted of two main points: in circumstances where political reform had been very evidently frustrated, it was thought that as long as market reform could proceed smoothly, the mechanisms of the state would undergo corresponding change, leading to the spontaneous growth of democracy. The true basis for democracy lay in the creation of a civil society, and once this came into being forms of social power-sharing would follow. I don't have the space here to analyze in any detail the theoretical ramifications of this discussion, but it is worth pointing out that the discussion represented a shift from the arguments over political transformation of the 1980s, from the notion of establishing democracy through the radical transformation of the political structure to the eventual achievement of political democracy through reliance on marketization, the formation of local and intragovernmental interest groups, and the unlocking of traditional resources embedded in such things as clan structures.

This discussion of civil society was not without value in the context of the effort to unlock popular resources, but as the extension of the rethinking of radicalism, it failed to analyze in any detail the mechanisms by which Chinese markets, Chinese civil society, and the middle class they hoped for were to be established. Nor did it analyze the role new interest groups were to play in social life, the exceedingly complicated relationships between these economic forces and the state, or the internal polizarizations within the state (such as center versus locality, the state versus interest groups, and the penetration of society into the state). As a consequence, this discussion had no way to foresee the problems inhering in this process, nor to analyze the social problems that had been gradually piling up since the 1980s. Even more important, the "civil society" that was imagined completely left out the huge working class and rural society, thus not only according perfectly with state policies that had the effect of drastically increasing the polarization between rich and poor, but also cutting off in principle the links between the ongoing progress of democracy and its true social foundations. This theoretical tendency was in complete harmony with the liberal critique of "populism" of the late 1990s: it was necessary to denigrate any social movement or protest that had its origin in the grassroots. Working from this premise, the development of Chinese democracy lost any practical impetus, not to mention any possibility of actual implementation.

The real question involved here is this: assuming that a rethinking of radicalism was necessary, this discussion of civil society on the one hand ignored the new alliance formed between the state and interest groups against the social movement while, on the other, it failed to take theoretical account of the major portion of the social movement itself. By setting "society" completely outside the realm of the state this way, this mode of thought could only imagine that the spontaneous action of the market would lead naturally toward democracy, thereby cutting off any broader political thinking about democracy. In moving from the reflection on radicalism to this discussion of civil society, the intellectual community was unable to tie the process of the movement itself to its democratic roots. The original purpose behind the thesis of civil society was to facilitate investigation into the possibilities and preconditions for democracy, but because it did not clearly distinguish between the standardized narrative and the course of actual history, the discussion easily fell into a theoretical impasse, namely, to conflate the demands of the theory itself with concrete historical developments, to the extent of taking the workings of uneven markets as the natural course leading to democracy.

Deng Xiaoping's Southern Progress of 1992 had reduced the tensions between the center and the localities (that is to say, non-Beijing-based organizations and interest groups) that had characterized the period of economic adjustment between 1989 and 1991, and the polarization of interests that resulted also disintegrated any possibility of a general social mobilization. As a result, I attribute the cessation of progress toward democracy in the 1990s to the following factors. First, the interaction between the social movement and institutional reform that had just come into being in 1989 had completely collapsed, and as a result, no segment of society was able to generate the force to make the state adjust relationships among interests. Second, the state had employed violence to remove the pressure exerted by social mobilization, but could not use the same means to promote democratic reform and synthesize democratic methods of supervising non-Beijing-based organizations and interest groups. These organizations and interest groups worked through the actions of the market to forge an even broader alliance with the state, such that interest groups no longer required any social pressure to further the process of the devolution of political and economic power; on the contrary, they were able to use the linkage of relationships of interest to influence public policy.[41] In light of this, any theory of political democracy must, as part of its mandate to protect the basic rights of citizens, develop an institutional means of preventing this double alliance between the state and interest groups; this is the fundamental premise of creating fair markets.

Thus, the contemplation of a mixed system with the participation of ordinary citizens at its core (that is, a tripartite arrangement among the state, elites, and the common people) is a democratic program well worth considering.[42] This notion of a tripartite structure emphasizes how to turn popular demands into national policy and thereby forestall both the creation of a new aristocracy and the dual alliance between the state and various interest groups. I think these explorations are worthy of attention and further discussion. On this point, it is particularly important to investigate how to create mechanisms of democratic oversight through the interaction between social movements and institutional innovation. That is to say, to look into how ordinary citizens through such means as social movements and public discussion might promote open dialogue on policy questions among different levels of society. This would mean not simply relying on the state to supervise the new aristocrats, but rather preventing the state from arrogating power to itself, as well as blocking corruption at the local level through democratic mechanisms installed at various levels of society. On this question, the creation of social movements and various levels of public sphere are an indispensable intermediary link, since public discussion and social movements do not take place solely within a national arena but also within a number of local public spheres, allowing ordinary people to discover in the public arena topics closely related to the concerns of their day-to-day lives.[43] This fostering of a public sphere is the way to ensure tangible significance to demands for democracy and freedom, and also an important method to avoid turning democracy and freedom into radical slogans that lack any actual content. This conception, produced in direct response to China's actual situation, is the diametrical opposite of a civil society thesis that presupposes the broadening of the gap between the state and civil society. This latter notion understands social democracy only as an apolitical and spontaneous process and thus collapses the affirmative interactive relationship between social movements and institutional innovation.

2. There was discussion on institutional innovation, theoretical innovation, and on matters having to do with the capacities of the state. Between 1993 and 1997, a number of critically minded intellectuals began to consider the question of social justice, beginning from differing perspectives and in the context of the experiences of the reforms in Russia and Eastern Europe and of enterprises both in the Chinese countryside and in Southeast Asia.[44] This discussion had points in common with the study of the capacities of the state that had begun slightly earlier (in 1992). This is not to say, however, that they aimed in the same direction, for there was an important difference in their theoretical framework. The question of the capacity of the state touched on a structural source of social inequality in the 1990s, that is, the relationship between the central government and local as well as government-ministry-based interest groups. In the discussions that took place between 1991 and 1993, the issue of "state capacity" was generally regarded as being a matter of policy

study with statist overtones, so most intellectuals did not respond directly to this broadly influential and exceedingly valuable research.[45] The irruption of the world economic crisis in 1997 caused people to think about the damage inflicted on societies and economies by the transnational mobility of floating financial capital, and brought a number of scholars to discuss anew the implications of "the state" from the standpoint of social security, to think about the relationship between democracy and the state, and to talk about the multiple roles of the state, the conflict implicit in the duality of state and capital, and the like.[46]

The question of the state should be considered against the background of two distinct phases: in 1991, the question of the state and state capacity was mainly concerned with the capacity of the central government in the context of reform policies that tended toward devolution of political and economic power and the consequences of that process, but after 1997 the core of the inquiry into the state turned toward the function and status of the state during the course of globalization. The two phases, however, have an obvious internal link. Questions concerning the contemporary Chinese state raise theoretical issues both highly sensitive and immensely complex: there are the closest of relationships between corruption, monopoly, the polarization between rich and poor, and the collapse of the system of social welfare on the one hand and authoritarianism, the huge apparatus of the state, and the consequences of its policies on the other (encapsulated in the notion of "the marketing of power and the empowering of the market"). It was, however, only the financial crisis and questions about social guarantees that brought up the question of the protective capacity of the state. There is a paradox here: the withering of the capacity of the state and the overinvolvement of the state in such matters as the workings of the market—at the grassroots level of society (including in making administrative divisions of the market), in the free market, and in the transnational movement—all seem on the surface to diminish the powers of the state; but, in fact, they provide the basic premise on which rests its very necessity. The historical circumstances of this paradox render it impossible for any democratic demands to separate a critique of the state from a critique of the move toward a market society.

In each of the discussions that took place between 1993 and 1996, the discourse on institutional and theoretical innovation was invariably its most penetrating component, as these touched on the real paradox of the post-1980 reform process from both theoretical and practical perspectives; they also were the areas where it was possible to take up the initiative to plan for even more democratic reforms.[47] The actual substance of this discussion was opposition to the systematic commodity fetishism of neoliberalism, opposition to the assumption that authoritarianism or a foreign system imposed by force were a nation's unavoidable fate, as well as inquiry into ways to democratize a market economy. Intrinsic to these discussions was the assumption that there was a diversity of economic systems and democratic experiences to be found in modern societies, thereby providing the theoretical possibility for choice and innovation within the context of particular historical requirements. Most important, this discussion critiqued the process of spontaneous privatization carried out by force that had already taken place in Russia and was just then occurring in China, in this manner revealing the antidemocratic character of this form of market economy as well as demonstrating the contradictions between the various programs of privatization that had been implemented recently and a truly democratic system. The discourse also provided a number of new directions for the participation by ordinary people in politics, for ways by which advanced and backward technologies could be allied, and for the reform of enterprises and political institutions.

3. There was discussion about the spirit of humanism *(renwen jingshen)* and postmodernism. In 1994 a number of young intellectuals published a series of dialogues in *Dushu* about the loss of the humanistic spirit. This was an intuitive response to the new commercial culture and the process of marketization, which, while affirming these new processes, sought to explore the morality and spiritual face of the

course of modernization so as to be able to safeguard the humanistic consciousness of the intellectuals. I believe that a certain amount of this discussion on the "spirit of humanism" in 1994–1995 was an instinctive reaction against the movement to expand markets, serving to remind the intelligentsia once again that it must not abandon its mission of critique in this new market context.[48] Like the discussions on civil society and radicalism, however, the conversation on the spirit of humanism did not analyze in any depth the social transformation that had taken place since the 1980s, and essentially continued along with the same presuppositions that had characterized the New Enlightenment of the 1980s. Echoing this discussion were the critiques of the market mentality by such authors as Han Shaogong and Zhang Chengzhi;[49] a number of their insights built an important bridge between the discussion of the spirit of humanism and the area of popular culture.

This discussion was attacked by a group of postmodernist critics that arose at almost the same time (or even a bit earlier).[50] Neither did the postmodernist critics comprise a uniform intellectual front, with a number of them taking direct aim at the development of contemporary society itself via a deconstruction of the narrative of modernity.[51] In the years between 1993 and 1995, however, the mainstream of the postmodernist movement took the discussion of the spirit of humanism as an elitist narrative, and they launched a defense of commerce and consumerism by means of a deconstructivist strategy that evinced a wholehearted embrace of the move toward markets. From this perspective, this impetus of postmodernism was indistinguishable from the object of the critique put forward by the New Enlightenment movement of the 1980s, that is the nation-state that had been produced in the midst of revolution and upheaval. Postmodern criticism and the discussion of the spirit of humanism were both marked by a number of intellectuals who touched on the profound crisis contained in China's process of reform, but both of these quite different discourses embodied an optimism similar to that of the advocates of the market.[52] It is worth noting in passing the attack on Zhang Chengzhi's work *History of a Soul* (Xinling shi) by both postmodern critics and commentators who were a few years older: no one paid any attention to the history of the relationships among different Chinese nationalities set out in this work, but took it instead as simply a legacy of the "Great Cultural Revolution," lambasting it as symbolic of the Red Guard spirit in particular.[53] This case powerfully exemplifies the most dangerous tendency among Chinese intellectuals: in relation to a matter as profoundly important as this, commentators not only failed to move the discussion forward, but even forgot what that question was in the first place—absolutely all their attention became fixated on how things were related to what they understood to be the "Cultural Revolution" or "anti-Cultural Revolution," "elite" or "anti-elite" and "secular" or "antisecular." The discussion of the "spirit of humanism" eventually turned into a debate on idealism, with a consequential abandonment of any analysis of the transformation of contemporary society and its internal contradictions, a direction both sides in the discussion moved toward.

4. There was also the discussion of postcolonialism, nationalism, and globalization. Between 1994 and 1995, the journals *Dushu* and *Tianya* (Frontiers) published a number of articles on Edward Said's *Orientalism* and American postcolonial criticism that consisted of sharp attacks on both the actualities and theories of Eurocentrism and the new cultural imperialism.[54] In this period also appeared essays that explained global relations and cultural theory from the perspective of dependency theory and notions of globalism, all of which provided leads for the reflections on global capitalism that were to come.[55] This tide of humanistic thought just happened to coincide with the discussions on globalism and nationalism that had been kindled by Huntington's "The Clash of Civilizations?" and it was thus inevitable that all these elements blended together in a fierce series of arguments. For those who were firmly committed to the market and to globalization, any criticism of Eurocentrism was nationalist, and it must be said that this criticism of Eurocentrism did in effect correspond to nationalism at the level of popular culture as well as to a

number of unrelated nationalist perspectives that had been inspired by the events described above—the publication of books like *China Can Say No* (Zhongguo keyi shuo bu) and *The Background to the Demonization of China* (Yaomohua Zhongguo de beijing) is a case in point.[56] These discussions interacted with a rethinking of tradition, as well as with theories on indigenous resources and the nature of modernity to bring about a thoroughgoing interrogation of the enlightenment framework that had dominated Chinese intellectual life since the 1980s.[57]

Almost all of the discussion of postcolonialism was limited to the introduction and elucidation of Western academic work, and it never looked very closely at China's position in the history of colonialism, the course of Chinese modernization, or the complex historical factors imbedded in globalization. Even more important, whether it was the postcolonial deconstruction of nationalism or the studies of nationalism and globalization inspired by the thesis of the clash of civilizations or other historical factors, none of them could provide an analysis of the multiple sources of "nationalism" nor of its character as a multifaceted historical phenomenon—such as the relationship among colonialism and nationalism, anticolonial nationalism, cultural and military nationalism, as well as between state nationalism and popular nationalism. Neither were they able to give a clear explanation of the relationship between nationalism and the process of globalization. This discussion eventually came to a halt owing to various sorts of "political correctness." In general, however, the discussions of this period had a positive significance in terms of China's intelligentsia extricating itself from a Eurocentric historical perspective and gaining a critical understanding of nationalism.

The discussions between 1993 and 1997 moved the locus of the discourse from the traditional grand narratives to the changes that were taking place in contemporary China and the world, providing an intellectual horizon and practical evidence for the more systematic critique of neoliberalism that was to come. The 1990s critique of Eurocentrism had a powerfully liberating effect, freeing people from the teleology of history and of their illusions about the West. Curiously enough, when the systemic crisis of contemporary capitalism engulfed the Asian region in 1997, it was labeled the "Asian financial crisis." The period between 1993 and 1997 happened to be the time of China's most rapid economic growth, and a number of economists and cultural commentators who were infatuated with Confucian capitalism and the East Asian model were left completely without any capacity to respond to the onset of this crisis or to evaluate the extent of the threat. This global crisis in itself posed a sharp challenge to the ideology of neoliberalism. If we assume that the discussion of the "spirit of humanism" was an instinctive reaction to this process, but one that never really explained the internal contradictions of this period of market advocacy, then the postmodern tide of thought that also sprang up in this brief period lost its vibrancy equally quickly. Neither of these ideas could provide a basic perspective for recognizing and understanding the internal crisis of contemporary capitalism, and, like the advocates of the program of radical privatization, who took the market as the best medicine for deconstructing the old era, they could thus never realize that their notion of the market was an even grander grand narrative. The postmodernists shared a number of assumptions with the neoliberals: their deconstructivist posture and some of their liberating effects coexisted with an implicit conservatism. I think that the most important intellectual development of this period was the theoretical reflection on the nature of modernity produced by the critique of Eurocentrism, as well as the intellectual exploration of institutional and theoretical innovation.

1997 to the Present: The Debate over Neoliberalism

The third stage is the period between 1997 and the present. The contentions of this period have been inappropriately described by some as a dispute between "liberalism and the New Left." In fact, the intellectual debates since 1997 have been set off by the sharpening contradictions within contemporary society, and have been endowed with a general global significance by the financial panic that has been labeled "Asian." During the course of this crisis, the economies of South Korea, Hong Kong, and the nations of Southeast Asia all suffered serious setbacks, while almost simultaneously Chinese rural enterprises fell into palpable recession even as the internal contradictions of the Chinese economy—particularly the financial system— were mercilessly exposed. Exactly what, however, were the factors that prevented China from suffering heavy losses comparable to those in many other parts of East Asia? In this context, one must honestly face up to the internal contradictions of the contemporary capitalist system, must earnestly think about the significance of the market process that has so long been held up as a model for China, and must look soberly at the attempts to legitimate established but covert interests under the representation of democratic demands for legislative reform—these all constitute the reasons for the need to critically examine the intellectual presuppositions that have gradually come to the fore since the 1980s. It was within this historical perspective that the actual implications of the "end of history" thesis were fully revealed and the contemporary significance of the question of democracy received its theoretical elaboration.[58] The war in Kosovo in 1998, the bombing of the Chinese embassy in Yugoslavia, the dispute over the WTO, along with the unemployment, layoffs, the increasing internationalization of institutional corruption (from smuggling to money laundering, from individual cases of malfeasance to organized wrongdoing), the growth in the gap between rich and poor, the environmental crisis, and all the other social problems that were exacerbated over the course of the reforms combined to shatter any naive illusions or theoretical fantasies about modern society.

This course of development is in itself sufficient to demonstrate that globalization is not something that is taking place external to Chinese society, but is, rather, a problem internal to it. The links between political power and market arrangements, the recent production of poverty and inequality, and the internal links between the old networks of power and the new expansion of markets have all provided new opportunities to rethink modern Chinese history and a new creativity in understanding the discussions of the legacies of the socialist system. The factors that were unconscious and had only a hidden potential in the 1989 movement are now gradually coming to light. As a consequence, on the one hand, there has been a tremendous amount of public debate and discussion that has been centered in the journals *Dushu* and *Tianya* on such issues as the economic crisis, the notion of development, political democracy, globalization, social equality, questions of women's rights, education, war and revolution, neoliberalism, and colonialism. On the other hand, accompanying the translation and publication of the classic works of neoliberalism (sometimes referred to directly as "classical liberalism"), along with the radicalization of the conservative direction taken by liberal commentators and their work, neoliberalism has clearly entered a period in which it is embarking on a full-scale explanation and propagandizing of its own ideological foundations.

Owing to these inquiries into assorted social and historical issues, the critical intellectuals as a body have greatly opened up space for thinking and speech, and they have come to believe profoundly that in a public sphere lacking constitutional guarantees, lacking serious pursuit of and struggle for freedom of speech and public discussion, there will also be no possibility for democracy and space for the existence of critical thought. As far as I am concerned, no matter what theory one uses as a point of departure, any proposition that devalues political freedom as being of secondary importance or a sham should be rejected. At the same time, social despotism itself does not originate merely from state power, but also arises out of the workings of certain social and intellectual groupings. In these complicated historical circumstances, critical intellectuals need to broaden the scope of their protracted struggle against different but interacting types of cultural despotism. There is another characteristic of the discussion as it has evolved since 1997 that is worth pointing out: namely, the appearance of a new critical space. Scholars and intellectuals from South Korea, Japan, the United States, as well as those from Taiwan and

Hong Kong all participate in the discussion by publishing directly in China mainland periodicals, and mainland Chinese scholars also participate in discussions that take place in other regions. As a result, an international perspective on China's problems has gradually emerged.

"Neoliberalism" is a broadly based ideology having a specific economic theory at its core. It has permeated into every corner of contemporary society and possesses a substantial organizational capacity. Because of this, the emerging critiques of neoliberalism/neoconservatism have had a number of different facets. In the past twenty years social thought on the Chinese mainland has never been as intricate and complicated as it is today, something that I believe to be a reflection of the crises and rifts that characterize the mechanisms and controls working in the contemporary world. Also because of this, before introducing these critiques of neoliberalism, it is first necessary to say that the issues addressed by them are extremely broad, and cannot be restricted to a theoretical critique of neoliberalism itself. The social relations that they do address, however, all have connections of one sort or another with neoliberalism. In addition, these criticisms are not of a piece, nor do they share a particular logic, and among themselves they frequently exhibit contradictions and divergent interpretations. They include elements from critical liberalism, from traditional Marxism, from internationalism and nationalism, and from traditional scholarship and culture as well as from postmodernism. As a result, we cannot regard the criticism of neoliberalism as a unified intellectual movement. The post-1997 discussion has concentrated on the following points:

1. There has been a discussion of the tradition of liberalism and its contemporary problems. Under the guise of introducing free markets, neoliberalism has engaged in a planned partition of society that has resulted in large-scale corruption and social polarization; this has, in turn, inspired efforts by some intellectuals to bring into play liberal concepts to expose the hypocrisy and coercion that have characterized the process of the commodification of power.[59] In contemporary Chinese discourse neoliberalism not only arbitrarily dismisses any the-

oretical critiques of itself, but is also completely intolerant of any alternative traditions within liberalism itself, such as the tendency toward egalitarianism characterized by Rawls and Dworkin or such related notions as communitarianism and republicanism. In a time of the commodification of power, and the use of privatization as a pretext to divide up public property, with its associated theories and arguments that so evidently pose freedom and equality, freedom and democracy, and the individual and society as being in opposition to one another, any opposition to the thesis that "democracy obstructs freedom" will prove significant in the long run.[60] Even in regard to Hayek's theories, the neoliberals only use his demonstrations of the legitimacy of a free market, demolishing any notion that any tradition of radically planned markets bears any relation to freedom, even as they resolutely dismiss any discussions of historicity in Hayek's theories. As part of its effort in the name of deconstructing the state to dismiss any exploration of the question of how democracy might work in the context of marketization, one of the characteristics of neoliberal theory is to deny the close relationship between the market and the political process.

It is against this background that a number of scholars have since 1997 begun to sort out the sources of the democratic tradition in an attempt to reveal from the standpoint of liberalism itself the extent of the antidemocratic sentiment within neoliberalism. This discussion has included an analysis of such thinkers as de Tocqueville, Berlin, Arendt, Hayek, Habermas, Rawls, and Charles Taylor and has constituted a reappraisal of the modern European liberal political tradition and contemporary liberal theory. At the same time that it has analyzed the internal dilemmas of this tradition, it has from a variety of different perspectives restored and developed the inclinations toward egalitarianism within liberal thought; in the process there has emerged what has been labeled "the liberal Left." Is the liberalism being professed by the neoliberals a liberalism for an aristocracy or one for the common people? Is it political liberalism or a conservative theory of modernization? Does it really value tradition, or is it a theory of market extremism that fragments all social relations? Does it represent the spontaneous generation of order, or does it break society into classes by human agency, planning, and coercion? The pursuit of these questions from the perspective of the liberal tradition itself overturns the rationality of neoliberalism, even as it reveals the internal predicament and crisis that liberalism is facing and injects new factors into the discussion.[61]

2. Since 1997 there have been discussions of the historical and theoretical analysis of historical capitalism. Neoliberalism assumed market systems to be "spontaneous and self-regulating," took free trade as the natural law of market economics, and took the maximization of profit as the only ethical standard of the era of markets. This theoretical perspective is, in fact, in the sharpest possible contrast to a polarization between rich and poor that was becoming daily more acute, an ever-deepening economic crisis, unending corruption, and the process of commodifying power. Throughout the course of China's reforms, this doctrine refused to consider the relationship between the creation of regulations for the market and general political participation and basic demands for equality. Instead, what took place was the creation of interest groups that colluded to use their power to divide up state resources, used monopoly power to earn super profits, and worked in concert with transnational or indigenous capital to seize market resources. Neoliberalism, whether self-consciously or not, has strengthened the tendency toward monopolization and restraint of markets. To take it to task only on moral grounds, however, is ineffectual, and is also the main reason that liberal economists use science as a pretext to reject this type of criticism.[62] In other words, transcending moral criticism by responding to the basic theoretical presuppositions of neoliberalism on the levels of theory, history, and practice has become an urgent task.

Extending the reflection on global relations and the problem of modernity of the earlier period, from 1998 on *Dushu, Tianya,* and a number of other journals have published a series of theoretical and historical investigations of historical capitalism, seeking thereby effectively to explode the market myth of neoliberalism from theoretical, historical, and practical angles—and from the perspective of the financial crisis in particular. In this discussion, the theories of Karl Polanyi and Ferdinand Braudel along with the tradition of Marxist political economy provided important intellectual resources. From the perspective of a critical political economy or economic history, these critical intellectuals sought to reexamine the main characteristics of historical capitalism and its links to the contemporary economic crisis, as well as to analyze the incommensurate views of neoliberalism toward politics and economics, the state and the market, nature and society, and state and society; neoliberalism's theoretical presuppositions were revealed to be ideological and historical illusions. These studies cleared a practical path toward formulating a direct critique of neoliberalism.[63] The discussion described above pointed out the intertwined relations between the capitalist market and power, violence, interference, and monopoly, and demonstrated the ceaseless interweaving among politics, economics, and culture. It also made the necessary distinction between capitalism and markets, and provided not only a historical perspective by which could be envisaged a democratic political structure and market relations based on equality and common participation, but also provided new possibilities for reevaluating the historical practice of traditional socialism.

3. Discussion took place in which the historical analysis of capitalism was directly related to inquiry into the WTO and developmentalism. It was this discussion that most clearly disclosed the interlocking relationships between neoliberalism on the one hand and the state, interest groups, and transnational capital on the other. The state and the media it directed undertook a long and one-sided campaign to publicize the WTO negotiations, which corresponded with reports in the American media on the same issue. A number of intellectuals used the Internet and academic journals to carry out serious research on the question of the WTO, but virtually no critical opinions on the WTO ever appeared in the public media, and there was thus no real public debate on the question. Neoliberalism regarded

the WTO as tremendous progress in their plans for a "free market," believing that this plan also paved the way for democracy in China. These political arrangements, however, which touched on the daily lives of hundreds of millions of people, received no public discussion at all, to the point that relevant information was never released even after the conclusion of the Sino–American negotiations.[64]

Very few people have, however, linked up this matter with questions concerning freedom of speech and open discussion. Why is this? Based on my reading, the majority of scholars who criticized the WTO agreement were not opposed in principle to China joining it, nor were they unconditionally or abstractly opposed to globalization. Their detailed analyses focused on two principal issues: Under what conditions should China join the WTO? And did there exist a public discussion, detailed analysis, and criticism of the world order represented by the WTO? In regard to this, the real question is one that concerns democracy: Was there open, democratic discussion and was there a democratic process that accorded with accepted international standards? I would like to ask whether the drawing up of the WTO regulations was open and democratic, and whether entry into the WTO followed the principles of democracy and public participation? In the absence of this sort of open, democratic participation, grandly talking about the relationship between globalization and democracy ends up being merely a democratic semblance legitimating an autocratic set of rules. From the discussion contained in any number of small specialist journals that are not widely influential (such as *Guoji jingji pinglun* [The review of international economics]), the Internet, and foreign journals, the theoretical and practical critique of the WTO—along with the sharp analysis of a minority of economists and political scientists—constituted an acute challenge to neoliberalism and the internal and international order it would support. It revealed the antagonistic relationship between radical theories of marketization and democracy.

4. The discussion outlined above echoes the discourse concerning developmentalism carried on by scholars of the humanities and social

sciences. Together they reveal how the myth of "transition" and the fantasy of development cover up the urgency of the need for political freedom and social democracy.[65] The criticism of developmentalism was not criticism of development itself, but rather an attempt to reestablish the connection between development and freedom and to reaffirm the importance of the roles of democracy and diversity in this process. Neoliberalism understands development narrowly—as being only a matter of economic growth—and disregards the connection between this growth and political freedom and social benefits, thereby intentionally or unintentionally ignoring the political preconditions for economic growth. In this context, the discussion of developmentalism concerns not simply economic growth and its paradigms, but includes the relationship between economics and politics. Developmentalism is not just the core of Chinese national policy, but also the basis for the plans for the contemporary world formulated by such international agencies as the WTO and the IMF; its theoretical underpinning is provided by the neoliberal notion of radical market expansion.

Developmentalism takes successful paradigms of development as being universal, thereby concealing their reliance on unequal center–periphery relations created by the paradigms themselves, which cut off any ties between development and freedom of choice. Even as these plans for a free market foster ecological crises and polarization between wealth and poverty, they also create various sorts of colonial relationships both within nation-states and on a world scale, rendering impossible democratic control of society.[66] The debate over the WTO most resonantly reflected the need for freedom of speech and public discussion. The appearance of the WTO controversy and other major social questions simultaneously placed new demands on the struggle by intellectuals for the right of free speech. In the exceedingly complicated circumstances of contemporary society, the struggle for free speech and a free press must be located in a broader democratic perspective, and the demands for constitutional rights and, indeed, for rights at every level of society closely linked to the social movement. The three key questions involved here are how to prevent interest groups from monopolizing these rights, how to prevent the refeudalization of the public arena, and how to substantially open up our social space.[67]

5. There has been since 1997 a discussion of nationalism. This at first was an extension of the discussion on nationalism and globalism that took place in 1993, but in 1999 it was rendered more pressing by the dramatic events of that year—the Kosovo war and the bombing of the Chinese embassy in Belgrade. The Kosovo crisis broke out after a Yugoslavia situated far away in Eastern Europe had endured a number of divisions. NATO, led by the United States, involved itself militarily in the name of humanitarianism. The tragedy that took place at the Chinese embassy on May 8 brought about protest marches by students and urban citizens in Beijing (and other cities) that ended up stoning the American and other NATO embassies. The post-1980 discussion of the May Fourth enlightenment movement occasioned much lamentation about how concerns for "[national] salvation overrode those for enlightenment," and this later event in 1999 was treated in almost the same fashion. Some people began to diagnose all the problems of modern Chinese history as resulting from two causes—"nationalism" and "populism"—but offered hardly any historical analysis of the complicated components of the social movement or its historical causes. A number of intellectuals expressed their opinions on the new situation, focusing also on the criticism of and encouragement for Chinese nationalism that had been uttered both at home and abroad. The first thing they took up was the nature of the NATO intervention: was it humanitarian or simply the embodiment of geopolitical interests, that is to say, a hyper-imperialist holy war? The high-tech weapons NATO brought to bear in this war, the mobilization of the media and the goals of the war, which differed from any that had come before, seemed to signal a difference from ordinary imperialism. None of this, however, could obscure its hyper-imperialist essence or the historical and theoretical connection between this military action and traditional imperialism.[68]

This group of intellectuals also took up the question of national self-determination and human rights. Between 1945 and 1960, the Western nations had consistently been indifferent to the provisions in the UN Charter regarding the right to national self-determination. By the time that national independence and liberation had become a worldwide trend, however, the Western nations shifted to providing the new sense of "internal self-determination" to the theory of "self-determination," thus linking the right of national self-determination to human rights and democratic elections. At the beginning of the 1990s, Slovenia and Croatia declared their independence by referendum and other means. After Croatian independence, there in fact took place instances of ethnic cleansing (or the forcible emigration of populations), but since Germany had recognized the results of the referendum, the Western nations eventually recognized Croatian independence. Because of this, when areas in which a number of ethnicities resided exercised their "internal self-determination" through referendum, there was a natural logic that brought about ethnic cleansing. Thus, democratic elections can only be used to decide matters within a given political configuration; they cannot be used to decide the boundaries of the configuration itself. Aside from the transformation of its internal political structure and relationships attendant on the dissolution of Yugoslavia (the 1974 constitution had already given each republic within Yugoslavia veto power over federal policy), the "shock therapy" that was part of the country's acceptance of IMF stipulations to contract the economy brought about economic recession and large-scale unemployment, which only intensified the tendencies to separatism. In order to guarantee Yugoslavia's ability to service its debt, the IMF in its "plan for structural adjustment" demanded that economic power become highly centralized, one of the direct causes behind Yugoslavia's rescinding of Kosovo's status as an independent province. The Yugoslavian crisis must not, therefore, be analyzed strictly within the context of nationalism, but looked at rather from the perspective of its position within the international political economy. The feeble link between a "humanitarian assistance" that took the form of wanton bombing and demands for human rights completely dissolves under this sort of scrutiny.[69]

The protest movement that was inspired by the war in Kosovo was entangled with various types of nationalism, so in order to prevent an analysis of that movement from lapsing into an account already determined by the political force of the status quo, it is necessary to distinguish both theoretically and historically the protest itself from ethnocentrism. It is also necessary to ask further: in circumstances where there is only partisan political reporting by state and Western media, is there a theoretical imperative to distinguish between protests against hegemonism and a state-mobilized nationalism? The state media that reported the bombing incident failed to deal with the internal crisis that Yugoslavia was undergoing, the gravity of the ethnic conflict, and the complicated social aftermath. The Chinese government used public opinion to bargain with the United States and other Western nations, but as soon as the protest movement showed signs of spreading, it immediately deployed means to attempt to organize it, limit it, and guide it. At the same time, the Western media failed to report the actual reason behind the bombing and the even greater "humanitarian disaster" brought about by the war, even as it depicted the response of ordinary Chinese citizens against violence as antiforeignism and nationalistic fanaticism.

In the context of the protest movement, it is thus necessary to explain theoretically the distinction between antiforeignism and protest against hegemonism and violence; it is also necessary to explain the significance of mass political participation and the social movement for the Chinese democratic movement. It is only by theoretically distinguishing between nationalism and the protest against violence that one will be able to provide affirmative support for and critique of the myriad possibilities inhering in the social movement. I think there is no reason whatsoever to idealize or romanticize the movement, and one should undertake an analysis of the conditions that occasioned any sort of social thought or movement, as these are the grounds on the basis of which one passes theoretical and practical judgment on it.

In this sense, to group all popular participation in and demands of the social process as well as all protest against hegemony under the rubric "populism" or "nationalism" or "radicalism," and then to banish them to the outside of the structure of reform would seem to be a viewpoint at odds with the nationalism propagated by the state, but in fact there is a consistent logic. For, from different directions, both these political inclinations disintegrate the democratic potential and the demands for equality latent in the social movement. If nationalism is treated as an historical phenomenon, it cannot be taken as only an intellectual trend; one must analyze it in light of the international relations that have control over events at the time. Those who monopolize the strength of the whole world in the name of globalism are actually the biggest nationalists. Thus, how to distinguish different nationalisms, how to analyze the historical conditions for nationalism, and how to reconstruct the historical tradition of internationalism in a period of globalization become the most urgent of theoretical topics.[70]

In discussions about nationalism, the discourse on gender issues and feminism provides a unique angle of vision and has the capacity to show in contemporary theoretical perspective the coercion and potential for violence that inhere in the agenda for a market society. The world order of neoliberalism not only creates a massive polarization between wealth and poverty, it also reopens the gulf between the genders and legitimizes this pattern in each of its grand narratives.[71] Out of concern over this, in 1999 the journal *Dushu* published a number of discussions of feminism that considered the relationship between gender and nationalism in India, Pakistan, Yugoslavia, and late Qing China, attempting to offer a sharp critique of those theoretical and social responses that place all contemporary problems within the framework of radical nationalism (these essays also offered the first Chinese behind-the-scenes looks at the Yugoslavian inter-ethnic conflicts). The above-mentioned discussion did not directly take up the analysis of gender issues in China, nor was it able to analyze the various historical contexts of "nationalism" and its diverging implications. The gender perspective, however, offers an indispensable reflexive viewpoint, spurring on those caught up in the tense and turbulent mood of contemporary China to consider again whether they have already fallen victim to violence and new forms of social and intellectual control. As far as I can tell, the Chinese intelligentsia's discussion of nationalism has become an active dialogue with the ability to combine onto one plane propositions concerning hyperimperialism and globalization, nationalism and internationalism, national self-determination and the global program of neoliberalism, and gender and feminism. This conceptual grouping has created a multiple perspective for comprehending the problem of nationalism and provided the intellectual resources to extricate ourselves from the old binary of hegemony and ultranationalism.[72]

6. There has been a discussion of the problems of Asia and of the Chinese revolution. Such matters not only provide a perspective for understanding modern Chinese history, but also allow one to break through the global perspective centered on the West, as well as the view of modern history created in the 1980s. Between 1996 and 2000, *Dushu* published a series of essays on Asian issues that included scholars from China, Japan, and South Korea and that also featured dialogue with related discussions in Hong Kong and Taiwan. This discussion on Asian issues took on added significance after the financial panic of 1997, giving rise to thinking about creating closer regional relationships that could resist pressure from global capitalism. Taking place as it did in the context of globalization and China's opening up to the West, the questions raised about Asia in this discussion were necessarily somewhat fuzzy, but nonetheless contained the seeds of revision and transformation of knowledge and intellectual interest.[73] I think that what was most worthy of attention in these considerations of Asia was not just the discussion of "Asian" culture, but the debates over war, colonization, revolution, and nationalism.

As an object of knowledge and as an interrelated, comprehensive concept, Asia is the product of a mixture of colonization, war, invasion, and revolution, and any discussion of matters pertaining to it cannot be separated from the specific historical factors spelled out above, nor can it be separated from a consideration of the different perspectives on this common history and the conversation among them. This discussion has provided a particular historical perspective on Asia, and on the future development of the East Asian region in particular. The reflections on the responsibility for World War II engaged in by Japanese scholars pointed out from yet another angle the necessity of a new understanding of modern Chinese history and revolution from outside the confines of modernization theory. In pursuit of the conditions that enabled these events and their historical implications, they strove to place this process in the context of the specific interrelationships of Asian as well as of global history.

In the discursive context of contemporary China, raising the questions of Asia, globalization, and the Chinese revolution seems like part of an historical cycle, but it has already become a critical process, and in no way can be said to be a simple replay of the revolutionary worldview. How to achieve a new understanding of the Chinese revolution, of the legacy of socialism, and of the achievements as well as the tragedies of this legacy are major questions urgently in need of address from Chinese intellectuals, but to which they have so far been unable to respond. This is because the ideology of neoliberalism and its legitimization were built on the total repudiation and moral condemnation of this legacy. From the end of the 1970s until the 1990s, the Chinese intelligentsia undertook a long process of digesting and rethinking the history of socialism, making critiques of every tragedy that marked its course. In this current reevaluation of the Chinese revolution, a basic tendency has been to substitute critiques of its consequences (that is, the new inequality and social despotism) for analysis of the historical factors behind it. The basic problem here, however, is not to defend in any way the tragedies of this revolutionary history, but how to understand the tragedy and its links to colonialism, the expansion of the capitalist market, and the historical conditions of Chinese society. In the course of implementing their demands for equality, both the social and the national revolutions to different degrees introduced unequal conditions into the new institutions they created.

Some people sum up the historical lesson of the last half century as being one of the dangers of egalitarianism, thereby conferring legitimacy on the unequal conditions of contemporary life. How do they deal, however, with what even Mao Zedong acknowledged as the "three great differences"?[74] Was it egalitarian for the state to institutionalize the difference between the city and the country in pursuit of its objectives of industrialization and modernization? At the beginning of the Cultural Revolution people were concerned about bureaucratization and the new social strata, which, in fact, provided some of the impetus for the social mobilization of the period. Was this sort of social order egalitarian? The thesis of blood lineage criticized by Yu Loke[75] was one of the legacies of the Cultural Revolution, and the tragedies this thesis brought about are there for all to see. But is the notion of blood lineage part of the demand for social equality or part of an ideology of social hierarchy? There are many profound cautionary tales to be learned from Chinese socialism, but these lessons have nothing to do with the realization of egalitarianism. Quite the contrary, they stemmed from the failure of its egalitarian objectives ever to be really implemented. In other words, what deserves criticism is not the victories won by the socialist movement in the realm of equality, but the new hierarchy and notions of social status that were created in the process. The complicated interactions between demands for equality and for various other things also need to be investigated.

Analyzing the conditions that brought about the Chinese revolution is not the same as calling for revolution and demands for social equality are not the equivalent of demanding revolution. The core of the matter here is to consider the possibilities and historical conditions for a free society enabled by democracy and equality via scrutiny of the actual conditions that gave rise to the revolution. Thus, rather than simply denouncing the value or the social experience of equality, the real question to ask is how a social movement whose object was equality managed within itself to produce a new system of hierarchy? What were the historical mechanisms involved? As long as we can understand the bitter experiences of China and the rest of the world since the colonial period, as long as we can understand the liberating effects produced by the Chinese socialist movement, and as long as we don't see the experiences and lessons of socialism through Cold War lenses, then we will neither gloat over the movement's failure nor engage in one-sided censure of socialism's history. This will also prevent us from too easily forgetting the wars, massacres, ethnic exterminations, and other acts of violence of the period of colonialism, and keep us from putting aside a thoroughgoing look at the history of Chinese socialism and all that transpired during the long course of this movement.

In the preface to my collection of essays entitled *Rekindling Dead Ashes,* I maintained that the focus of the contention over neoliberalism lay in the questions of social equality and justice. These entailed questions of national and international equality, economic equality, and of other social relations (such as gender relations, national relations, political relations, relations between city and country, and between humans and nature). This is why the discussion of such issues as feminism, nationalism, postcolonialism, Asia, ecology, and development can all be regarded as far-ranging critiques of neoliberalism. Based on this notion, I take the body of thinkers engaged in these types of critique as constituting a critical intellectual movement that is at once broad, internally differentiated, and working in a discursive space that is not completely uniform; neither are its discussions restricted only to economics and politics. The characteristic shared by all members of this critical group is a determination to reveal the links between politics and economics, as well as to reveal the internal relationship between the forms of thought and ideas of the intellectuals and the unequal process of development. This is undertaken in order to extend political demands for democracy to the realms of economics and other areas of society—to seek out a path of reform that is more fair, more democratic, and more humanitarian. In this context, equality and fairness are not *a priori* propositions, but rather criticisms of the policies and theories of neoliberalism that are being put into practice by the state and other interest groups. From the perspectives of both theory and practice, the basic difference between Right and Left in today's China is closely related to their respective understandings of the notion of democracy. Critical intellectuals stress that the market and the urban movement have never been and indeed never can be separate from the particular political structure under which they exist, so the task of social reform is to create mechanisms for political participation. In its theorization, on the other hand, the New Right stresses the autonomy and apolitical nature of the market and of civil society, and accordingly places demands for freedom ahead of those for democracy. In my opinion, the core of the issue is the need to give substantive content to political freedom, not to abandon the basic demand for it.

In the context of contemporary China, opposing freedom to democracy and using individual rights to critique the notion of equality cannot be considered merely as part of a discussion of the theory of liberalism, as these are so closely related to the expansion of unequal markets that is going on today (the question then becomes one of the process by which a minority freely and legitimately expropriates public property): is this a political or an apolitical process? If one takes political freedom as nothing more than an independent process, or takes political reform as meant only to protect the fruits of economic reform and at the same time fails to pay attention to the links between politics and economics, fails even to consider the connections among politics, new developments in the economic arena, and various other areas of society, then this is tantamount to saying that the arena in which economics is articulated with other areas of society transcends politics. It can only be a matter for self-adjustment for the "autonomous and spontaneous market order." Using this perspective, there is no way to discuss the numerous theoretical and practical questions that have been with us since the 1980s.

The Chinese intelligentsia's understanding of the contemporary situation demonstrably deepened between the rethinking of radicalism that followed 1989 and the debates on liberalism that have been going on since 1997. After 1989, however, since intellectual deliberation had begun from a reconsideration of the radicalism of the social movement, and because this reconsideration was in certain respects based on a number of premises taken from conservatism and neoliberalism, study of the interaction between the social movement and social reform never received the theoretical attention it deserved. Questions concerning the interests of workers, peasants, women, and other social groups gradually came to the surface in intellectual discussion, but the connections between structural reform and the movements for self-protection on the part of these groups never received theoretical elaboration. The post-1978 reform movement was to a certain extent a process of the specialization of the division of labor as well as a process of the redifferentiation of social strata. As a social entity that benefited from the reforms, the intelligentsia was gradually integrated into professions within such endeavors as state employment, education, research units, commercial activity, high-tech, and the media. The historical relations this group had with the workers and peasants seem to have been completely severed. The intellectuals were thus concerned to achieve such constitutional rights as freedom of thought, expression, and association, but were unable to make any close links between these demands and the demands of other social groups connected with their struggle for existence and the advancement of their rights.

Even the critical intellectuals concerned with the movement to protect social safeguards have been unable to find an effective way to establish links among the implementation of their theories, institutional innovation, and the social movement itself. I think that because of this, thinking about institutional and theoretical innovation, about bringing into being structures enabling widespread economic and political participation, has remained at a relatively abstract stage, even as contemporary social contradictions have reached new levels of severity. I raise this point here not to negate in any way the importance of theoretical work nor to support unconditionally the social movement (as the experience of 1989 tells us, the movement itself contains a number of complicated components and tendencies). Rather I believe that it is precisely this inability to theorize the connections between the social movement and institutional reform that has prevented us from seeing the real junctures that link up theory and practice, that has prevented us from establishing an historical understanding of the social movement and social change, and finding a genuine democratic path to forestalling social polarization and collapse.[76]

Alternative Globalizations and the Question of the Modern

Such matters as free markets versus state intervention, globalization versus antiglobalization, and the right of private ownership of property versus state ownership constitute some of the focal points for the debates as well as for some of the activities of the left and right wings. If, however, these debates and actions are placed in the context of the actual process of historical development, then abstract notions like free markets, state intervention, rights to private property, and globalization all emerge as a tangle of completely different types of complex relationships. From my perspective, one of the ways to link up the inherent connections between theory and practice is to examine actually or historically the process by which the new political and economic order was able to constitute itself. This would entail proceeding from a practical reliance on the web of connections within the historical developments themselves rather than from such categories as the free market/state intervention and capitalism/socialism.

Based on my analysis of the 1989 social crisis, the year 1989 can be regarded as a time of a temporary suspension of the process of Chinese market reform. This suspension coincided with the period of policy adjustments undertaken by the state in its response to the first round of crises at that time, and also as a necessary preparatory stage in the further expansion of markets. This fact is pregnant with rich historical and theoretical implication. First, market expansion took the form of coercive intervention by the state, and because of this, the notion of a binary market/state opposition was shattered. After June of that year, those who thought that the movement had speeded up the process of Chinese democratic reform discovered that they had been abruptly dragged back into an era they thought was passing away—the old language, old patterns, old characters, old announcements, and old faces that should have retired from the scene all took the stage once again. These old patterns created a hallucinatory effect, such that no one became conscious of the fact that the actual function of the repressive measures was precisely to reestablish the links among market mechanisms that had begun to fail. Nor did anyone reckon that violent repression and the reactionary period that followed would provide moral legitimacy for the creation of an era of markets. Just as people have forgotten the sound of social fragmentation echoing behind the excitement at Tiananmen, neither can people remember that the market era referred to today as "neoliberalism" is hiding behind the political specters of those on the square and has only in this way secured an exemption from social protest against it. In addition, these very specters of the past era are today's stage properties. The old violence and the old language have conferred on the present era of dramatic polarization a reputation for being progressive.

Those in charge of implementing the last will and testament of the revolution carry out their dual responsibilities in an absurd fashion: on the one hand they clownishly bury all of the reasonable aspects of the revolution and of socialism, while on the other they employ state violence and monopolization to guarantee the smooth transition of a Chinese economy in crisis to one based on market mechanisms, in the process wrecking all of the equitable features of the social guarantees contained within the old system. As a result, behind the continuity of the political structure there is a profound process of transformation of social forces: the face of the old system put an end to its own moral legitimacy by the very act of successfully repressing the social movement, even as it established the foundation for the hegemonic position of the new social order. Meanwhile, radical changes were set in motion in the social conditions existing under the state structure, such that there took place a profound reorganization of the social structure itself and of the relationships of social interest it represents. This process is the historical premise that underlay the open national call for capitalists to join the Communist Party some twenty years later. In light of this, it is fundamentally impossible to use the binary of socialism/capitalism as a framework for historical analysis in the discursive context of China today.

In reconfiguring the relations between society, the state, and the market, the historical role played by the 1989 social movement was epochal. As outlined above, the creation of the Chinese market system had two basic thrusts. Internally, by means of the devolution of economic and political power, the state furthered a process of privatization by such means as enterprise autonomy and the reform of the financial system; it developed market relations in every sector of social life and, even as it achieved huge economic growth, it dissolved the system of social guarantees and restructured the relations among Chinese social classes and strata. Externally, via reforms of foreign trade and the financial system, the state gradually brought China into the set of global market relations governed by the WTO and IMF, then reorganized the legal and contractual relations of society in concert with the economic order of neoliberalism. The events of 1989 along with the changes that have transpired since then demonstrate the paradoxical relationship between the state and market expansion: on the one hand, lacking the policy adjustments, legal system, and political guarantees of the state, it is almost impossible to imagine the cultivation and expansion of the market system; on the other hand, the reliance of the market system on the state is also the precondition for the commodification of power.

From this perspective, we can see the integral historical relationship between the reforms of the 1980s and the period that followed 1989 and the singular form of the interactions between the traditional socialist system and the creation of markets: the expansion of markets brought about social fragmentation and disorder, which in turn cre-

ated the reason for violent state intervention, an intervention resulting in the state's becoming a political structure that "established market mechanisms." Finally, the hegemony of market mechanisms was
pivotal to the transformation of the sources of state legitimacy. In
1989, the social movement attempted to facilitate an organic interaction between state and society via mass participation, but after 1989
mechanisms of interaction between state and market came to substitute for those between state and society. As part of this historical process, the concept of society was gradually replaced by the concept of
the market and the basic motive power behind promotion of the
transformation of the mechanisms of the state and the reform of the
legal system was no longer "society," but internal and external markets. As a result, the very implications of the term "politics" underwent a huge shift: the state became the defender of market mechanisms and the principal administrator of the legal system along lines
set out by the WTO. From this historical perspective, the links
among the social movement, the crisis of reform, and the role of the
state need to be reexamined.

Looking at the historical process that unfolded around the events
of 1989, the dramatic pace of change does not mean that the creation
of market conditions was the sudden result of a single historical
event, nor does it mean that it was the natural extension of a particular historical process. What it does show is that the actualities of market economics and the process of globalization cannot be implemented other than by state intervention. Without the national
economic system and the state capacity that had already taken shape
prior to the reforms, without the reform policies that had been gradually put into effect since 1978 and, while abounding with twists and
turns, had been generally quite effective, and without global political
and economic relationships and their transformations there is no way
for us to understand the historical conditions that enabled the establishment of China's market system. In this sense, the process of
marketization also contained within itself the forces of "anti-
marketization," as the process of globalization relied upon the forces

of "antiglobalization." In following Hayek's views—however much they misread them—the neoliberals used notions about markets and free trade and corresponding political theories to critique the economics of socialist states that had planned economies at their core. They went on to regard the market order as one that was spontaneous and self-regulating, thereby obscuring the meta-market forces on which the market order depended. As markets expanded, polarization between wealth and poverty, capital flight, social inequity, the environmental crisis, unemployment, corruption, and similar phenomena rapidly spread and the social need for the protection of basic fairness (that is, social benefits and insurance) became more acute by the day. This finally reached the point that neoliberalism was obliged to employ the theory of "transition" to maintain its myths of free markets and globalization.

In this context it is necessary to make three basic distinctions. First, there needs to be a distinction between the notion of free competition or self-regulating markets and the formation and historical functioning of the actual market economies that we have today. Second, there needs to be a distinction between the market ideology of neoliberalism (which normally is characterized by demands for the complete withdrawal of the state) and the actual policies and market system of neoliberalism (which normally is expressed through state policy and its reliance on coercion). Third, there needs to be a distinction between the categories of market and society. According to these distinctions, the formation of a market society and its rules results from a complex process of interaction among state intervention, institutional innovation, monopolies, social custom, and historical factors; free competition makes up only a portion of the mix. As a result, a critique of an actual market society and its crises cannot be equated with repudiation of the mechanisms of market competition, as the principal task of critical intellectuals is to disclose the antimarket mechanisms within market society and to bring to bear a democratic and socialized conception of markets to counter the antimarket logic of actual market society. In accordance with the second distinction made above, the ideology of neoliberalism makes demands on the state to implement policies of *laissez-faire*—that is, that the state abandon its responsibilities for social benefits and the system of social insurance—while demanding that the state abandon the economic means of regulating market activity; it even demands that the links between politics and economics be cut.

To abandon these responsibilities, however, would be a set of policy and institutional plans in itself. For example, the crises faced by Chinese state enterprises and the agricultural sector are the consequence of activist and systematic policy plans, while the slogan of opposing state intervention just happens to constitute the precondition for state policy, which is, in fact, another form of activist intervention. The agricultural crisis that will be brought about by entry into the WTO is a good example of market planning. It not only uncovers the close links between the state and the rules of the international market, but also proves the inconsistencies between the concept of a self-regulating market and the actual working of the contemporary market economy. In accordance with the third distinction above, stipulations for the market cannot be equated with stipulations for society, and mechanisms for social democracy cannot be equated with mechanisms for the functioning of markets. Thus, the path toward national democracy cannot be equated with a transformation of political functions that would lead to establishing mechanisms of the market. The 1989 crisis demonstrated how the expansion of markets under state direction could produce a social crisis, and how this social crisis could become the occasion for the state to take complete control of society—and not just the market. Thus the rules of the market could be established because of the complete withdrawal of society—rather than the state—from the political sphere.

Because of this, rather than use the separation of economics from politics (or the state) to characterize the process by which the market economy was created, it would be more realistic to bring to bear an historical perspective to outline the interpenetrating links between politics and economics that give rise to market systems. In *Capitalism and Material Life, 1400–1800,* Fernand Braudel employs a detailed historical analysis to prove that unequal relationships of exchange cannot be explained by economic laws (that is, the rules of the market), because economic inequality is simply a reproduction of social inequality. This intellectual perception is directly reflected in the fundamental distinction he makes between capitalism and market economics: the market economy is the bond between production and consumption, but capitalism is only concerned with the value of the exchange; the market economy is governed by competition, with the result that exchange under the conditions of a market economy is equal. For its part, however, capitalism creates and uses its monopoly positions to bring about inequalities of exchange. As a result, first, capitalism is an antimarket system that always relies on and tends toward monopoly. Second, whether the category used is everyday life, market economics, or capitalism, there is no way to generalize about particular social formations or processes, because the material relations described by these categories all have long individual histories. For instance, the feudal society described as being precapitalist and the socialist China described as being postcapitalist both encompass various sorts of market relations as well as various sorts of market monopolies (that is, things characteristic of capitalism). Third, economics is imbricated within the activities of the political system, law, everyday life, and cultural habit; and any attempt to abstract the market from the processes of politics, law, and custom is in itself a political process, and it must thus be negated by political means.

On this last point, the possible choices include: resisting the monopolies of capitalism by preserving the value of everyday life, opposing the union between the state and interest groups or transnational capital by relying on social movements and true competition, preserving free competition and social equality by relying on active state regulation and industrial policy, and resisting the so-called economic totalization program of neoliberalism through state and local cooperation. At the level of the system, people can on the one hand protect the rights of workers and the freedom of contract by defending constitutional rights, and on the other resist the tyranny of the neoliberal market by safeguarding customs, manners, and traditional relationships.

In line with the above analysis, I here outline a few possible tendencies that might develop. First, capitalist monopolies are always closely related to inequalities in politics, economics, culture, and other spheres, so the struggle for freedom—including the freedom of labor contract, exchange relations, politics, and the like—must at the same time also be a struggle for social equality; all forms of discourse that are dead set against demands for freedom and for equality must be rejected. Second, because of the distinction between markets and capitalism, resistance to the despotism of market domination and monopolization should no longer be seen as an "antimarket" struggle, because this social struggle in itself contains the seeds of a search for fair competition. Third, resistance to economic hegemony and transnational monopoly is not the same as isolationism, and trade protection cannot be taken as "antimarket." The social movement that has sprung up in response to the WTO, and the contention between the rich and poor countries that has taken place in the course of the negotiations over the WTO negotiations have revealed a new form of struggle. This is not a struggle against international organizations and international regulation in toto, but rather a participatory movement aimed at pushing international organizations (including the WTO) and international regulations in a democratic direction, with the intention of linking domestic economic justice to international economic justice. Fourth, since the workings of the economy are invariably imbricated in political, cultural, and other social conditions, the fight for fair competition in the market cannot be equated with breaking away from the national political system, social customs, or the various mechanisms of regulation. Quite the opposite, the effort to perfect market competition must move in the direction of reforming, limiting, or expanding these systems in order to create the conditions for fair exchange.

The struggle for social justice and fair market competition is not, therefore, opposed to state intervention, but rather seeks social democracy in order to use the democratic control of society over the state to oblige the state to implement social insurance and to prevent it from becoming the protector of domestic and transnational monopolies. The key here is using democratic means to secure the institutional basis for guaranteeing free competition and fair exchange, and the means employed here must include the powers of the society, the state, and the localities to further the democratization of the international economic order itself. In other words, no matter what the context, whether it is the context of the nation-state or that of the world market, the struggle for freedom must express itself as a struggle for democracy and equality. I generalize all these tendencies as part of a meditation on a democratic market system, and as a meditation on social development that is not restricted merely to economic development. It is only within such a framework that the struggle for economic justice can become at the same time a struggle for social justice and political democracy.

State, Locality, and the New Internationalism

The success of capitalism's expansion worldwide was only achieved by the expansion of the system of nation-states; without the political and military structure provided by this system, the global division of labor would never have been able to take place. The expansion of markets and of the capacity of the state were parallel historical phenomena in the development of capitalism, a fact quite at odds with the neoliberal historical narrative. The economic development of the United States, Germany, and Japan was in each case facilitated by a long period of protectionism, and even today the role played by the state in economic life should not be overlooked. Excepting China and other East Asian nations, the experience of the vast majority of developing nations that have pursued free-market theory and policies of complete economic openness has been highly problematic, and many Latin American nations (such as Argentina) are on the verge of bankruptcy. Neoliberalism uses its program of market totalization to call for completely open markets and to deny any function for the state in regard to social guarantees and economic regulation. From the international perspective, this position rests on a completely new concept of globalization that takes the free circulation of capital—especially financial capital—as its historical foundation, and which then powerfully coordinates the economies of developing nations with a free-market order promoted and regulated by the World Bank, the IMF, and the WTO. From the domestic perspective, this position represents a radicalization of the reform policies of devolving political and economic power, which then seeks to use new rules to completely restructure the legal system and the entire economic order, including urban–rural relations.

As I analyzed above, on the one hand, the 1989 social crisis and the post-1989 period of rapid growth marked by structural corruption and polarization of wealth occurred under the guidance of national policies that were part of the neoliberal trend. On the other hand, Chinese economic development had benefited from a successful national industrial policy, and China successful weathered the financial panic of 1997 with the assistance of a national financial policy and its associated financial protections. In addition, the amelioration of a Chinese system of social guarantees that was facing crisis depended on a national policy of social benefits and the capacity of the state. Thus, national policy itself in fact faces in two directions and the ideology of neoliberalism cannot be naively equated with current national policy, even as critiques of neoliberal ideology and a national policy tending in the direction of neoliberalism cannot be equated with complete repudiation of the state itself. That China's opening was able to secure economic gains is not attributable simply to the opening itself. According to Chu Wan-wen and other economists, these gains are actually owed to successful industrial policies and state regulation implemented by the East Asian nations, including China, which allowed the risks inhering in the process of market expansion to be contained.[77] The ability for the state to regulate the economy and to set appropriate industrial and financial policy are fundamental conditions guaranteeing economic growth and social stability. It is precisely because of this that all critical social movements since the nineteenth century have taken the nation-state as the only effective arena of political struggle, even as they have linked this struggle to their inclinations toward internationalism. From the perspective of the interactions between the movement and the state, the real question here is how to effect by social power and structural reform the transformation of the state from an apparatus that "establishes market mechanisms" into an administrative mechanism of mass social participation, even as it dissolves the too-frequent alliances between state power and market monopolies.

If we say that the core issue for nineteenth- and twentieth-century social struggles has been "how (and to what degree) to use the democratic structures and powers based on the nation-state to shape and control global capitalism and to thereby produce the forms of economic growth that society hopes for,"[78] then can "democratic structures and powers based on the nation-state" still be used effectively to shape the forms of social and economic progress, even after China has joined the WTO and other international economic structures? Or, more succinctly, in the era of transnational capitalism, how can we harmonize domestic social equality with social justice in the world at large? In order to respond to this question, we need to analyze at least three aspects of this question. First, what exactly is the relationship between the nation-state and a "globalization" that has its historical foundation in the free circulation of financial capital and the development of high-tech industries? Second, is the retreat of the state's social role beneficial to social democracy and economic justice? And third, how does democratic power based in the nation-state manage to maintain links between domestic and international democracy, and economic justice within one country and in the world as a whole?

Let us initially examine the first question. The main indicator of contemporary economic globalization is the massive circulation of financial capital. According to statistics compiled by the Bank of International Settlements, in 1983 total turnover per day was 2 billion

U.S. dollars, which had risen to 20.7 billion by 1987 and 82 billion by 1992; by 2001 the daily turnover had reached 130 billion dollars. At this rate, the annual rate of capital turnover of international financial capital is 40 trillion dollars, of which only 800 billion is needed to support international trade and all funds used for investment—the rest is all used for speculation. Given this, the transnational circulation of massive amounts of financial capital and the global expansion of information technology cannot be seen as simply built on nothing, as many of the planet's people live in the corporate world, and not, as people did in the past, in a "country." This does not mean, however, that there is no role left for the nation-state. To begin with, the nation-state still has a decisive function in such areas as implementing an active industrial policy, managing wage relations, limiting the mobility of labor, and carrying out programs of social insurance. The globalization notions of neoliberalism have as their core narrative element the weakening of the nation-state or the minimization of the state, along with demands that the state abandon its policies of intervention and systems of social insurance, and that market rules replace social development, while relations based on capital take possession of the social sphere. As a result, the core of the neoliberal conception of globalization described above no longer recognizes the division between politics and economics characteristic of the nineteenth century, but rather envisions the workings of the economy, markets, and capital as replacing the political and social spheres. Thus, the view of "freedom" in neoliberalism has replaced the political realm with a concept of "pure economics," which has become in the process the antithesis of political and social freedom.

The development of high technology and the military structure of the nation-state have become closely interrelated. Without massive financial outlays from the American defense establishment, the economic miracles of Silicon Valley and other high-tech areas would have been impossible. So even as neoliberal economists hold forth on the unification of the global market and the decline of the nation-state, a new form of globalization is gradually coming into being: a globalized military with the United States and NATO at its center. In the Asian region, this process of military globalization continues the structure of the Cold War; it seeks to make permanent the partitioning and military confrontation on the Korean peninsula and in the Taiwan Straits. This American led process has thus become the motive force behind isolating certain areas and maintaining the pattern of the Cold War. In this respect, this "globalization" is in actuality a force for "antiglobalization" in the world, a sort of hypernationalism masquerading as globalism. The process of military globalization that has accompanied economic globalization very clearly demonstrates the hegemonic quality of the neoliberal economic order.

Let us now take up the second question, that of whether the withdrawal of the nation-state will benefit social justice and economic development in the developing countries. From the perspective of rural development, contemporary Chinese agriculture, the rural townships, and the rural population in general have all become enmeshed in a serious crisis. The growth of the gap between city and country, the substantial expansion in the number of the poor and of the floating population, and the destruction of land, water, forest, and other natural resources are all directly related to the withdrawal of the state's role from rural areas. Because China's rural population lacks any real representation at the level of state policymaking, the state in the course of its negotiations with the WTO made huge concessions on agricultural questions to the United States, Europe, and other nations, demonstrating the close links between the reduction of the role of the state and the global economic order. From the perspective of the urban economy, if it is possible to say of political and economic devolution that as a reform policy it stimulated entrepreneurial and local government activity and creativity, when this devolutionary process turned into pure privatization, a great deal of state property was lost, vast numbers of workers were faced with the threat of unemployment, the system of social guarantees (such as healthcare, housing, and retirement) verged on collapse, and social corruption proved impossible to choke off. The principal social crises facing contemporary China all derive from these factors, and they illustrate the predicament created by the neoliberal program for the withdrawal of the state. It is precisley because it is under pressure from these dual pressures that, in order to prevent the predicament described above from plunging society into a situation of collapse and crisis, the state needs once again to adjust its economic and social insurance policies and in a significant way to refuse the radical program of neoliberalism. From a historical perspective, the state must shoulder responsibility for guaranteeing domestic and international social justice.

As for the third question, there can be little doubt that the state has broad political responsibility for the domestic economic order and for social justice. In an era in which the processes of production, the circulation of commodities, and consumption have all been globalized, however, there is no united world government to coordinate global industrial policy, financial security, and equitable economic distribution, so every national government should take responsibility for creating some sort of social justice and economic order that would supersede the scope of the individual nation-state. As Thomas W. Pogge has pointed out, however, there are frequent conflicts between the imperatives of these two spheres (that is, between the imperatives of nationalism and internationalism), since were the wealthy nations to pursue a global economic order of greatest advantage in preventing world poverty or preserving the global environment, then there would certainly be no way for them to put the advantage of their own people first.[79] In the bilateral or multilateral negotiations over the WTO, the negotiating strength of the economically developed nations was superior to that of the developing nations. As a consequence, world polarization between rich and poor is certain to intensify further. In its negotiations to join the WTO, China had to make major concessions to the United States and European nations, and these concessions are bound to make the gap between rich and poor within China even wider—particularly as this is measured between city and country. At the same time, the scale of China's economy, whether in Asia or in the world at large, has already reached a substantial level, and the logic of development may push China toward repeating the developmental logic of the economically advanced nations, thereby creating new economic conflicts.[80] This illustrates the necessity to link the democracy and justice of one society to demands for democracy and justice on a global scale. So, aside from confirming the role of the state in domestic relations between politics and economics, we must also again posit the role of the state within a new trend of participatory internationalism. We must thus ask that, within the world economic system, the various states organize a global force to reduce the polarization of north and south, protect the global ecology and push for a fair world order, rather than working to oppose these ends.

As we can see from our discussion of the three questions raised above, the state must take on the serious responsibility of ensuring social justice, coordinating the market system, and setting up a fair and democratic world order. Even coordinating the function of international organizations like the WTO is premised on the participation of the nation-state, which in turn explains how those social movements that have alternative globalizations as their goal must not overlook the nation-state and its role in industrial, social, and environmental policy. Thus, the question becomes one of how to guarantee that the state is not in collusion with monopolistic, coercive, and unequal systems, but is instead taking up the social responsibilities described above; this is the principal task of all social movements that have as their goal domestic and international democracy. In other words, regardless whether it is the theoretical critiques of the intellectuals or the political practice of social movements, neither of them can abandon the arena of political struggle represented by the nation-state. Since every nation-state has a different position and interests within the global economic context, and a national policy that might be able to bring about domestic economic justice might well be in conflict with international economic justice, any struggle for democracy and social justice within the nation-state must be integrated into a new international perspective. For example, in 2001 the administration of George W. Bush refused to sign the Kyoto Treaty, something that may be of benefit to domestic economic development and the employment situation within the United States, but which poses a threat to the global environment and to fair-market competition. If the American labor movement stands only for the advantages accruing to a single nation-state and lacks any inclination toward internationalism, then it might repeat the logic of colonialism—damaging and expropriating the economies, societies, and environments of other countries. This logic applies as well to other countries, including China, and is thus the motive power behind the creation of the new internationalism.

The logic of transnational capitalism demands the globalization of labor movements, but the reality we are facing is this: a global labor movement has yet to take shape, while the evidence of cooperation and collusion between transnational capital and the nation-state is visible everywhere. From looking out on the current situation in China and Asia, it would seem that the perspective of an open Asia is worth considering. This is because, first, the transnational nature of contemporary economic activity has rendered preexisting forms of the nation-state no longer able to adapt comfortably to the needs of the market, and regional unity has thus become necessary for economic development. In spite of layer upon layer of difficulties, the regional coalition with the Association of South-East Asian Nations (ASEAN) at its center has maintained regional vitality and elicited the serious attention and active participation of China, Japan, and South Korea. An even closer regional structure in northeast Asia that would include Japan, South Korea, mainland China, Taiwan, and Hong Kong (as well as Mongolia and North Korea) and that could resist the political, economic, and military order of an American-led neoliberalism has already been discussed by many scholars and politicians. Second, there are close economic, cultural, and political relations among Asian nations, and the circulation of labor among them is also quite well developed, with the consequence that the region as a whole is facing directly related economic and social problems.

Third, during the process of economic globalization, the economic links in the Asian region have grown closer by the day, but this does not imply that a united or more internally consistent "Asian" or "East Asian" regional grouping will be able to emerge. For one thing, economic interdependence has been simultaneously accompanied by the intensification of economic competition among the neighboring Asian economies, such that any regionalism or transnationalism in the realm of foreign trade is inevitably accompanied by nationalism and protectionism in that same realm. For another, economic interdependence does not necessarily bring about greater political unity, and the intensification of competition can, in fact, promote political and even military conflict. Thus, if we say that the market and the state are the motive forces behind furthering the imagining of a region, then they also make up a force limiting this imagining.

At this point I would like to mention two factors that are particularly worthy of attention. First, should neoliberalism's market program suddenly result in an economic crisis, it could lead to calls for protectionism and isolationism. The historical experiences of Asia and Europe all show that the strengthening of economic relations does not necessarily lead to peace, unity, and integration, and the crises created by market ideology can frequently lead to conflict and isolation; all sorts of "sacred alliances" have been formed with resistance, throttling of competition, protectionism, and war as their motives. Thus, criticism of neoliberalism is not a rejection of free exchange and free trade, but rather rejection of the closures, protectionism, isolation, and tendencies toward conflict concealed in its developmental logic. Second, "Asia" or "East Asia" has always been an open region with complex historical links to other regions, so the stability, peace, and fair development of the Asian region are not matters that can be restricted to one self-sufficient area. The Asian economic predicament is a function of the subordinate position the region has in the political, military, and cultural arenas worldwide, in which Asia's tense situation is a product of the continuation of the Cold War. It is precisely the Asian region's subjection to the dual pressures of neoliberalism and the continuation of the Cold War that facilitates the link between the intellectuals and the social movements in the area, and that causes them to share a common historical sense and set of social goals. In fact, in the global context, because of differences and contradictions in goals, national discourses, and in other areas, it is impossible to constitute a social movement with the goal of seeking an alternative globalization that has any internal strength. Thus, regional links may be the bridge to combining the critical force that characterizes the political arena of the nation-state with such a critical force on a global scale.

Why Start from the Question of Modernity?

In contemporary Chinese discourse, the criticism of neoliberalism grew gradually out of a rethinking of the question of "modernity," which is a broad and complicated issue that contains much ambiguity. What lay behind the rethinking of this abstract theoretical principle? To begin with, the reflections on socialism that took place in the 1980s unfolded in the context of a binary juxtaposition of tradition/ modernity, with the result that this critique of the problems of social- ism could not be extended into rethinking the process of reform and the Western model of modernization after which it patterned itself. On the contrary, the critique of socialism turned into a post–Cold War self-justification. From the perspective of rethinking modernity, socialism and its crisis was understood as part of the crisis of moder- nity, and it was not possible to place all contemporary manifestation of the crisis outside the scope of our reflections and criticisms. It was precisely because of this that the close connections between socialism and the contemporary crisis came to light through the vector of the problem of modernity. The Chinese socialist movement was one of resistance, but was also one of modernization that unfolded via a na- tion-building movement and the process of industrialization, so its historical experiences and lessons are all closely linked to the process of modernization itself. Inquiry into the process by which the demands for freedom and equality that characterized this movement slipped into institutional inequality and a rigid hierarchy thus could not be separated from the reconsideration of the process of modernity (that is, nation-building and industrialization) itself. So even though we take the repudiation of this movement as the start of the modernized history of the contemporary period (the New Era), from certain perspectives we are still enmeshed in the same historical process. Thus, we cannot on the one hand critique and reject our socialist history while, on the other, use this same critique and rejection to justify our process of modernization in the contemporary period.

Second, in the 1980s and, indeed, ever since May Fourth, the Chinese intelligentsia's thinking on the problems of Chinese society has developed in the context of a China/West binary, so any consideration of China's problems could not be extended to reflection on the knowledge and truths provided by a colonialist history and its related enlightenment movement. On the contrary, critique of the Chinese tradition became the justification for adherence to the model of Western modernization and its model of modern history. From the perspective of reflecting on modernity and how the problem of Chinese modernity can be regarded as a part of the general crisis of modernity, the history of European capitalism and its expansion throughout the globe cannot only not be taken as the self-evident standard by which to gauge China, but must be the object of critical reflection in itself. Thus, it is only within the perspective of modernization that the close links between issues concerning China and historical capitalism become manifest, and that China's historical legacy and its modern experience, along with their contemporary significance, can garner the respect and understanding they deserve. As a result, the reconsideration of modernity is not only a process of critique, but also a process of uncovering new historical meanings and possibilities.

Third, in light of the above, the reflection on modernity is not a complete rejection of the experience of modernity, but quite the contrary, a movement for liberation, a movement of liberation from

modes of thought based on notions of historical teleology and deter-
minism, a movement of liberation from the fetishism of other systems, and an effort to use the history of China and of other societies
as sources for theoretical and institutional innovation. From an
epistemological standpoint, the reflection on modernity is primarily a
reflection on various historical paradigms, as well as a quest to render
the actual process of history as the object of historical understanding.
For example, ever since the nineteenth century, classical economists
have established any number of theoretical concepts and paradigms in
order to study capital and the movement of the market; they have
used these to explicate price systems, the free market, the maximization of benefit, and a number of other such principles. Over a long
historical period, these theories not only provided the theoretical underpinning for colonialism, but also served as models for modernization movements in other parts of the world. What these concepts
actually provided, however, was a completely theoretical teleological
narrative, not a description of actual historical interactions, and
the discourse of the so-called market ideal served to cover up historical relationships that were in fact antimarket. Thus, criticism of neoliberalism is to begin with an historical criticism, a process that sets
out from the actual course of history to critique the master narrative
of modernization.

Fourth, raising the issue of modernization implies a critique of theories of modernization, a complex consideration of the modernization paradigm, and a reflexive attitude toward Chinese society from
the late Qing onward [that is, from ca. 1900] as well as toward the
various initiatives undertaken by Chinese intellectuals over the years
(not, however, to be confused with a simple posture of rejection).
Absent this theoretical perspective, there is no way for the contemporary Chinese intelligentsia to go any farther in the theoretical analysis
of such matters as developmentalism and nationalism. As for their
sharp criticism of developmentalism, intellectuals' analysis has revealed the coercive, violent, and antidemocratic essence implicit in
the logic of development, whether in China or in the global arena.

They have joined to this critique reflections about ecology, the environment, the links between development and freedom of thought, as well as inquiry into the broadening of democracy in the context of the present. The question of development is not one that can be isolated to economics or society alone; it must be undertaken simultaneously at a global level and at the level of specific social experience. It is because of this that the reflection on modernity can be linked up extremely naturally to a global perspective, and must in no way be restricted to the framework of a totalistic notion of the nation-state. Within this broad perspective, thoughts about nationalism, the right of national self-determination, democratization, market relations, development, individual rights, and cultural diversity can only take on their full significance when placed in an extensive network of relations and in historical sequence—where thinking about any one of these notions will require considering others at the same time. I believe that in our present circumstances lack of this broad perspective will make it impossible to present the interrelations and complexities of these problems, while raising the possibility of unknowingly falling into a new essentialism.

The problem of modernity constitutes our point of departure here, and it must open up into all sorts of more specific discussions. This is my hope: it is a hope to transcend formalistic theory and to open up the examination of the actual relationships of history, a hope to transcend the gulf between theory and practice, and a hope that we may get beyond our various prejudices. In the end, however, the discussion of practical matters cannot avoid returning to more theoretical and comprehensive reflections, since the crux of today's problems cannot be separated into isolated components. The discussion must root itself deeply in the internal logic of modern society, because if it fails to think things through at this level, a social movement of resistance and the critical thinking that goes along with it run the risk of slipping into the logic of that which they are resisting in the first place. As is the case with my attitude toward history, I have never taken a nostalgic or romantic view of theory, reflection, or even of intellectual exchange itself. History, experience, and knowledge are the sources we must use constantly to transcend ourselves, but at the same time pose limitations we can overcome only with great difficulty.

This, then, is the nature of our freedom and of the limitations on it.

CONTEMPORARY
CHINESE THOUGHT
AND THE QUESTION
OF MODERNITY
(1997)

Translated by

Rebecca Karl

The year 1989 was a historical watershed; nearly a century of socialist practice came to an end. Two worlds became one: a global-capitalist world. Although China's socialism did not collapse as did the Soviet Union's or Eastern Europe's, this was hardly a barrier to China's economy from quickly joining the globalizing process in the arenas of production and trade. Indeed, the Chinese government's persevering support for socialism does not pose an obstacle to the following conclusion: in all of its behaviors, including economic, political, and cultural—even in governmental behavior— China has completely conformed to the dictates of capital and the activities of the market. If we aspire to understand Chinese intellectual and cultural life in the last decade of the twentieth century, we must understand the above transformations and their corresponding social manifestations.[1]

Before moving into an analysis of contemporary Chinese thought, we must first explore several premises that bear an intimate relationship to thinking within intellectual circles in the 1990s.

First, the 1989 Tiananmen incident did not change the fundamental reform path China has followed since the end of the 1970s; to the contrary, under state promotion, the pace of the reforms has been faster than even during the most open period of the 1980s (by reforms, I refer primarily to the adaptation to marketization and to the process of economic and legislative structural reforms). Through the stepped-up reforms in the systems of production, trade, and finance, China has increasingly entered into the competition of the world market, with the result that the restructuring of the domestic social and production mechanisms has been undertaken under restrictions imposed by the contemporary market system. Moreover, commer-

cialization and its attendant consumer culture have thoroughly pene-
trated every aspect of social life, thereby demonstrating that the
painstaking creation of markets by the state and by enterprises is not
merely an economic phenomenon. Rather, this social process ultimately seeks to use market rules to regulate all social life. In this context, not only have the original social and professional roles of the intellectuals profoundly changed, but so has the state, particularly the
social and economic roles the government plays at every level—by
daily becoming more intimately related to capital.

Second, in the 1990s, Chinese intellectual voices have not all ema-
nated from China; rather, they also come from abroad. The 1989
Tiananmen incident precipitated a large westward outflow of prominent intellectuals; in addition, many scholars and others went abroad
for different reasons and then either stayed or chose to live in exile.
At the same time, a number of those who went to study in Europe,
the United States, and Japan under the state policies on study abroad
of the late-1970s have now received their degrees. Of those, there are
some who are employed abroad and some who have returned to
China. From the perspective of intellectual subjectivity, these two
generations of Chinese intellectuals have undergone different experiences, but both have had the opportunity to fundamentally understand Western society and intellectual trends. They have brought
their observations on Western society to bear on their analyses of
Chinese questions, thus opening up a different perspective on China
from that of those who stayed at home. From the perspective of the
institutionalization of knowledge, contemporary education and research in China have gradually become structurally transnational, that
is, the production of knowledge and research activities have been incorporated into the globalization process.

Third, after 1989, intellectuals in China could not help but rethink
their historical experiences. Under pressure from the harsh environment and through their own choices, a large majority of intellectuals
engaged in the humanities and social sciences gave up their 1980s
New Enlightenment mode. After discussing the problem of intellec-

tual norms and taking up increasingly specialized research, they clearly turned to a more professional mode of work. Owing to the dissolution of intellectual groups such as those devoted primarily to the introduction of Western scholarship under rubrics like "Culture: China and the World," and the appearance of such periodicals as *The Scholar* that had research on Chinese history and thought at their cores, some people saw the intellectual activity in the 1990s as moving toward a revival of "Chinese studies" (*guoxue*). This characterization is, however, inaccurate, no matter from what perspective one approaches it. To begin with, the 1989 incident obliged the scholarly world to review the implications of the intellectual movement of the 1980s and to reflect on the relationship between Chinese history and the cultural movement in which they had participated. Because of this, the scholarly gaze turned toward the practical demands implicit in Chinese history rather than to the revival of any sort of pure scholarship. Second, even though research on the history of academic thought became for a time the principal focus of intellectual effort, it would be hard to categorize the work of this new generation of scholars as simply being "Chinese studies." It is worth pointing out that although this epistemic shift was most directly registered as a move of intellectual interest from the "West" to "China," these efforts at self-adjustment were at the time based on Weberian theories of "academic professionalization." After 1992, the process of marketization accelerated the tendency toward social stratification, a tendency seemingly in accord with the internal professionalization of scholarship; the progress of professionalization and institutionalization of intellectual life gradually effected a fundamental change in the social role of the intellectual. Basically, the intellectuals of the 1980s were gradually transformed into experts, scholars, and professionals.

Of course, there are many other circumstances that could be listed here; in general, however, it is possible to say that the above three conditions produced a vastly different cultural space from that inhabited by intellectuals of the 1980s. Not only has this profoundly altered the relationship of intellectuals to the state, but the unity of the intellectuals as a group no longer exists. Chinese intellectuals have responded to these transformations in various ways: some have turned to the pursuit of traditional values; some, to appeals to the spirit of humanism; some, to a self-conscious sense of professional responsibility; and some have called for a renewal of the sense of the intellectuals' mission. On the one hand, these different and contradictory efforts have allowed Chinese intellectuals to maintain their critical and moral condemnation of contemporary society; on the other hand, these very attitudes have become the basis for their own social reorientation. Intellectuals during the 1980s saw themselves as cultural heroes and trendsetters; 1990s intellectuals are urgently seeking new ways of adapting. Facing a pervasive commercial culture, they have become painfully conscious of the fact that they are no longer contemporary cultural heroes or arbiters of value.

Contemporary Chinese society has entered a complex era, and the views of social issues held by intellectuals as a group have become ambiguous. Throughout the modern period the reflections of China's intellectuals have centered on how China can modernize and the reasons for its failure to do so. During the 1980s, intellectual critiques focused on a reevaluation of Chinese socialism, which was generally denounced as antimodern in its very methods. In reality, though, the clarification of thinking came from the elucidation of social questions. For intellectuals, modernization was on the one hand a search for wealth and power along the path to the establishment of a modern nation-state; on the other hand, it was the process of reevaluating their society and tradition against the yardstick of Western society and its cultures and values. Therefore, the most conspicuous feature of the Chinese discourse on modernity is its location within the "China/West" and "tradition/modernity" binaries.

Those young intellectuals who reside in the West (particularly the United States) and have come under the influence of Western critical theory, however, have become dubious about the so-called Western path as a model of China. For intellectuals residing in "the market with Chinese characteristics," the goal of reform has become similarly ambiguous. The "good society" promised by the Chinese enlightenment thought of the 1980s has not only failed to accompany the market economy in coming into existence, but the market society has given rise to new and in some ways even more intractable contradictions.[2] The globalization of capitalism signifies not only the breakdown of the borders of the nation-state in the realms of the economy, culture, and even politics, but also the clarification of the benefits to the people in both global and domestic economic relations. It is worth noting that the advance of economic globalization is still guaranteed politically by the system of nation-states, so that even though the function of the nation-state has changed, its significance as a unit that benefits from the advance of economic globalization is even more important. To a very real extent, the clarification of the relations of interest in the international economic system has assisted the internal integration of the nation-state. In China's case, the tension between state and society engendered by the 1989 incident have to a certain extent actually been alleviated.

From the ideological perspective, the problems facing Chinese intellectuals in the 1990s have become much more complex. First, the cultural and ethical crises of contemporary society can no longer be attributed to manifestations of an outmoded Chinese tradition (even as there are those who maintain to the contrary that these crises are the result of the decline of Chinese tradition); many of the problems are produced by the process of modernization itself. Second, China's problems cannot be simply blamed on China's socialism, as economic reforms have already brought into being an essentially market society. Third, since the disintegration of the Soviet and Eastern European socialist systems, global capitalism has advanced to a new historical stage and China's socialist reforms have already led to the complete incorporation of the country's economic and cultural processes into this global market. Under these conditions, China's sociocultural problems—including the very behavior of the government—can no longer be analyzed from the position of a single context. In other words, in rethinking Chinese society, the usual targets of criticism can no longer explain contemporary difficulties. In the historical context of the rise of Asian capitalism, tradition can no longer be used as a self-evidently derogatory term; in the context of the globalization of production and trade, the nation-state is also no longer a self-evident unit of analysis. (This does not imply that the contemporary world has succeeded in establishing a supranational political system. On the contrary, the transnationalization of production and trade has been guaranteed by the original form of the nation-state. The problem is that the nation-state system is less and less able to adapt itself to the process of globalized production and culture. It is in this sense that the nation-state system and the capacity of nation-states to control sociopolitics are facing profound transformation.) With the complete interpenetration of the activities of capital and social life, the government and the behavior of all other organs of the state, as well as the workings of state power, have also been tightly linked to the market and to capital; it is thus insufficient to apply a simple political perspective to the problem. (This does not imply that political analyses are not significant or valuable.)

So, just what are China's problems? Or, what methods or even language should be used to analyze them? In a time when the various theoretical stances of pluralism, relativism, and nihilism have eliminated the possibility of the resurrection of any unitary parameter of value, the proponents of various alternative theories, the major characteristic of which is their critical edge, have begun to recognize in the course of their heated debates that the very idea of critique is gradually losing its vitality. It is thus necessary to first confirm the premises of critique. At present, however, the binaries of reform/conservatism, the West/China, capitalism/socialism, and market/planning are still hegemonic concepts, and in such a discursive situation the problems described above can hardly even be brought to light.

Contemporary Chinese intellectuals have abandoned their analysis of the workings of capital (including the complex relationship between political, economic, and cultural capital); they have also abandoned research into the interpenetrating and mutually conflicting relations between the market, society, and the state. Instead, they have confined their gaze to the level of morality or to the ideological frameworks of modernization, something especially important to note.

Contemporary Chinese social and cultural problems are linked to the question of Chinese modernity in a number of complex ways, but my question is simply this: if China's historical practice of socialism is the major characteristic of Chinese modernity, why have the New Enlightenment intellectuals who have borrowed from Weber and other theorists to critique socialism not been logically led to a critical reflection on the question of modernity itself?

In the context of contemporary global change, Chinese reforms have on the one hand profoundly reorganized the basic structures of Chinese society. (That the intellectuals have been forced to affirm themselves is itself a demonstration that they have moved from being central subjects of society and culture to being marginal. This alteration in the fixed positions of social classes is clear evidence that the social structure is being reorganized.) On the other hand, the Chinese reforms have also contributed in unknowable and unspecifiable ways to the direction in which global capitalism itself is developing. (Debates on the uniqueness of the Chinese path have in the end only managed to address the questions of whether there can be a modern society that deviates from the historical model of capitalism or whether there can be a process of modernization that causes a rethinking of the concept of modernization itself.) I think that the above questions are implicit in the moral stance of contemporary intellectuals and are more profound then the stance itself. The questions themselves reveal the ambiguous historical reasons for the current state of contemporary thought.

Three Versions of Marxism

Prior to any discussion of the decline of critical discourse in contemporary Chinese thought, it is necessary first to understand the historical relationship between Chinese Marxism and modernization. Those

Western scholars who rely on modernization theory to analyze Chinese history reduce the problem of Chinese modernization to a problem of scientific and technological development, that is, to the transformation of an agrarian economy into an urban industrial one.[3] Because modernization theory derives from the historical development of European capitalism, modernization has often been understood as the process of becoming capitalist. Marxism, too, sees modernization as the mode of capitalist production. However, China's situation is different not only because the question of its modernization was posed by Marxists, but because Chinese Marxism itself is an ideology of modernization; not only was the goal of the Chinese socialist movement modernization but the movement itself constitutes the main characteristic of Chinese modernity. Although the popular understanding of modernization in China focuses primarily on the process of transforming the state, the economy, the military, and science from backwardness to an advanced condition, this concept does not merely set technological goals, and it does not point only to the formation of the nation-state and a modern bureaucracy. Rather, it also includes a teleological historical perspective and worldview. It is a type of thinking through which China's social praxis is understood as a path toward an ontological historical goal, which in turn fosters an attitude that links existential meaning to the historical period in which one finds oneself. As a result, socialist modernization is a concept that not only points out the difference between the institutions of Chinese modernization and capitalist modernization, but that also provides a whole set of its own values.

Thus, the "modernization" in Chinese discourse and the "modernization" in modernization theory are different. This is because inherent within the Chinese concept of modernization is a tendency toward values based on a content of socialist ideology. Mao Zedong believed in irreversible historical progress and used revolution and the methods of the Great Leap Forward to push Chinese society along the modernization path. He used the socialist system of public ownership to establish a prosperous and powerful modern nation-state while at the same time working toward his principal goal of equality by striving to eliminate the "three differences"—between workers and peasants, between town and country, and between mental and manual labor. Through the movement to nationalize the economy and particularly through the establishment of People's Communes, Mao led his primarily agricultural nation to social mobilization; he thus successfully subsumed society under state goals. Internally, this resolved the tax-collection problems that were a legacy of the late Qing and Republican periods; resources for urban industrialization were now to be secured by exploiting production and consumption in the countryside, which was organized according to socialist principles. In this sense, public ownership in the countryside was premised on even more inequality between the urban and the rural sectors.[4] Externally the effective subsumption of society under the state enabled China's backward society to coalesce into a united force to finish the unfinished task of nationalism. Mao often said that his socialist revolution was the heir to and the development of Sun Zhongshan's [Sun Yat-sen's] democratic revolution; in reality, he saw his revolution as the final resolution to the modernization movement that had been ongoing since the nineteenth century and as having set its future direction.[5]

Mao's socialism is both an ideology of modernization and a critique of Euro-American capitalist modernization. But this critique was not a critique of modernization itself. Quite the contrary: it was a critique of the capitalist form or stage of modernization based on a revolutionary ideology and a nationalist standpoint. For this reason, on the perspective of history and values, Mao's socialism is a modernization theory opposed to capitalist modernization. From the perspective of its political impact, Mao's elimination of the "three differences" in actual practice eliminated the possibility of the existence of a public sphere autonomous from the state. This not only produced a huge structure of unprecedented size and overarching scope, but brought all social activity under the organization of the vanguard party.

This "antimodern theory of modernization" is a characteristic not just of Mao Zedong thought, however; it is one of the major characteristics of Chinese thought from the late Qing onward. The tendency to "anti-modernism" was not only a function of what people refer to as traditional factors, but was even more importantly a result of the fact that the discourse on China's search for modernity was shaped in the historical context of imperialist expansion and a crisis in capitalism. Thus, those intellectuals and state officials who promoted modernization in China could not help but consider how China's modernization could avoid the multiple abuses of Western capitalist modernity. Kang Youwei's one-world utopia *(datong)*, Zhang Binglin's egalitarianism, Sun Zhongshan's principle of the people's livelihood *(minsheng zhuyi)*, and the various socialist critiques of capitalism all went hand in hand with programs and plans for the construction of political, economic, military, and cultural programs and plans. (Including those for a modern national political system, economic forms, and cultural values). It is even possible to say that the basic characteristics of Chinese thought on modernity are doubt and critique. As a result, at the heart of the search for Chinese modernity in Chinese thinking and in some of China's most important intellectuals stands a huge paradox.

Modern Chinese thought includes critical reflection on modernity. Yet in the search for modernization, among the profound ideas that this particular discourse has produced are both antimodern social practice and utopianism: fear of a bureaucratic state, contempt for the formalization of legal structures, an emphasis on absolute egalitarianism, and so forth. Indeed, in China's historical context, the struggle for modernization and the rejection of rationalization have proceeded together, something that has produced profound historical contradictions. For example, on the one hand, Mao centralized power to establish a modern state system; on the other hand, he launched the Cultural Revolution to destroy that system. On the one hand, he used People's Communes and collectives to promote

China's economic development; on the other hand, he designed the social distribution system to avoid the severe social inequalities of capitalist modernization. On the one hand, he used the nationalization of the economy to subsume society under the state goal of modernization, in the process stripping individuals of their political autonomy; on the other hand, he abhorred the use of state mechanisms to suppress the autonomy of "the people." In sum, inherent in the practice of China's socialist modernization is a historical anti-modernity. This paradox has cultural roots, yet it is even more important to search for an explanation in the double-edged historical context of Chinese modernization (namely, the search for modernization and reflections on the various historical consequences of Western modernization).

The end of the Cultural Revolution marked the end of a socialism characterized by perpetual revolution and the critique of capitalism. In 1978, the socialist reform movement that has lasted to this day began. On the level of ideology, the criticism of the prior socialism focused first on its idealistic system of public ownership and egalitarianism, both of which led to a decrease in efficiency, and second on the dictatorial methods that caused political damage to the whole country. At the same time as the evaluation and the historical summing-up were proceeding, China's socialist reforms, with improved efficiency as their central focus, were launched. They began with the disbanding of the agricultural communes and their replacement by the responsiblity system in the countryside. Gradually, these were extended to responsibility and shareholding systems in the urban industrial sector. In addition, in the course of reform and opening up, China was gradually absorbed into the global capitalist market.[6] These reforms have plainly advanced economic development and re-shaped the preexisting social structure, but what they have abandoned is Mao's idealistic modernization methods while continuing the goal of modernization; the socialism of the contemporary reforms is at the same time an ideology of Marxist modernization and pragmatism. Different from prereform modernization, the most important characteristics of the socialist reforms that China is now implementing are marketization in the economic arena and the convergence of the Chinese economy, society, and culture with the contemporary capitalist system. In contrast to prereform socialism, while contemporary socialism is a type of Marxism as an ideology of modernization, it has already in effect been stripped of the antimodern character of the prior socialism.

The astonishing achievements brought about in China by the contemporary socialist reforms are not limited to the economic arena, but also entail profound political implications. The socialist reform has, through economic development, moved the country one more step toward completing the unfinished nationalist project of the modern period; at the same time there is deep belief that, along with the development of science and technology, the transition to a capitalist commodity economy represents great historical progress. The slogan "allow some people to get rich first" clearly demonstrates that China's socialist reformers consider that the policy is an expedient measure that bears neither on fundamental changes in the relations of production nor on the equal distribution of social resources. People generally use the formation of "mechanisms of competition" or "increased efficiency" to explain the great success of "the household responsibility system" in agricultural reform. This overlooks the principles of equality embedded in the redistribution of land, and the gradual equalization of urban–rural relations that was part of this process. The facts demonstrate that justice and equality were the basic factors that furthered the efficiency of Chinese agriculture. According to the research of agricultural economists, the income difference between city and country decreased between 1978 and 1985, only to increase again after 1985. Between 1989 and 1991 agricultural income essentially was stagnant, and the inequality between urban and rural income returned to the levels that had existed prior to 1978. After 1993, because the state raised the price of grain, the rapid advance of rural enterprises, and the increase of income of rural migrants to urban areas, rural income grew relatively quickly, but in circumstances of a great surplus of urban labor, this situation began to change.[7] The status of rural economic development is directly related to the corresponding issue of social equality—the equality of urban–rural economic relations in particular. In contrast to the reform in rural areas, in urban areas the process of market reform and privatization that has redistributed social wealth (particularly state-owned assets) has not been carried out on the principle of a level playing field, where ownership is assigned to the original owner, but rather on a de facto basis that grants it to the last owner.[8] What is often neglected is that the pragmatism that focuses solely on efficiency has created the conditions for social inequality, and it also poses obstacles to political democratization. Had the redistribution of social wealth been implemented openly or with some degree of popular supervision, the partitioning of national assets that is its characteristic could not have proceeded so unequally. People currently place their hopes for solving our contemporary social contradictions on the legitimization of private property rights, but if this privatization is carried out under undemocratic and unjust circumstances, this "legitimization" will guarantee only an illegitimate process of distribution. Since 1987, there have been many debates about reform. The heart of these debates has not been the question whether to modernize; rather, it has been the question of modernization methods. In general we can characterize this as a struggle between Marxism as an antimodern ideology of modernization and Marxism as an ideology of modernization. As things stand now, however, this debate has been unable to encompass the essentials of the contemporary economic and political struggle.

A third kind of Marxist modernization ideology is utopian socialism. By this, I mean what has since 1978 been called "authentic socialism" by some Marxist intellectuals in the CCP. Its major characteristic is the use of humanism to reform Marxism. Such a "humanistic Marxism" was mobilized as a critique of the ideological mainstream of the prereform period and could have become the theoretical foundation for the contemporary socialist reform movement. This trend was part of the "thought liberation movement" in China at the time. On the one hand, humanistic Marxism criticized state socialism's disregard for the Marxian ideals of individual freedom and liberation, which was responsible for the cruelties of the social dictatorship that arose under the aegis of "the people's democratic dictatorship." On the other hand, it was in direct contradiction to socialist reform thinking, a contradiction I regard as a conflict between utopian socialism and the pragmatism of socialist reformism. The core of China's humanistic Marxism is Marx's theory of alienation, as outlined in his *Economic and Philosophical Manuscripts of 1844*. The early Marx took this concept of alienation from Feuerbach and other Western humanist philosophers and used it to analyze the problem of labor in capitalist production. He pointed very specifically to the problem of the alienation of laborers in capitalist relations of production. Chinese humanist Marxists wrested this concept from the historical context in which Marx used it to critique capitalism and turned it into a tool for the critique of traditional socialism. This trend of thought specifically critiqued Mao's theories of dictatorship as the historical legacies of tradition and feudalism; it also engaged the problem of alienation in socialism itself. However, these Chinese humanist Marxists offered no critical reflection on the question of modernity.

Just as with the Western humanist attack on religion after the Enlightenment, China's humanistic Marxist critique of traditional socialism has accelerated the "secularization" of society—the development of capitalist commodification. In certain contexts, Marx's critique of Western capitalist modernization has been transformed into an ideology of modernization, and has become an important part of contemporary Chinese New Enlightenment thinking. Thus, the major task of China's humanistic Marxism has been to analyze and critique the historical experience of Mao's antimodern modernization. Yet in the context of the capitalist opening in China's socialist reforms, abstract theories of human freedom and individual liberation in the end have become the very definition of the values of modernity. In other words, humanistic Marxism itself has become a Marxist ideology of modernization. For this reason, it cannot possibly launch either an appropriate analysis or a critique of the multiple social crises that have resulted from modernization and the capitalist market. In a context in which the market society and its norms are increasingly dominating discourse, the type of critical socialism that primarily targets the traditional socialist historical experience is already obsolete.[9] If Chinese humanistic Marxism wants to revivify its critical power, it must take leave of its humanistic tendency and refocus its attention on people to concentrate on a political economy that takes account of the current situation.

Enlightenment as an Ideology of Modernization and Its Contemporary Form

The most dynamic intellectual current of the entire 1980s was the New Enlightenment movement. Initially, it proceeded under the banner of humanistic Marxism, but after the Spiritual Pollution Campaign of the early 1980s that was aimed at humanistic Marxism, the New Enlightenment movement gradually was transformed into an intellectual movement with radical demands for social reform that increasingly took on a popular and anti-orthodox pro-Western tendency. The New Enlightenment movement is by no means unitary; its literary, philosophical, and political aspects have no direct relationship to one another. However, I wish to particularly point out that to regard China's New Enlightenment thought as simply an intellectual trend in opposition to the goals of the state and China's New Enlightenment intellectuals as simply political dissidents makes it impossible to explain the basic sequence and logic of Chinese thought in the new era. Despite the fact that the history of the New Enlightenment movement is confusing and complex and that serious divisions had emerged by the end of the decade, nevertheless, in historical perspective, it is clear that the movement has served as the foundational ideology of the reforms. Indeed, the split between the New Enlightenment intellectuals and the state establishment emerged gradually from their intimate relationship to one another.

The intellectual fountainhead of New Enlightenment thought derives from Western (especially Western liberal and modernization) economics, political science, and legal theory. This was all posed in opposition to orthodox Marxist ideology and is directly attributable to the fact that the Chinese reforms were striding toward globalism via a process of commodification. In this respect, it is impossible to explain the split between New Enlightenment intellectuals and the state establishment simply as an opposition of civil society and the state. Quite the contrary, from an overall perspective, the efforts of the intellectuals and the goals of the state were completely compatible with one another. The active intellectuals in both the intellectual and cultural spheres in China in the 1980s (some of whom went into exile after 1989) occupied leading positions in state institutions, including universities. In the 1990s, some of them have become leading officials in the state's legislative bodies.[10] A more complicated aspect of the problem is that the process of reform has transformed not only society, it has transformed the state. It has created cracks in the internal structure of the state and deepened factionalism among the ruling elites, which has led to the formation of different political cliques. The apparent opposition of some intellectuals to the state in essence reflects these internal structural divisions. This complexity was concealed by the post-1989 political situation and the transformed position of exiled intellectuals. Actually, it is precisely this conscious or subconscious concealment of the internal divisions within the state and their complex relationship to the activities of New Enlightenment intellectuals that has already become a huge obstacle to the analysis of the 1980s Chinese intellectual situation overall.

The theoretical fountainhead of the Chinese New Enlightenment movement was not socialism but early French Enlightenment thinking and Anglo-American liberalism. Its critical stance toward Chinese socialism was understood as a critique of tradition and feudalism. Consciously or unconsciously, New Enlightenment thinking pursued Western capitalist modernity. In other words, the New Enlightenment critique of politics (and of the state) was couched in an allegorical critique of Chinese socialism as feudal tradition; it thus avoided discussing the modern content of this historical experience. The result of this allegorical strategy is that reflections on China's modernity (whose major characteristic is socialism) are subsumed under the tradition/modernity dichotomy, where modernity is completely reaffirmed. In the movement for the liberalization of thought of the 1980s, intellectual reflections on socialism were undertaken under the slogan of antifeudalism, thereby avoiding any discussion of how the difficulties of socialism were part of a "crisis of modernity."

In its self-understanding as part of the tradition/modernity dichotomy, the New Enlightenment overlooked the fact that the state system, party politics, industrialization, and the social despotism and inequality that resulted are in themselves products of "modernity." In many respects, particularly in its desire to incorporate China into the global capitalist economic system, China's New Enlightenment has many points in common with the socialist reforms. Painting traditional socialism as a relic of feudal tradition was not merely a tactic on the part of the New Enlightenment intellectuals, it was also a means of self-identification. It allowed them to identify themselves with the antichurch and anti-aristocratic European bourgeois social movement. However, such a self-understanding obscures the fact that both the New Enlightenment movement and Marxism, as ideologies of modernization, have many common values and common modes of historical understanding: belief in progress, acceptance of modernization, belief in the historical mission of nationalism, and particularly, belief in the ideals of freedom, equality, and universal harmony. These latter ideals are linked to individual struggle and the existential significance of the individual—both hallmarks of the modern attitude that understands the present moment as the temporal transition to a better future. To point out this link is not an attempt to erase the gradually emerging contradiction between the two, nor is it to deny the status of the New Enlightenment intellectuals as a group distinct from the state at this particular time. Still less is it an attempt to deny an independent value orientation on the part of the intellectuals. What I am talking about here is an actual historical relationship. If the intellectuals build their self-identity on an imaginary relationship, then no matter how much they stress their independence, it will be in doubt. This is because we have a hard time believing that those who cannot accurately know themselves can accurately grasp reality.

China's New Enlightenment movement, unlike Marxism, is by no means a coherent or unitary intellectual system. In reality, it is a far-flung and jumbled social trend that is constituted by various and sometimes incompatible elements. These elements were initially united by their shared critique of traditional socialism, a unity forged in the process of their common support for the goals of "reform." Nevertheless, we can risk some generalizations about the basic features of this social trend because the mutually exclusive yet mutually linked trends of thought that constitute it take as their basic task the advocacy and establishment of a Chinese modernity. The core of their modernization project lies in their support for the establishment of "autonomy" or subjective freedom in the economic, political, legal, and cultural spheres. In the economic sphere, through its condemnation of traditional socialist economic planning, the New Enlightenment movement reaffirmed the rightful position of the market economy and its associated law of value in commodity exchange; it upheld the market (understood as the free market) and private ownership of property as elements of a universal, modern economic mode; and it sought thereby finally to integrate the Chinese economy with the world capitalist market (which it takes as economic freedom). The ideas behind the economic reforms gained their initial impetus from the notions of value in classical economic theory (particularly Marxist economic theory). The critique of capitalism embedded in the theory of value in classical Marxist economics, however, gradually disappeared and the theory of value on the ideological level eventually became identical to that of the market in capitalism. As a result, this idea lost its profound capacity to reveal structures of monopoly.[11]

In the political sphere, it demanded the reestablishment of formal legal frameworks and a modern civilian bureaucracy; it also demanded the gradual establishment of human rights and a parliamentary system to limit the power of the rulers through the expansion of freedom of press and speech (this was understood as political freedom).[12] Because of a fear of the mass movements of the Maoist period, however, the understanding of political democracy on the part of many people was limited to "formal democracy," and the establishment of the rule of law in particular. They thus took the broad social question of "democracy" as applying only to plans for reform coming from the higher reaches of society and to suggestions for revisions to the law from experts. They thereby not only overlooked the fact that widespread participation is a necessary constituent of democracy, but also failed to realize that a positive interaction between widespread participation and the legislative process is the very hallmark of modern democratic change. What was particularly surprising was that some scholars ignored the mutual implication between direct and indirect democracy in modern constitutional democracies—no matter what forms this entailed. In thus completely excluding the significance of direct democracy to democratic practice, these scholars even came to regard the widespread participation of the populace as the hotbed of authoritarianism. This sort of "idea of democracy" runs in complete opposition to any actual understanding of the spirit of democracy.

In the cultural sphere, some scholars have used the scientific spirit or scientism to adopt Western modernization as the yardstick for the reconstruction of world and Chinese history, thereby basing their critique of traditional socialism on a total critique of Chinese feudal history and social structure.[13] Other scholars, by contrast, have used philosophy and literary criticism to raise the question of subjectivity to call for personal freedom and liberation while trying to establish social norms and values based upon individualism, something understood as individual freedom. The notion of subjectivity includes certain misgivings about the procedures and ideologies of modernity. In this context, however, subjectivity means both individual subjectivity and the subjectivity of the human species, where the former is counterposed to the dictatorial state and its ideology and the latter is counterposed to the natural world. Its positive significance lies in its provision of a philosophical foundation for the notion of postsocialist political rights. This theory is suffused with the optimism of the eighteenth- and nineteenth-century European Enlightenment and is couched in the binary framework of subjectivity/objectivity.[14] It is worth noting that in the quest for individual autonomy and subjectivity, New Enlightenment thinkers have derived inspiration not only from Western Reformation thinking and classical philosophers (particularly Kant) but also from Nietzsche and Sartre. Yet in the Chinese appropriation of Nietzsche and Sartre, the latters' critique of Western modernity has been conspicuously ignored, and they are seen simply as symbols of individual autonomy opposed to a powerful state.[15] The internal conflict in Chinese New Enlightenment thinking is thus often reflected in a split between classical liberalism and radical individualism. While the notion of subjectivity holds real potential for the present, if we cannot liberate it from the dichotomy described above and situate it in our new historical circumstances, then the idea might calcify into one without critical potential. In general, in the 1980s the critical potential implicit in New Enlightenment thought brought forth a flourish of ideas, but in the process of being deployed and reduced to the ideology of modernization, this critical potential has gradually lost its force. We can thus say that, however large the internal conflicts and contradictions within the New Enlightenment movement, and regardless of the degree of consciousness the proponents of the New Enlightenment movement have about its social effects, Chinese New Enlightenment thinking is without a doubt the most influential of all ideologies of modernization, and in a short historical period it has been transformed from a mode of ardent critical thinking into the pioneering voice of contemporary Chinese capitalism.

In the latter half of the 1980s, because of the real decrease in social controls, divisions within the New Enlightenment movement gradually came to the surface. After the earthshaking changes of 1989, the essential unity of that movement could not be restored. Because the Chinese New Enlightenment Movement and the socialist reforms had many points in common, the conservative wing of the movement was absorbed by the reform faction of the state to serve as technocrats or theorists of neoconservatism, the official ideology of modernization. The radical wing gradually formed itself into a political opposition, focusing on promoting the liberal idea of human rights and pushing for political reform in the direction of Western democracy. Culturally, the radical faction of the New Enlightenment movement (here, "radical" indicates a cultural attitude toward tradition) began to become conscious of the possibility that the social goal of modernization could become (or could already be) a crisis in values. Within this group a number of insightful young scholars used Christian ethics to highlight crises in morality and belief in modern Chinese society.[16] The derivation of this question clearly came from the transmission into Chinese intellectual circles of Max Weber's *Protestant Ethic and the Spirit of Capitalism*. The book's most important message (in this context) was: if the spirit of capitalism arises from the Protestant ethic, then the process of modernization in China must undertake some fundamental cultural transformations. In general, while the 1980s New Enlightenment intellectuals wholeheartedly believed in a Western-style path to modernization, their hopes were built on an idealistic individualism or subjectivity and based on universalism.

It was only in the course of the split in the movement that doubts about universalism cropped up. Its first manifestation was in the emergence of relativism. By this, I mean that in the early 1990s some of the early New Enlightenment scholars resorted to traditional values, particularly to Confucianism, to question whether the Western model of development was appropriate to Chinese society and culture. This trend of thought was strongly encouraged and inspired by the experiences of Japan and the so-called Four Small Asian Dragons—Korea, Singapore, Taiwan, and Hong Kong—whose successful modernization had been called a victory for "Confucian capitalism." This concept of Confucian capitalism conceals three basic matters: first, the completely divergent paths of development and the cultural and historical differences within the Confucian cultural sphere; for example, if Japan, Korea, Vietnam, and China all belong to this sphere, why have their historical paths diverged so widely? Two, this idea takes capitalism as the sole form of modernity, and in this articulation of Confucianism to capitalism, Confucianism is no longer regarded as an obstacle to modernization but rather as a key motivating factor for its realization. In other words, this nostalgia for Confucianism has nothing to do with traditionalism, nor is it a cultural barrier to capitalism. Indeed, in the eyes of these scholars, Confucianism plays the same role as that assigned by Weber to Protestantism in the development of Western capitalist modernity. Three, this idea obscures the unbreakable connection between the entire process of modernization and the history of colonialism. If one takes Confucian capitalism as an outstanding example of a norm, one obscures the basic motive power of the formation of modern history: the regulation and standardization imposed by the global market on the economic relationships of nation-states has been a much more important historical factor than anything else. Clearly, "Confucian capitalism" is an ideology of modernization. In its rejection of Western values, Confucian capitalism enables exponents to embrace the capitalist mode of production and the global capitalist system—phenomena born of Western historical specificity—while adding a layer of cultural nationalism on top. In this context, "Confucian capitalism" and the contemporary Chinese socialist reforms are simply two sides of the same coin.

A derivative of "Confucian capitalism" is the theory put forth by some scholars that emphasizes the role played by lineage organizations and localism in Chinese economic life. These theorists argue that rural enterprises based on various types of social collectives are leading China along a unique path of modernization that is neither capitalist nor socialist.[17] To be sure, this theory of rural-enterprise-led modernization has an important empirical base, and these types of local and collective formations have indeed wrought economic miracles in many places. Yet revisionist Chinese New Enlightenment thinkers want to render rural industry as a unique model of modernization to avoid a theoretical confrontation between capitalism and socialism and to find within the discourse of global capitalism a non-Western path to modernization. From 1993 to 1995, some Chinese social scientists undertook full-scale research programs and came up with striking results. The basic questions these scholars asked were: After the dismantling of the People's Communes, did the peasants become autonomous and unorganized social actors? Is relying on the collective to reach prosperity the same as recollectivization? Is an economy of individual entreprise tantamount to the beginning of privatization? In the wake of the development of a market economy, do there still exist organizational forms akin to the People's Communes' "three-in-one" structure? What changes have there been in these? Is there essential order or disorder in the articulation of various rural social organizations? What is the general characteristic of village social organization?

The researchers analyzed and described in detail the changing relations between the collective and the individual after the dismantling of the People's Communes, the relationship between individual peasant activities and socialized rural production, and the transformation of rural organizations and rural organizational networks. They mapped out the trends in rural social organization and localization, from which they derived the concept of "new collectivism." In their view, the organizational methods of new collectivism reflect the principles of competition in the modern market economy and are entirely compatible with the current social system and its efforts toward shared prosperity. Moreover, as a continuation of the quintessence of traditional lineage culture, they reflect the essence of China's "collective society" and the unique characteristics of China's current path of social development.[18]

Neither the theory of modernization via rural and township enterprise nor the concept of new collectivism has neglected the historical lessons of the era of People's Communes, and their delineation of "collective" is rigorously differentiated from the collectivism of China's socialist period. The most important difference is in the emphasis given to "individual interests"; indeed, the new collectives are founded on the premise that they are the product of a voluntary cooperation among individuals based on their individual interests. The collective and the individual are linked by mutual benefit based on localism and local feeling; the goal of cooperation is to adapt to the conditions of the market economy, through which the new collectives attain the most effective economic results.

The emergence of the theory of modernization via rural and township enterprises and the theory of new collectivism has implications for theoretical and systemic innovations amid the historical conditions of global capitalism. The revived use of such concepts as "collective," "cooperation," "localism," "local feeling," and so forth clearly emphasizes the problems of "fairness" and "equality" in social production and distribution. Under new collectivism, Chinese peasants, seemingly through the revival of traditional forms, are for the first time moving out of their centuries-old isolation and rapidly developing rural industries. They have developed markets and promoted urbanization (not goaded by the state but created by the locality) and have become in the process an important motivator of and stable basis for the expansion of China's economic reforms to the urban industrial sector. This is the first time that the Chinese countryside has led in economic reform and has been the primary motive force for the nation's modernization.[19] Yet the study of individual cases of "new collectivism" and the theory of modernization via rural and township enterprises both have clear tendencies to generalize and idealize particular situations.

Because these theories rather too urgently wish to promote "non-Western paths of modernization," they both suffer from the same problem as modernization theory itself, that is, they treat modernization as a neutral technical indicator. They thereby evade a central problem, namely, the relationship between the modes of production of rural enterprises and the international and domestic capitalist market, as well as their relationship to the state goal of marketization. From a technical perspective, both theories want to see in village enterprises a unique modernity in their mode of production and social organization, and they ignore the different modes of development such enterprises have taken in different regions of China[20] and seriously overlook "the after-effects of modernization," the environmental degradation, and the neglect of labor protection that have come in the wake of their pursuit of efficiency first.

Through its idealized description of and disregard for the serious internal contradictions in the production relations of rural industries, the theory of modernization via rural and township enterprises has effectively discarded the New Enlightenment critique of traditional social relations as well as allowed for the idea that capitalist privatization is not necessarily the only alternative to socialist public ownership. It has seemingly opened the possibility for a third road to modernization. There are solid grounds for setting out to understand the question of Chinese modernity through the experiences of China's rural and township enterprises. Yet because this theory does not take into account the fact that China's economy is already a very active part of the global capitalist market and because it takes modernity as a neutral technical indicator, it has been unable to make appropriate diagnoses about either modernity or modernization. We cannot help but ask whether rural industries, for all their uniqueness as a social model, have behaved in unique ways after joining the marketplace. Positing the internal uniqueness of rural industries does have the understandable intellectual attraction of rejecting global capitalism's social predictions; this can then be mobilized along with cultural data to explain China's unique path to modernization. But the inventors of this theory have forgotten that the very uniqueness of which they speak (I am not denying the existence of uniqueness, just as I would never deny that China, Japan, the United States, and England are all different) is today made possible only because of its relation to global capitalism. There can be a "theory of modernization with Chinese characteristics" only where the notion of modernization is teleologically assumed.

Over the past several years of social development, the rural industries in many regions—including Jiangsu and Guangdong—have undergone profound transformations; one of these is the privatization of collective enterprises, another is their transformation into [Sino–foreign] joint ventures, in which a new economic system is being forged in collaboration with multinational capital. It remains to be seen whether rural industries are a transitional avenue to modernization or whether they constitute a new model of modernization. Moreover, I think that the rural industries that have led Chinese modernization have trodden a path that is quite different from the industrialization paths of Western and other countries. To use this, as does the theory of modernization via rural and township enterprises, as the basis for a critique of the Eurocentrist notion that there is only one model of modernization has great theoretical value and significance. But this theory still uses efficiency as its yardstick; it is silent on the questions of whether the system of production and distribution in the rural enterprises promotes the expansion of economic democracy, whether their culture is conducive to a political democratization that will guarantee economic democracy, whether their mode of production can protect the environment, whether their organizational methods are conducive to political participation, and whether, in the context of global capitalism, they are capable of setting the systemic and ethical foundations of economic equality, both domestic and international. The critical quality of this theory has, however, been sharply limited. In short, this theory has failed to identify targets of criticism in the economic and political processes of modern society.

The New Enlightenment thinking of the 1980s provided an enormous source of liberation for the reform of Chinese society and it dominated and still dominates intellectual discourse in China. But in the rapidly changing historical context, what used to be China's most vigorous source of ideas has increasingly descended into equivocation; it has gradually lost not only its ability to critique but also its ability to diagnose problems in contemporary Chinese society. This is not to say that the issues raised by New Enlightenment thought have lost their significance, nor is it to say that the intellectual movement of the 1980s has already attained its goals. My point is simply that China's New Enlightenment movement now faces a fully capitalized society: the market economy is increasingly the dominant economic formation, and China's socialist economic reforms have already brought China completely into the global capitalist mode and relations of production. As part of this process, the state and its capacities have witnessed corresponding and extremely important changes, even if they have not been complete. Capitalist relations of production have already created their own spokespeople. New Enlightenment intellectuals, as the definers of values, face a profound challenge. More important, New Enlightenment intellectuals, while deploring commodification, moral bankruptcy, and social disorder, cannot help admitting that they are in the middle of the very process of modernization that they have longed for.

China's modernization (or the process by which capitalist markets were created) has enlightenment as its underlying ideology and cultural harbinger. Because of this, the abstract concept of human subjectivity and the concept of human freedom and liberation, which played significant roles in the critique of Mao's socialist experiment, lack vigor in the face of the social crises encountered in the process of capitalist marketization and modernization. Some humanists committed to the notion of enlightenment have attributed the crisis to an abstract "decline of the spirit of humanism."[21] They have gone back to Western and Chinese classical philosophy to seek moral norms and final answers; in the end, they reduce the problem to one of the moral foundation of selfhood. At this historical juncture, New Enlightenment thought has seemingly become a spiritual moral stance (whereas formerly its hallmark was to condemn moralism). Its abstract and indistinct categories are incapable of critically examining the activities of a ubiquitous capital and actual economic relations; it has thus lost its ability to diagnose and criticize the problems of a Chinese modernity that is already part and parcel of a global capitalist system.

An even more important question is what is this spirit of humanism, and how has it been lost, if it has? The wild hopes that Chinese New Enlightenment intellectuals harbored about this process of "reason"—that it would lead to the control of nature, to the formation of subjective freedom, to the progress of morality and justice, and to the happiness of human beings—are now subject to large doubts. As a result, if we wish to explore the "loss of the humanistic spirit," we must first understand the historical relationship between this loss and the efforts of the New Enlightenment intellectuals during the modernization movement.

The recent discussions on the humanistic spirit began in 1994 and lasted for more than a year. There were many participants, but they did not even touch on the following problem: if this so-called humanistic spirit is directly linked to the intellectual activity of the 1980s, how have the dramatic social changes since 1989 collapsed the category of the "intellectual"? Changes in the social position of the intellectual in China include a higher degree of division of labor and a concomitant professionalism, increased stratification within corporations and enterprises, the technocratization of the state machinery, and consequent changes in many of society's values. The original intellectual stratum is now dividing into experts, scholars, managers, and technocrats and is subjected to the same relentless process of stratification as everyone else in Chinese society. The ascribing of the changes among intellectuals to a loss of "spirit" and their silence on the social conditions that lead to stratification can be attributed to the fact that New Enlightenment intellectuals have an extremely contradictory and equivocal attitude toward these social processes.

China's "postmodernists" have exploited this ambiguity in their deployment of Western postmodernism as a tool for the critique of New Enlightenment thinking, even though China's postmodernism is even more ambiguous than the latter. I cannot undertake a full-scale analysis of Chinese "post-ism" *(houxue)* here, because it contains so many factors and complexities. What I analyze here are some of the principal essays of "post-ism" by some of the representative players. Postmodernism in China emerged under the influence of Western, and particularly U.S., postmodernism, but Chinese postmodernism's theoretical intentions and historical contents are very different from the West's. I consider Chinese postmodernism to be a supplement to the ideology of modernization. Its major sources are deconstruction, third-world theory, and postcolonialism. Yet Chinese postmodernism has never carried out a full-fledged historical analysis of Chinese modernity, nor have I ever seen any adept of Chinese postmodernism subject the relationship between Chinese modernization and Western modernization to serious historical analysis. In the field of literature, the historical target of postmodern deconstruction and that of the New Enlightenment thinkers is the same—namely, China's modern revolution and its historical roots. The one difference is that postmodernists sneer at the New Enlightenment concept of subjectivity without taking into account the historical context of this concept's emergence. When Chinese postmodernists mock the historical position of enlightenment, they are merely saying how as a historical process and social movement enlightenment is outmoded in a postmodern society dominated by the mass media and consumerism.

For its part, postcolonialism can be seen as the cultural self-criticism of the West (principally in the United States), a critique launched from the perspective of peripheral cultures against the culture of Eurocentrism. It reveals the extent to which colonialism is implicated in culture and thought, and it also indicates the complicated process through which colonized peoples used Western theories to resist their colonizers. In Chinese postmodernism, postcolonial theory is often synonymous with a discourse on nationalism, which reinforces the China/West paradigm. For example, there has not been a single Chinese postcolonial critique of Han centrism from the standpoint of peripheral culture. What is particularly amusing is that Chinese postmodernists turn the postmodernist critique of Eurocentricism on its head to argue for Chineseness and to search for the prospects for China repositioning itself at the center of the world. In this typical metanarrative of modernism (even though it proceeds under the banner of postmodernism), the vision of the future of Chineseness not only says nothing about the change in China's position within a process of globalization but is also silent regarding any predictions and hopes for the twenty-first century. The Chinese postmodernists' vision not surprisingly replicates those of the traditionalists.[22]

Another of the most salient features of Chinese postmodernism is that in its treatment of popular culture, it misrepresents the production and reproduction of desire as peoples' "needs," and it interprets the marketized social mode as a neutral and ideology-free "new mode" *(xin zhuangtai).*[23] In this type of analysis, there is neither differentiation between levels and aspects of popular culture, nor any attempt to undertake a hermeneutic and critical appraisal of the ideology of consumerism and commercialism. Rather, postmodernism appears as the champion of the people and popular culture and as the defender of their neutral desires and their "unmediated state." It is used to attack other intellectuals and as a legitimation of market ideology and consumerism. At the same time as it deconstructs all values, postmodernism jeers at the serious sociopolitical critical intent of the New Enlightenment intellectuals while ignoring the formative role of capitalist activity in modern life and neglecting consideration of the relationship between this capitalist activity and China's socialist reforms.

In constantly pitting popular culture against official culture, the postmodernists fail to see that the complex relationship the two have developed through the mediation of capital is one of the main features of contemporary Chinese society and culture. Actually, the hopes of the postmodernists ride on commercialism: "'Marketization' means the weakening of anxieties over 'Othering' and the possibility for the confirmation of the self through national culture. . . . The result of marketization is the inevitable transcendence of the imbalance produced by the old metanarrative and the possibility that the shocks produced by these imbalances and by cultural decline can be realigned. . . . It also offers the possibility of new choices, a new path towards self-confirmation through nationality and self-discovery."[24] Their so-called marketization is not simply an affirmation of the market, but represents an effort to subsume all the rules of social activity to the functions of the market. As a result, the scope of this marketization is not limited to just the economic sphere, but includes politics, society, and culture as well. In the 1990s Chinese context, the rise of consumerist culture is no longer merely an economic event, it is also a political event because the penetration of such culture into people's daily lives is carrying out the task of the reproduction of hegemonic ideology. In this process, it is the interaction between popular and official culture that is the main feature of contemporary Chinese ideological hegemony, and what is being excluded and ridiculed is the critical consciousness of elites. The academicism of some of these postmodern critiques conceals their cultural strategy of embracing popular culture (as the defender of neutral desire and the commercialization of culture) to adopt a posture of negating elite culture in order to effect a conquest of the cultural center stage. This is none other than the socialist market with Chinese characteristics. Some postmodernist critics have effectively participated in the establishment on the Chinese mainland of a unique market ideology.

In contemporary China, the responses to the above problems in intellectual circles is quite without vigor. Some Western-trained mainland Chinese scholars in conjunction with their mainland collaborators have been exploring new theoretical approaches (such as Marxism) to these problems. The understanding of these young scholars of modern Chinese conditions leaves something to be desired. Nevertheless, I think that their consciousness of these problems has poignant relevance and their mode of thinking has transcended to some extent the West/China binary that remains the focal point of New Enlightenment thought. Intimately linked to the end of the Cold War, their point of departure is that old concepts and categories born of the Cold War era are no longer sufficient to accommodate the realities of post–Cold War China or the world. A new world situation demands new theories. A number of them want to apply insights gained from "neo-evolutionism," analytical Marxism, and critical legal studies to China's situation by building on the foundation of new systems and structures within China that then nourish their theoretical innovations.

So-called neo-evolutionism seeks to transcend the traditional dichotomy of capitalism/socialism to introduce theories that can explain the institutional innovations, such as rural enterprises, in the legacy of the socialist economic system. Analytical Marxism, a theory promoted by U.S. scholars such as John Roemer and Adam Przeworski, has been imported to China with the goal of rigorously explicating Marxist positions on the possibilities for the realization of the all-round liberation of human beings and the development of individual potential. Its core theory is that the historical emphasis of socialist ideals has promoted the expansion of mass economic democracy in opposition to economic benefit for the few and as a way to prevent the monopolization of social resources by an economic and political elite. Clearly, this theory stems from opposition to the large-scale privatization of state property that has already been completed in Russia and is well under way in China. Analytical Marxists believe that political democracy is necessary so that the few can be prevented from becoming the exclusive beneficiaries of privatization; if "capitalist democracy" is a compromise between capitalism and democracy, then socialism is synonymous with political and economic democracy. As for critical legal studies, its major theoretical contribution lies in its discovery that the basis of Western civil law since the end of the eighteenth century—that is, the concept of absolute property rights, or the exclusive right of disposal by the "final owner" of a property—has collapsed. In the Chinese context, the significance of this theory is once again connected to the expansion of economic democracy and restraint of the privatization movement. It seeks to transcend the private/public ownership dichotomy and to focus on "the separation and reconstitution of the cluster of powers over property," to expand economic democracy, and to give priority to the right to life and freedom over the right to property in the constitution. In sum, Chinese scholars subscribing to neo-evolutionism, analytical Marxism, and critical legal studies strive to transcend the either/or binary theoretical model and to highlight the interdependence of economic and political democracy as the guiding principle for institutional innovation.[25]

Whether one uses concepts from socialism or from capitalism is not important. The current situation in China does not easily lend itself to either. The main questions are whether the social problems China now faces will be confronted and whether careful analysis can be made of the concrete situation. The emergence of neo-Marxism in China is part of a trend toward the revival of Marxism in economics, sociology, and legal studies in U.S. universities. This can be seen as an example of "traveling theory" in the new conditions of globalization. However, a shortcoming of Chinese neo-Marxism, apart from its simplistic borrowing of Western theory not grounded in empirical study of Chinese history and contemporary reality, is its exclusive focus on the economy with little reference to culture.[26] If one can say that Chinese neo-Marxism has already brought the problem of economic democracy to attention, it has still not begun a discussion of the problem of cultural democracy. In the present market conditions, however, the possession of cultural capital is an important part of social activity. Control of cultural capital and of the media determines the general orientation of culture and mainstream ideology. For example, the most important arm of the media today is television; in addition to state control of the media, the production of television dramas is becoming marketized. In the space between popular culture and state-controlled programming, might we be able to offer this as an internal possibility for the democratization of culture? Many Chinese intellectuals optimistically, but quite naively, assume that marketization will naturally lead to the resolution of the problem of social democracy in China. Today, when popular culture and the media are already extensively developed and especially when cultural production is already completely linked to international and domestic capital, to abandon an analysis of cultural production and cultural capital is to miss completely the opportunity to understand the complexity of contemporary Chinese society and culture.

Neo-Marxism focuses almost exclusively on economic democracy and rarely if ever touches on the problem of cultural democracy; this is to some extent a reflection of the lingering influence of China's goal-oriented modernization theory. In the present context, the complex interpenetration of the state machinery and the capitalist market means on the one hand that the state is completely involved in cultural production, and on the other hand that cultural production is limited by the activity of both capital and the market. Clearly, in the present circumstances, cultural production is part of social reproduction. Therefore, cultural studies must transcend the Marxist base/ superstructure dichotomy to treat culture as an organic part of social production and consumption. In other words, for Chinese scholars, cultural criticism must be thoroughly integrated with political and economic analysis, and this integration must be sought in methodological practices. In this respect, there are few scholars who have developed systemic theories to deal with the problem, for this type of theory requires large amounts of empirical information and historical research, both of which are still lacking. This does not, however, prevent us from reaching a basic conclusion: namely, that the struggles for economic, political, and cultural democracy are all essentially the same fight.

In the Chinese social context, discussions of economic democracy inevitably must involve discussions of the system of social distribution and production; as such, they cannot but include discussions of political democracy as well. Discussions of economic and cultural democracy can thus provide the substance for discussions of political democracy. Since the 1990s, there has been a clear decline in discourse on political democracy. This is not only because it remains a taboo topic, but also because in the post–Cold War context, how to define democracy and how to plan a realistic historical outcome have become questions in need of discussion. Political democracy is both the goal of social praxis and the topic of cultural reflection. The interpretation of political democracy is determined very much by cultural values; it also is influenced by the intimate relationship between politics and economics in the international sphere. In the context of China's unique market society, there is no longer any question of a political democracy that can be abstracted from economic and cultural democracy. Nor is there any question of an economic democracy that can be abstracted from cultural and political democracy. As a result, on the one hand we can say that in the 1990s the question of democracy has a new social context, and, on the other, that discussion of economic democracy cannot avoid a discussion of political democracy.

The debates on Chinese democracy have concentrated on how to guarantee individual autonomy and individual political participation. Chinese intellectuals have approached the problem from two angles. The first is the discourse on economic liberalism. Privatization, the development of rural enterprises, and the presence of multinational corporations have made the Chinese economy exceedingly complex. Yet many economists still believe that as a "natural process," market activity alone is sufficient to lead to the emergence of democracy. They argue that because "the logic of the market is a free exchange of individual rights" and "the state represents the coercive implementation of public rights," and because "the former is premised on the assertion and protection of individual freedom and rights, while the latter is founded on the result of public choice," the development of the market itself constitutes a guarantee of individual freedom and rights.[27] In this discourse of economic liberalism, individual rights are guaranteed by the logic of the market, and even though the market and the state have a complicated relationship, the market nevertheless puts certain restrictions on the excessive expansion of state power.

We can understand this idealistic discourse as targeting state interference in the market and in society. If the state is not, however, simply seen as completely exterior to the market and as the direct antithesis of the individual, then how are we to categorize the internal forces of market distribution? The discourse of economic liberalism obscures the relationship between state plans for reform and the creation of markets in China, giving rise to a notion of natural "markets" that forfeits any ability to analyze the power relationships within these markets' systems of distribution. These power relationships are not just the principal sources of social corruption, but also the basic premise behind the unequal distribution of social resources. Within the dichotomy of planning/market, the notion of the "market" has been assumed to be the source of "freedom." This notion, however, blurs the distinction between markets and a market society. If we can say that markets are transparent and function in accordance with the price mechanisms of the marketplace, then a market society would use market mechanisms to govern the realms of politics, culture, and all other aspects of life—the working of market society cannot be distinguished from a monopolistic superstructure. It is in just this way that the notion of markets obscures the inequalities of modern society and its unequal structures of power. As Immanuel Wallerstein pointed out in summing up the contributions of Fernand Braudel, "Without political guarantees, there is never any way to control the economy. . . . If anyone thinks that without state support or from a position of opposition to the state that he can become a capitalist (in Braudel's sense of the term), this is an absurd presumption."[28] If the state is a constituent element in the implementation of capitalism, should not the imagery of economic liberalism that governs the contemporary Chinese intellectual world be rethought? In attempting to use the degree of state interference in the economy to explain economic and political democracy, should not one first reevaluate just who it is that stands to benefit from the activities of the state?

The second angle proceeds along the lines of the discourses on civil society and the public sphere. More and more people have recognized that the market is not exterior to the state and that between the market and the state is "society." As a middle force, society can maintain the balance of power between state and market. Under the influence of Habermas, many people have turned their attention to civil society and the public sphere. They believe that a Western-style civil society is emerging in China, or at least they call for its emergence as a defender of the civil rights and freedoms of the individual against the excessive interference of the state. If we take this discussion as a set of norms to be employed in appealing for political democracy, then we can understand it, sympathize with it, and even give it considerable support. But if this formal research agenda is taken as a concrete path and actual experience, then the theory becomes self-contradictory. But market reforms in China were initiated by a strong state from the very beginning; it is doubtful that a state-sponsored civil society could provide an effective counterbalance to the state in this state/civil society dichotomy.[29] For example, members of the political elite or their families directly participate in economic activity and have become agents for large corporations and industries. Can we call them representatives of civil society? In China, political and economic elites have been completely conflated, and they participate in international economic activity. The worst scandals in the economic sphere exposed thus far have all involved top-level bureaucrats and their dependents. Even more important is the question asking what is implied in the fact that most of this discussion focuses on the capacities of "society" and very little is directed to the "state" that stands in opposition to society. Is this state situated in a fixed position outside of or on top of society, or does it interpenetrate with society? Are there specific spaces implicit in the notion of the "state"? Do these spaces constitute potential areas of critique under certain circumstances?

These questions involve the issue of how to create space for social and political critique. Some scholars have turned their attention to the sphere of cultural production such as the media and print culture, because in this realm contemporary China has produced a number of "unofficial" periodicals, "independent" producers, and other cultural products. Several "civilian" or "independent" journals emerged after 1989. The first was *Xueren* (The scholar), followed by *Zhongguo shehui kexue jikan* (Chinese social science quarterly), *Yuandao* (Inquiry into the way), and *Gonggong luncong* (Public forum).[30] A number of semi-official publications such as *Zhanlue yu guanli* (Strategy and management) and *Dongfang* (The Orient) also appeared.[31] In addition, state-owned China Central Television (CCTV) began broadcasting the program *Dongfang shikong* (Oriental time and space), which was made by freelance producers. All this has changed the cultural scene considerably. But there are two things to be noted about these "unofficial" publications. First, they are published by state-owned publishing houses (in the absence of nonstate publishing houses), and second, their legal status is quite ambiguous, since they have no proper ISBN identification. Significantly, they are usually more cautious about printing critical material than official publications because of their greater vulnerability and lack of systemic protection. *Dushu* (Reading) is a case in point. Generally seen as the standard-bearer of free thinking, this journal is by no means an unofficial publication; it is published by a state publishing house and administered by the Bureau of Journalism and Publications. *Dongfang shikong* is another case in point. This sort of television reporting, even in the hands of independent producers, is still the product of a combination of the organs of the state ideology and huge advertising revenues. To be sure, because of the participation of unofficial elements, it is quite different from the monotonous and superficial state news programs in its use of imagery, language, presentation style, and content. Nevertheless, it is under strict state control and must fulfill the task of creating and promoting the state ideology. Thus, the public sphere in China is not a mediating space between state and society, but rather the result of the interpenetration of society and part of the internal structure of the state. These cultural products do have a general significance in extending cultural space in Chinese society, but since they exist in the space between state and society (and also within the state's space), they have no real power to resist state intervention.

Since the 1990s, many scholars from the United States, Taiwan, Hong Kong, and China have imported Habermas's concept of civil society into China. According to Habermas, the public sphere of early liberalism had a close relationship with civil society, stood between civil society and the state, and exercised supervision over both. What Habermas has constructed is an ideal norm, and he pays particular attention to the transformations and distortions of this ideal norm through the course of modern history. This is what he calls the "refeudalization" of the public sphere, that is, the media and other parts of the public sphere fall under the sway of the state, political parties, and the market. By the basic logic of this theory, we can say that, first, in mainland China, the public sphere emerged before a mature civil society, and in many ways it exists very much within the state apparatus. Its existence in this position is facilitated on the one hand by the financial assistance offered by international and domestic markets and on the other hand by the needs of the state and the creation of space within the state. Because of this, this public sphere never exhibited the characteristics that Habermas identified as peculiar to the early bourgeois public sphere; the position of the media in the social structure forcefully points to the vast differences between China's public sphere and the public sphere in Europe, of which Habermas speaks. We can also see how in this context the media was never a realm of free discussion and the creation of public opinion. If anything, the media was just the opposite: an arena in which hegemonic powers contended. It is thus important to do more research into the complex relations between society and the state in contemporary China; it is also important to recognize that, within this complexity, neither the market nor society is a "natural" deterrent to state power. This highlights the fact that economic and cultural democracy are inseparable from political democracy; it also demonstrates that the hope that the market will somehow automatically lead to equity, justice, and democracy—whether internationally or domestically—is just another kind of utopianism.[32]

The decline of the New Enlightenment movement marks the end of the most recent phase of Chinese thought. Yet, we can also say that this represents the historical victory of the ideology of modernization shared by socialism and the New Enlightenment movement. These two mutually conflicting yet mutually supportive modes of thought have produced a rationalization and a legitimization of China's modernization and have illuminated the path for a Chinese society facing global capitalist marketization reforms. In this era of multinational capitalism, the New Enlightenment movement was able only to produce a critique internal to the nation-state and particular to state behavior. It was unable to turn its critique of state dictatorship toward a timely critique and an analysis of the changing relationship between state and society and the conditions of changing state behavior in a market economy. It also was unable to come to an understanding of the fact that China's problems are also the problems of the world capitalist market and that any diagnosis of those problems must come to terms with the steadily increasing problems produced by the globalization of capitalism. Finally, it was unable to recognize the futility of using the West as a yardstick in the critique of China. The discourse of the Chinese New Enlightenment movement is built on the basic goal of the modernization of the nation-state, a goal whose origins are in Europe and have by now become the global prescription of the capitalist process. The new problem facing New Enlightenment thinking is how to transcend this goal and formulate a diagnosis and critique of the problem of China's modernity in the era of global capitalism. In the wake of the decline of New Enlightenment thinking, what we see are its remnants; on these ruins rests the capitalist market that crosses all national boundaries. Even the state behavior that was the primary target of New Enlightenment thinking has been constrained by this huge market. Thus, at the close of this century, there are those who have already announced an end to history.

Critical Thought in the Era of Global Capitalism

The two most important events of the end of the twentieth century were the failure of Eastern European socialism and the reorientation of China toward the global market through its "socialist reforms." They brought to a close the Cold War conflict between two opposing ideologies. Standing at this crossroads of history, there have been all sorts of prophecies about the twenty-first century: it will be the era of a new revolution in production; it will be the century in which population and living-standard problems will be resolved; it will be the era of cultural and religious renaissance; it will be the era when economic activity centers on the Pacific rim. Samuel P. Huntington of Harvard University in his 1993 essay "The Clash of Civilizations?" said that the major arena of conflict between peoples in the contemporary world is no longer ideology or economics, but rather cultural. In world affairs, the nation-state is still the major actor, but the principal conflicts in global politics will occur between peoples and states from different civilizations. Conflict between civilizations will thus dominate world politics.

I do not intend to discuss these predictions here (others have already touched on questions such as whether, in the context of world politics, it is possible for states to put cultural values above economic and political interests). I simply want to raise a question. In the post–Cold War era, China and other socialist countries have become important, or even the most dynamic, components of the world capitalist market. Indeed, East Asia could be turning its accustomed peripheral position in the former world capitalist system into the economic center of the new world capitalist order. Under such circumstances, what are we to make of the internal contradictions of the capitalist mode of production in the twenty-first century? For example, in the course of marketization in China, what will the relationship be between state, private, and foreign capital? What will the relationship be between new classes and other social groups? What of the relationship between agricultural and urban populations? Between the developed coastal regions and the backward hinterland? All of these social relationships must be placed within the context of new relations of production and particularly in the context of their relationship to the market. The fundamental question is how changes in these relations will impinge on Chinese society and the world capitalist market. In the era of multinational capitalism, do these "internal relations" matter any more? I am reminded here of the warning of that giant of liberal theory, Max Weber, who said that the rationality of modern capitalism would inevitably lead to a system in which some people rule over others; in this context, nothing, he said, would be able to root out faith in and hope for socialism. Is there still any relevance to these words, now that the traditional socialist movement has brought about a deep social crisis even as it seems to have ended in failure in the course of the Cold War?

The problem's greater complexity lies in the fact that as both a method and an embodiment of China's modernization, Chinese socialism did bring social organization. In fact, in the matter of state domination over society and people, it was even harsher than anything that ever existed under capitalism. Weber's and Marx's critiques of modernity were based on their observations and understandings of capitalism. Today, we must link our critique of the history of Chinese socialism to a critique of modernity and to the fact that the problem of modernity was first raised as a problem of European capitalism and its culture. The expansion of market society and its monopolization of social resources will as a matter of course be accompanied by a spontaneous and unplanned movement for the protection of social rights. The conflict between these forces provided the motive force for the most serious social crises of the nineteenth and twentieth centuries—including the two world wars. They also provide the basic momentum for efforts at self-reform on the part of modern social systems. The modern socialist movement was brought about by an analysis of the internal contradictions of capitalism and by the aspiration to overcome these contradictions, but the practice of socialism not only failed to complete the task of this aspiration, but it ended by being absorbed into global capitalism. At the same time, capitalism derived from socialism and from various movements for the protection of social rights opportunities for reform and self-critique, to the point where today, it is impossible to define socialism or capitalism in their original senses on the basis of the autonomous unit of the nation-state.

In this sense, when we use concepts like globalism or global capitalism to describe the changes to the contemporary world, this in no way implies that the structure and functioning of monopoly capitalism can represent the contemporary world in its entirety. This is because the social systems and public policies of Europe and America have already come to include elements from socialism or these movements for the protection of social rights. Aside from these elements embedded in social practice, we can also detect features of what Braudel calls "material civilization," or those things that have persisted in basic life and have through long historical duration created enduring associations. In this regard, because we are still at the stage where modernization is the historical goal, a rethinking of Chinese socialism entails not just its past experience, but also questions about its present and predictions of its future. Traditional socialism has not been able to resolve the internal crisis of modernity, and both Marxism and New Enlightenment thinking, as ideologies of modernization, are virtually devoid of force and unable to formulate appropriate approaches to contemporary world developments. It is here that the imperative to rethink the China question is located.

Chinese intellectuals are now engaged in discussions of the question of globalization, in contrast to the Western media's discussion of Chinese nationalism. Most Chinese intellectuals, however, understand globalization within the context of the Confucian ideal of universal harmony. In my opinion, this type of universalism is nothing more than another version of the century-long modernist dream of "meeting the world."

In this, it is still possible to discern vague features of "the prospects for world Confucianization." Another group of young people in a spirit of commercial speculation concocted best-sellers like *China Can Say No,* eliciting from an already extremely unstable Western society apprehensions about Chinese nationalism and notions of a plainly exaggerated "China threat." The success of the commercial speculations on the part of this latter group has caused some of the foreign media to believe that the tide of Chinese nationalism has taken on an extreme xenophobic quality. In making this assumption, however, they are forgetting the commercial aspect of the publication and circulation of this book. As long as the nation-state system does not completely collapse, then nationalism as the essential basis of national unity will not disappear.

Even more importantly, however, the politics of contemporary nationalism bear significant differences from traditional nationalism. Rather than seeing it as something in opposition to globalization, it would be preferable to view it as a by-product of globalization. Discussion of nationalism must be linked to the global political and economic order; it cannot be explained in isolation from this. In the twenty-first century China may become a developed market society, but it is not possible for it to become a new global hegemon. The economic, political, and military positions of the United States and the Soviet Union were the products of the Cold War, and after the dissolution of the Soviet Union, NATO has become the overwhelming military force in the world. In the foreseeable future, there is no other country capable of developing this sort of hegemonic military power. If one fails to think about contemporary nationalism from the perspective of the global political, economic, and military structure, then it doesn't matter if one actively supports nationalist movements or strongly opposes them—both positions neglect the crux of the question. Those scholars who regard globalization as a new world order forget that this order has been long in the making; as a process set in motion by the rise of capitalism, it has already passed through several stages. In the period of commercialism prior to the Industrial Revolution (1500–1800), commercial capital dominated the Atlantic, turning parts of it into European peripheries (for example, the Americas); during the so-called classical period brought into being by the Industrial Revolution (1800–1945) accompanying the development of Western capitalism, Asia (excluding Japan), Africa, and Latin America came to occupy the periphery of Western capitalism and were integrated into the global division of labor through agriculture and mining. It was during this period that an industrial sector began to develop within each bourgeois nation-state and that national liberation movements simultaneously arose in the peripheral countries. The dominant ideology of these movements was their single-minded pursuit of modernization and the establishment of a wealthy and strong nation-state; they took "catching up" as synonymous with progress and equated industrialization with liberation. From the end of World War II until today, the peripheral states have undertaken industrialization under globally disadvantageous and unequal conditions. China, along with many other Asian, African, and Latin American countries, did indeed achieve political independence, yet in the process of the globalization of capitalism, the self-sufficiency of their national industries gradually collapsed. These countries all found themselves being reorganized into a unified world system of production and trade.[33]

Globalization evidently cannot resolve the multiple social problems we now face. From the perspective of the development of the modern world, the globalization of production and trade has not spontaneously produced new political and social institutions capable of transcending the organizational forms of state and society within nation-states, nor has it been able to address the political and economic problems of the peripheral regions of Asia and Latin America. It has been even less able to bridge the so-called north–south gap. It is also clear that the weakening of the nation-state has not changed nation-states' political, economic, and military domination over their own societies. Because of this, in order to eliminate the negative effects of nationalism, we must explore the possibility of fairer and more peaceful political relationships from the broadest of global perspectives.

As for China, the interpenetration of and mutual conflict between international and internal control of capital that has resulted from China's increasingly deep involvement in globalized production and trade has led to increased complexity in the domestic economy and to inevitable systemic corruption. (It should be recalled that in China, as in other Third World countries, those who control domestic capital are in fact the same as those who control political power.) This corruption has seeped into every aspect of the political, economic, and moral spheres, giving rise to serious social inequities at every level. Even from the standpoint of pure efficiency, if institutional innovations are not able to stop the disintegration of society, such systemic corruption will constitute a major obstacle to economic development and will encourage a destructive consumerism that will rapidly drain national and social resources.

The upshot is that the teleology of modernization that has dominated Chinese thinking for the past century is now being challenged. We must reconsider our old familiar premises of thought. Even though there is no one theory that can explain the complex and often mutually contradictory problems that we now face, it nevertheless behooves Chinese intellectuals to break their dependence on time-honored binary paradigms, such as China/West and tradition/modernity, to pay more attention to the factors that might contribute to institutional innovation within society, to attend to the capacity for renewal within civil society, and to move on to a reexamination of the historical methods and conditions under which China has sought modernity. The reconsideration of China's problems by placing them in the context of globalization is an urgent theoretical problem. Socialist historical practice is part of the past; the future designs of global capitalism, by the same token, do not promise to overcome the crisis of modernity that Weber wrote about. The modern era, as a historical phase, continues. This provides the impetus for the continued existence and development of critical thought; it may prove for Chinese intellectuals to be a historic opportunity for theoretical and institutional innovation.

NOTES

Introduction

1. Perhaps the most lurid example of the final type is Richard Bernstein and Ross H. Munro, *The Coming Conflict with China* (New York: Knopf, 1997), a book that commanded a great deal of attention when it was first published.

2. The classic early study is Harold R. Isaacs, *Scratches on Our Minds: American Images of China and India* (New York: John Day, 1958).

3. Davies notes that there has been a "general lack of engagement in Anglophone cultural studies with Chinese critical inquiry despite the availability of many relevant China-related texts (including those in translation) published in important cultural studies journals as *Social Text, Boundary, positions, Postcolonial Studies,* and *Critical Inquiry.* In this context, it is worth noting in passing that an absence of engagement can be read as an exemption from critical review, which is really a polite form of exclusion." Gloria Davies, "The Self-Made Maps of Chinese Intellectuality," in G. Davies, ed., *Voicing Concerns: Contemporary Chinese Critical Inquiry* (Lanham, Md.: Rowman and Littlefield, 2001), p. 38.

4. Wang Hui, "La défaite du mouvement social de Tiananmen: Aux origines du néolibéralisme en China," *Le Monde Diplomatique,* April 2002, pp. 20–21.

5. Wang Hui, "Dangdai Zhongguo de sixiang zhuangkuang yu xiandaixing" (Contemporary Chinese thought and the question of modernity), *Tianya* (Frontiers) 5 (1997): 133–150. A translation by Rebecca E. Karl appeared in *Social Text* 55 (Summer 1998): 9–44, and is included as the second essay in this book.

6. Several of these articles have been translated into English. See, for example, "The Fate of 'Mr. Science' in China: The Concept of Science and Its Application in Modern Chinese Thought," *positions: east asia cultures critique* 3.1 (Spring 1995): 1–68; and "Zhang Taiyan's Concept of the Individual and Modern Chi-

189

nese Identity," in Wen-hsin Yeh, ed., *Becoming Chinese: Passages to Modernity and Beyond* (Berkeley: University of California Press, 2000), pp. 231–259.

7. "In Search of a 'Third Way': A Conversation Regarding 'Liberalism' and the 'New Left Wing,'" trans. Geremie R. Barmé, in Davies, *Voicing Concerns*, p. 203.

8. Chow Tse-tsung's *The May Fourth Movement: Intellectual Revolution in Modern China* (Cambridge, Mass.: Harvard University Press, 1960), now more than forty years old, still contains the best summary and analysis of this important event and its aftermath.

9. A number of books published in the United States have stressed the relationship between the intellectuals and the state, and a sample of their titles indicates the complexity of the relationship: Merle Goldman, *China's Intellectuals: Advise and Dissent* (Cambridge, Mass.: Harvard University Press, 1981); Carol Hamrin and Timothy Cheek, eds., *China's Establishment Intellectuals* (Armonk, N.Y.: M. E. Sharpe, 1986); Merle Goldman et al., eds., *China's Intellectuals and the State: In Search of a New Relationship* (Cambridge, Mass.: Council on East Asian Studies, Harvard University, 1987).

10. Appropriately enough, it is impossible to assemble a straightforward account of the advent of postmodern theory in China. It began in the early 1980s as a vague concept more often than not conflated with modernism, but was provided with a clearer definition in a series of lectures that Frederic Jameson presented in China while teaching a course at Beijing University in the fall of 1985. The transcribed and translated lectures were subsequently published in 1987 as an extremely influential book entitled *Houxiandai zhuyi yu wenhua lilun* (Postmodernism and cultural theory). Much of the early discussion of the theory was published in film studies journals, and included Jameson's "Third-World Literature in the Era of Multinational Capitalism" (originally published in *Social Text* in 1986). In the years that followed, translations of essays by Ihab Hassan, Jean-François Lyotard, William Spanos, Douwe Fokkema, Jonathan Arac, Linda Hutcheon, and Hans Bertens were published in China. It is probably safe to say that widespread critical awareness of the notion of the postmodern was only brought about by the 1994 debates between the advocates of a new humanism and the self-described advocates of the postmodern who opposed it. A notable feature of the postmodern discourse in China is that its popularization in China coincided with the introduction of Edward Said's concept of "Orientalism" via the translation of his book of that title. Since then, notions of "postcoloniality" have been inextricably entwined with theories of postmodernity. The clearest account in English of this process is to be found in Wang Ning, "The Mapping of Chinese Postmodernity," in Arif Dirlik and Xudong Zhang, eds., *Postmodernism and China* (Durham: Duke University Press, 2000), pp. 21–40.

11. The standard account of the political repression of dissent by the Communist Party through the 1950s is Merle Goldman, *Literary Dissent in Communist China* (Cambridge, Mass.: Harvard University Press, 1967).

12. David Zwieg, *Freeing China's Farmers: Rural Restructuring in the Reform Era* (Armonk, N.Y.: M. E. Sharpe, 1997), pp. 3–7.

13. Quoted in ibid., p. 26.

14. Jonathan Spence, *The Search for Modern China* (New York: W. W. Norton, 1990), p. 574.

15. For a clear summary of the political debates and moves surrounding collectivization, see Roderick MacFarquhar, *The Origins of the Cultural Revolution*, vol. 1, *Contradictions among the People, 1956–1957* (New York: Columbia University Press, 1974), pp. 122–138.

16. On the 1970s devolution, see Lynn T. White III, *Unstately Power: Volume 1: Local Causes of China's Economic Reforms* (Armonk, N.Y.: M. E. Sharpe, 1998).

17. For a full analysis of this speech, see MacFarquhar, *Contradictions among the People*, pp. 184–200.

18. See Maurice Meisner, *Mao's China: A History of the People's Republic*, 3d ed. (New York: Free Press, 1999), pp. 165–188.

19. Ibid., pp. 195–196; MacFarquhar, *Contradictions among the People*, pp. 278–281.

20. Spence, *The Search for Modern China*, p. 572.

21. Meisner, *Mao's China*, p. 231.

22. For a detailed account of this famine, see Jasper Becker, *Hungry Ghosts: Mao's Secret Famine* (New York: Henry Holt, 1998). It should be noted that while details of this famine are widely known and actively discussed in China— including in a number of college classrooms—no written account of the disaster has been permitted to be published.

23. On the question of ultra-leftism, see William A. Joseph, *The Critique of Ultra-Leftism in China, 1958–1981* (Stanford: Stanford University Press, 1984).

24. For the official role in this critique of Mao, see Meisner, *Mao's China*, pp. 462–464.

25. For more detail on the 1980s, see Dorothy J. Solinger, *China's Transition from Socialism: Statist Legacies and Market Reforms, 1980–1990* (Armonk, N.Y.: M. E. Sharpe, 1993).

26. An excellent summary of these developments can be found in Zwieg, *Freeing China's Farmers*, pp. 12–23.

27. For the perspective of a prominent American sinologist on these events that is in general consonance with that of Wang Hui, see Maurice Meisner, *The Deng Xiaoping Era: An Inquiry into the Fate of Chinese Socialism, 1978–1994* (New York: Hill and Wang, 1996), pp. 471–523.

28. Ibid., p. 467.

29. Between January 18 and February 21, 1992, Deng Xiaoping paid an extensive visit to southern China, visiting Canton, Shanghai, and Wuhan, as well as the special economic zones in Shenzhen and Zhuhai in Guangdong Province.

While he had already retired from all public office at this time, the statements he made on this visit about encouraging economic development were treated as policy directives by the government. On the background to this, see ibid., pp. 478–480. *Nanxun* has been generally translated as "Southern Tour," but I have chosen "Southern Progress" to emphasize both the linguistic and procedural similarity between Deng's 1992 visit and the imperial progresses to south China made by the Qing sovereigns, a similarity that immediately strikes any educated speaker of Chinese.

30. See, for instance, Xudong Zhang, "Intellectual Politics in Post-Tiananmen China: An Introduction," *Social Text* 55 (Summer 1998): 3.

31. In his "Nationalism, Mass Culture, and Intellectual Strategies in Post-Tiananmen China," *Social Text* 55 (Summer 1998): 119–126, Xudong Zhang goes into this discussion over humanism in some detail.

32. See Wang Hui, "Dangdai Zhongguo de sixiang zhuangkuang yu xiandaixing" (Contemporary Chinese thought and the question of modernity), included as the second essay in this book. Geremie Barmé notes the agenda-setting importance of this essay both in his *In the Red: On Contemporary Chinese Culture* (New York: Columbia University Press, 1999), p. 355, and in his "Time's Arrows: Imaginative Pasts and Nostalgic Futures," in Davies, *Voicing Concerns,* p. 230.

33. A good summary of Wang's thoughts on this can be found in Joseph Fewsmith, *China since Tiananmen: The Politics of Transition* (Cambridge: Cambridge University Press, 2001), pp. 113–114.

34. Wang Xiaoming, "Manifesto for Cultural Studies," in Chaohua Wang, ed., *One China, Many Paths* (London: Verso, 2003).

35. Note Barmé's scathing words on neoliberalism in "Time's Arrows," pp. 227–228. For another description of the difference between the "liberals" and the "New Left," see Luo Gang, "In Search of a 'Third Way,'" p. 206.

36. On the neo-authoritarians, see Fewsmith, *China since Tiananmen,* pp. 86–93.

37. Gan Yang, "A Critique of Chinese Conservatism in the 1990s," trans. Xudong Zhang, *Social Text* 55 (Summer 1998): 45–66.

38. See Fewsmith, *China since Tiananmen,* p. 129.

39. Zweig, *Freeing China's Farmers,* p. 5.

40. Hardt and Negri, *Empire* (Cambridge, Mass: Harvard University Press, 2000), pp. 109, 113. Note also the critique of Arif Dirlik in "Revolutionary Hegemony and the Language of Revolution: Chinese Socialism between Present and Future," in which he says that where a situation is constructed in which "national struggle against global capital" becomes the dominant discourse, the result is "not a socialist language but a dialect of capitalism. This is the language that dominates Chinese socialism today." In Dirlik and Maurice Meisner, eds., *Marxism and the Chinese Experience* (Armonk, N.Y.: M. E. Sharpe, 1989), p. 38.

41. Hardt and Negri, *Empire,* p. 95.

42. An excellent early study on the Chinese determination to emulate the Western nation-state can be found in Benjamin Schwartz's *In Search of Wealth and Power: Yen Fu and the West* (Cambridge, Mass.: Harvard University Press, 1964).

43. For an account of some of these, see Fewsmith, *China since Tiananmen,* pp. 93–95, 143–146.

44. Other summaries can be found in Ben Xu, "Contesting Memory for Intellectual Self-Positioning: The 1990s New Cultural Conservatism in China," *Modern Chinese Literature and Culture* 11.1 (Spring 1999): 157–192.

45. M. E. Sharpe has recently published translations of two important books by the Chinese social analysts Wang Shaoguang and Hu Anguang evaluating the contemporary Chinese situation. They are *The Political Economy of Uneven Development: The Case of China* (Armonk, N.Y.: M. E. Sharpe, 1999) and *The Chinese Economy in Crisis: State Capacity and Tax Reform* (Armonk, N.Y.: M. E. Sharpe, 2001).

46. Michael Leeden, "From Communism to Fascism?" the *Wall Street Journal,* 22 February 2002.

47. Fewsmith, *China since Tiananmen,* p. 114.

48. Indeed, Gloria Davies exhibits a defensiveness on this point at several places in the introduction to her collection of translated essays. For instance, she allows for "[t]he perceived or perhaps even demonstrably 'theoretically underdeveloped' status of the Chinese humanities" even as she tries valiantly to argue why this judgment should not be made. See the introduction to *Voicing Concerns,* p. 15.

The 1989 Social Movement

1. The Chinese word for "groupings" is *quanzi,* which refers to voluntary groups of intellectuals, generally in Beijing, who function as "opinion leaders" in the intellectual community.—*Trans.*

2. The socialist tendency I am referring to here does not refer to any form of state socialism characterized by a planned economy, but rather to the movement for social self-protection that took place as the new marketization expanded. It naturally tended toward appeals for social equality and justice, and set out demands for social democracy on this basis. Working within a postsocialist environment, the mobilization of this movement was influenced by the value system of socialism.

3. In December of 1986 there was a brief student movement demanding more democracy that began at the University of Science and Technology in Hefei, Anhui Province, from which it eventually spread to Shangahi by December 20. Although the movement faded away, Hu Yaobang's apparent ties with some of its

leaders led to his dismissal from his post as general secretary of the Communist Party in January of 1987. For more details, see Maurice Meisner, *Mao's China and After: A History of the People's Republic*, 3rd ed. (New York: Fee Press, 1999), pp. 486–488.—*Trans.*

4. According to research by sociologists, the urban–rural divide manifests itself in five major ways. First, a difference in political power in which the farming population is completely directed by the government in all realms, whether political, economic, or cultural, and none of these representatives of the government are rural people. Second, a difference in economic status in which there is "scissors differential" in prices between agricultural and industrial products in order to accumulate capital for urban industrial development. At the same time, the government monopolizes economic resources and opportunities for development even as it limits rural industrialization. Third, a difference in income such that urban incomes are from three to six times greater than rural incomes. Fourth, a difference in social benefits in which the major portion of urban residents (whether the whole population, or the employees of collective or state-owned enterprises, or state cadres) enjoy life-long free medical care, retirement pay, and guaranteed rations of meat, oil, and grain; rural residents enjoy none of these benefits. Fifth, a difference in social status, in which the position in society of urban residents is much higher than that of rural residents. See Wang Hansheng and Zhang Xinxiang, "Jiefang yilai Zhonguo de shehui cengci fenhua" (The differentiation of social strata in China since liberation) *Shehuixue yanjiu* (Sociological Research) 6 (1993); Li Qiang, "Dangdai Zhongguo shehui fenceng jiegou bianqian baogao" (A report on the transformation of the structure of social differentiation in contemporary China), in Li Peilin, ed., *Zhongguo xin shiqi jieji jieceng baogao* (A report on the differentiation of class in China in the new period) (Shenyang: Liaoning renmin chubanshe, 1995), pp. 65–67; and Zhang Wanli's summary and commentary, "Zhongguo shehui jieji jieceng yanjiu ershi nian" (Twenty years of research on class differentiation in China), *Shehuixue yanjiu* 1 (2000): 26.

5. Contracts were phased in after 1978 to replace state management of mandatory sales quotas. Negotiations over price and amount of rural product resulted in contracts being given to rural producers for specified amounts of product. For a summary of this process, see David Zweig, *Freeing China's Farmers: Rural Restructuring in the Reform Era* (Armonk, N.Y.: M. E. Sharpe, 1997), pp. 151–160. See also Maurice Meisner, *The Deng Xiaoping Era: An Inquiry into the Fate of Chinese Socialism, 1978–1994* (New York: Hill and Wang, 1996), pp. 227–231.—*Trans.*

6. Lu Xueyi has broken down the rural population into eight strata: agricultural laborers, rural workers, hired workers, intellectual employees, individually employed workers, business people and laborers, private entrepreneurs, and managers of collective enterprises and of the rural social apparatus. Lu Xueyi,

"Chongxin renshi nongmin wenti" (Rethinking the issue of the rural population) *Shehuixue yanjiu* 6 (1999).

7. This view was set forth in 1980 by Liao Jili and was affirmed by Xue Muqiao. At its core lay the notion that agricultural development depended on state policy to raise the level of rural initiative and economic diversity—a national policy that required few additional resources or investment. See Guo Shuqing, *Jingji tizhi zhuangui yu hongguan tiaokong* (Retracking the economic system and its macro-controls) (Tianjin: Renmin chubanshe, 1992), p. 175.

8. Zhang Wanli sees two parts to this. One is the groups outside the original system and the great increase in the resources they control, such as individual managers, autonomous professionals, private entrepreneurs, high-level employees in cooperative, foreign or private enterprises, entrepreneurs outside the system of public ownership, and the like. The second is made up of groups that had been part of the original system, but whose social position had begun to change and become polarized, such as farmers, cadres, various professionals, and workers. Zhang, "Twenty years of research on class differentiation in China," pp. 29–30.

9. Wang Shaoguang, "Jianli yige qiangyouli de minzhu guojia—jian lun 'zhengzhi xingshi' yu 'guojia nengli' de qubie" (Establish a rich and powerful democratic nation—including discussion of the difference between "type of regime" and "state capability"), *Dangdai Zhongguo yanjiu zhongxin lunwen* (Essays from the Center for Research on Contemporary China) 4 (1991): 15–17.

10. Wang Shaoguang concluded: "The guiding reform policy of 'The devolution of political and economic power' did not diminish the power of the public sector (each level of government and their various branches) to distribute the national income, but merely decreased the power of the central government to distribute it. . . . Following the expansion of the fiscal authority of local governments, their ability to interfere in economic life through administrative measures not only did not weaken, but actually grew more powerful. Moreover, this economic interference was even more direct than had been the economic interference of the central government in the past. The reform guideline of 'devolving political and economic power' did not lead to the extinction of the tradition of a command economy, but did reduce the scale of the traditional system." Ibid., p. 20.

11. On the income disparity that first manifested itself in increasing disharmony between incomes in individual and national enterprises, see Zhao Renwei: "Zhongguo zhuanxingqi zhong shouru fenpei de yixie teshu xianxiang" (Some characteristics of income distribution in China's transitional period) in Zhao, ed., *Zhongguo jumin shouru fenpei yanjiu* (Studies on the income distribution of China's people) (Beijing: Zhongguo shehui kexue chubanshe, 1994); on internal disparities manifesting themselves in increasing differences among management, technical personnel, and workers, see Feng Tongqing et al., *Zhongguo zhigong*

zhuangkuang, neibu jiegou ji xianghu guanxi (The situation of Chinese workers: internal structures and relationships among them) (Beijing: Zhongguo shehui kexue chubanshe, 1993); on the position and benefits of employees, including lack of guarantees on hours worked, job protection, and labor contracts, and on the inability of those with weakening labor power to secure appropriate initial compensation, see Zhang Wanli, "Twenty years of research on class differentiation in China," pp. 29–30.

12. People customarily take Wu Jinglian as the representative of those who simultaneously advocated price and enterprise reform, while Li Yining is recognized for having in 1980 advocated the issuing of stock. In 1988 Wu compiled the comprehensive report on the intermediate period of the reform program, *Zhongguo gaige da silu* (The thinking behind China's reform) (Shenyang: Shenyang chubanshe, 1988). Related materials include, *Zhongguo jingji gaige zongti guihua ji* (Essays on the overall plan of Chinese economic reform) (Beijing: Zhongyang dangxiao chubanshe, 1987); *Zhongguo jingji gaige de zhengti sheji* (The integrated design of China's economic reform) (Beijing: Zhanwang chubanshe, 1990); and "Jiage gaige he tizhi zhuangui de chenggong baozheng" (Guarantees for the success of price reform and systemic transformation), *Gaige* (Reform) 6 (1988).

13. Guo Shuqing, *Jingji tizhi zhuangui,* p. 181.

14. On the principal goals of this "administrative rectification," see "Zhonggong zhongyang guanyu jinyibu zhili zhengdun he shenhua gaige de jueding" (The decision on advancing administrative rectification and extending reform taken by the Central Committee of the Communist Party) in *Zhongguo jinrong nianjian (1990)* (China's fiscal yearbook, 1990); and *Shinian jihua tizhi gaige gailan* (Survey of a decade of reform of the planning system) (Beijing: Zhongguo jihua chubanshe, 1989).

15. As Wang Hui explains below, the term "rent seekers" *(xun zu)* refers to those who were able to exploit the difference between the fixed price of commodities that were part of the economic plan and the higher price available on the free market.—*Trans.*

16. Hu Heyuan, "1988 nian Zhongguo zujin jiazhi de gusuan" (Estimate of the value of rent in 1988), in *Jingji tizhi bijiao* (Comparative economic systems) 7 (1989).

17. On the changes to the cadre stratum before and after the reforms, see Li Qiang, *Dangdai Zhongguo shehui fenceng yu liudong* (Social differentiation and mobility in contemporary China) (Beijing: Zhongguo jingji chubanshe, 1993).

18. The "floating population" *(liudong renkou* or *youmin)* refers to people who have left rural areas of China to seek employment elsewhere, generally in the relatively prosperous cities of the southeast. For the circumstances that nurtured this population movement, see Meisner, *The Deng Xiaoping Era,* pp. 232–233.

As Meisner notes, "the numbers of those who make up this 'floating population' of migrant workers fluctuate greatly, depending on economic conditions."— *Trans.*

19. During the historical era that is customarily referred to as "the new period" (1978–1988), the vast majority of the older and middle-aged intellectuals who played a leading role (including economists, political scientists, philosophers, historians, and literary critics) were leading figures from within the university and research institute system. For instance, a number of the disputes among economists had their origin in arguments over national policy. In this period, as well, "Left" and "Right" within Chinese thought in fact originated in factional disputes within the state system. And because these were people of position and reputation, divisions among them were frequently understood as the division between Left and Right among the intellectuals as a whole. Even today there are people who understand the Left and Right produced by the process of social differentiation on the model of intraparty political struggle, and there are even those who seek to eliminate opposition by using the model of the struggle over the correct line.

20. This is not because people approved of a planned economy, but rather because the practical problems grew out of the process of transformation, so that the questions were directed first at that process itself.

21. The Chinese government and ruling party continued to use the political system established in 1949 as the premise of its own legitimacy, and people thus were accustomed to viewing the Maoist and Dengist periods as a continuum. This was also one of the primary reasons that people blamed their discontent with the current situation on the Maoist period and its planned system. The state of the reform period and its leading policies, however, contained important differences from the state of the Maoist period. It was precisely for this reason that, when the organs of the state ideological apparatus insisted on ideological continuity, the internal contradictions between the ideology and the policies and practices of the reform period were fully exposed. The state ideological apparatus and the dual sources of the ruling party's legitimacy (that is, its simultaneous status as a Marxist political party and as the promoter of market reforms) resulted in ambiguity underlying the movement to critique the state: it often criticized current state policies and practices under the name of criticizing the old system. As for 1989, the critical movement launched that year in opposition to such things as "official peculation," "corruption," and "the princely party" cannot be understood as a simple critique of the traditional socialist state. Rather, it was a critique of the reform state, or a dual critique.

22. Companies like these were enterprises with extremely high official connections, often through the mediation of the children of the national leadership. The Kanghua Company, for instance, was founded by Deng Pufang, Deng Xiaoping's son, who was able to build it into a "multibillion-dollar conglomerate specializing

in international trade." See Meisner, *The Deng Xiaoping Era,* pp. 325–329.— *Trans.*

23. For example, the fact that the student hunger strike in May of 1989 began after a meeting of intellectuals convened by the *Guangming Daily* and its subsequent publication of a manifesto is a case in point.

24. This so-called neoliberalism refers to a type of ideology. Even though there are many points of overlap between this ideology and the views of the individual scholars cited in this essay, the focus of my analysis here is not on any individual scholars. The concept of ideology refers to a governing mode of thought, which can turn into a means by which people make judgments. For instance, when China and the United States signed the World Trade Organization (WTO) agreement, almost the entire media reported it from the same perspective, which gained a hugely positive response throughout society. The ordinary people, and even the intellectuals, however, knew nothing whatsoever of the content of the agreement, so why the mass enthusiasm? It would be almost impossible to imagine this phenomenon absent the ideologies of the market and of development. After 1989 the ideological apparatus of the Chinese state continued to operate, but compared to the Maoist period, this state ideological apparatus could no longer function as effectively as before, not even being able to manage "infractions" whether through administrative or coercive measures. We can say, at least, that the state ideology faces in two directions at once, one looking toward the ideologies of the market and development, and the other toward the ideology of traditional socialism. The latter has metamorphosed into an exceedingly brittle propaganda, lacking any persuasive force.

25. This also helps to explain why the critique of the devolution process was not thoroughgoing. Against the background of the failure of the traditional planned system, devolution was both inevitable and necessary. The questions remaining, however, included how to guarantee the transparency and fairness of the redistribution of social property via a democratic policy process; how, under the principles of social democracy, to guarantee that the process of power sharing would not lead to the reconcentration of social benefits at another level; and how to establish a balance between state regulation and the market.

26. The "income distribution" task-force (Zhao Renwei et al.) of the Institute of Economics at the Chinese Academy of Social Sciences has made the following estimates of the income difference between rural populations engaged in agriculture and those engaged in other occupations: the incomes of those working for rural enterprises is one to two times greater than those in agriculture, whereas those working in commerce or the service industry have incomes two to five times as great, while those involved in transportation and the rural construction industry have incomes five to eight times larger. In 1980, the national average rural income was ¥191.33 per capita, with the ratio of distribution among the eastern, central and western sectors being 1.39:1.11:1 (with the western region being 1).

By 1993, the national average rural income had risen to ¥921 per capita, while in the same period the ratios of distribution among east, central, and west had risen to 2:25:1.75:1, the different figures being ¥1,380, ¥786, and ¥604. The difference in income between employers and the employed varied in accordance with the number employed, but that difference also grew dramatically.

Differences in urban incomes also grew overall, primarily in the following ways. First, differences among regions expanded, with, for example, the differences in average annual disposable income among western, central, and eastern urban residents being eighty and fifty yuan (i.e., ¥458, ¥493, and ¥543, respectively). By 1994, however, the respective average annual incomes of urban residents in the three regions were ¥2,402, ¥2,805, and ¥4,018, the differences having risen to ¥1,616 and ¥1,213, or 14.2 and 32.3 times as great. Second, the income difference among different categories of employment grew, with, for instance, incomes in the financial and insurance sectors surpassing those in the old high-income sectors such as electric power and gas and fisheries; it had risen to be 2.4 times that of those engaged in agriculture, forestry, herding, and fisheries, with the absolute differentials being even greater. Third, the income differential among those working under different systems of ownership increased. For instance, in 1986 the annual per capita income for those employed in enterprises with foreign participation was ¥1,527, 1.14 times the national average in comparable enterprises that year, with an absolute differential of ¥200. By the beginning of 1994, the average income of workers in enterprises with foreign participation had continued to rise, and while the rate of wage increase in China as a whole rose by 26.3 percent, the rate of increase in foreign-affiliated enterprises reached 92.2 percent, an increase that was 41.7 percent higher than the year before. By the year 2000, the income of employees of foreign-affiliated and rural enterprises had reached a level at least two or three times that of party and State functionaries and employees of research units. Fourth, the differentiation of incomes among different groups within the same enterprise had grown. There are two different situations here: one is the income differential between employers and employees in private and foreign-affiliated enterprises and the other is the income differential between factory heads and managers and workers in publicly held enterprises. The average annual income of Chinese managers of foreign-held companies in China has already reached US $6,600, ten times that of ordinary employees, and the income differential between managers and administrators in publicly held enterprises has reached substantial levels, while it has become common practice for these managers and administrators to receive a number of benefits beyond their salary. Fifth, the appearance of a new stratum of poor people refers primarily to those laid off as a result of enterprise reform, the hidden unemployed, employees of enterprises that have either partially-ceased production or ceased altogether, the retired, a segment of public employees, as well as a floating population in urban areas of poor people from the countryside. By 1994, the proportion of workers having subsistence problems had risen from 5 percent to 8 percent, with 100 million people—or 8 percent of China's population—mired in poverty. These are the research results of Zhao Renwei and his group as published in *Zhongguo jumin shouru fenpei yanjiu* (Studies on Income Distribution among the Chinese People) (Beijing: Zhongguo kexue chubanshe, 1994). Zhang Wanli, "Twenty Years of Research on Class Differentiation in China), p. 36.

27. Lu Mai, "Shizhong buneng wangji nongcun de fazhan" (Never forget rural development), cited in Luo Yuping's interview in *Sanlian shenghuo zhoukan* (Sanlian life weekly) 14 (1998): 26 (31 July 1998, issue no. 68 overall).

28. In recent years, more and more scholars are focusing on trends toward "urbanization" and "deruralization," one of the principal reasons for which is that economic recession has rendered the surplus of rural labor a huge social problem. In such circumstances discussion aimed at what the sociologist Fei Xiaotong dubbed the "big problem of small towns" has been gradually replaced by this discussion of urbanization. See Wang Ying, "Chengshi fazhan yanjiu de huigu yu qianzhan" (A review and a forecast of studies of urban development), *Shehuixue yanjiu* 1 (2000): 65–75.

29. Lu Xueyi, "Zouchu 'chengxiang fenzhi, yiguo liangce' de kunjing" (Getting out of the impasse of "different systems of urban and rural governance: one country with two policies"), *Dushu* (Readings) 5 (2000): 3–9.

30. China's rural reforms and the rural crisis have long been the focus of study for a few economists and reformers, but it was not until the 1997 financial crisis, with its slowdown in China's economic growth and persisting deflationary environment, that rural problems received widespread attention. A substantial number of the scholars who became interested in the problems facing the rural population, however, did so from the perspective of such issues as stimulating economic development and reducing the pressure on urban areas. They were interested neither in the question of the rights of the rural population nor in the matter of social inequality, but rather raised the problem of the countryside and its population only from the perspective of the question of economic growth, and of urban economic growth in particular. In other words, such matters as the freedom of labor contracts for workers from rural areas and social equality received attention only insofar as they were perceived to impinge on economic growth.

31. In September of 1988, Yu Ying-shih presented a talk entitled "Zhongguo jindai sixiang shi zhong de jijin yu baoshou" (Radicalism and conservatism in modern Chinese thought) that prepared the ground for the battle over radicalism and conservatism that developed after 1989. Gan Yang's "Yangqi 'minzhu yu kexue,' dianding 'ziyou' yu 'zhixu,'" (Sublate "democracy and science," establish "freedom" and "order"), *Ershiyi shiji* (Twenty-first century) 3 (1991): 7–10 is another essay that was widely influential. Essays on radicalism from the early 1990s appeared primarily in *Ershiyi shiji*, including Lin Gang's "Jijin zhuyi zai Zhongguo" (Radicalism in China), 3 (1991): 17–27; Yu Ying-shih's "Zhongguo

zhishifenzi de bianyuanhua" (The marginalization of Chinese intellectuals), 6 (1991): 15–25; Jiang Yihua's "Jijin yu baoshou: yu Yu Yingshi shangque" (Radicalism and conservatism: a discussion with Mr. Yu Ying-shih), 10 (1992): 134–142; Yu Ying-shih's "Zailun Zhongguo jindai sixiang shi zhong de jijin yu baoshou: Da Jiang Yihua xiansheng" (Radicalism and conservatism in modern Chinese thought revisited: a reply to Mr. Jiang Yihua), 10 (1992): 143–149; Wang Rongzu's "Jijin yu baoshou zhuiyan" (Superfluous words on radicalism and conservatism), 11 (1992): 133–136; Xu Jilin's "Jijin yu baoshou de mihuo" (The conundrum of radicalism and conservatism), 11 (1992): 137–140; Li Liangyu's "Jijin, baoshou yu zhishifenzi de zeren" (Radicalism, conservatism and the responsibility of the intellectuals), 12 (1992): 132–134; Wang Shaoguang's "'Baoshou' yu 'baoshou zhuyi'" ("Conservatives" and "conservatism"), 12 (1992): 135–138; Hu Cheng's "Jijin zhuyi yihuo baoli zhuyi?" (Radicalism or an ideology of force?) 13 (1992): 139–145; and Liu Shuxian's "Duiyu jijin zhuyi de fansi" (Thoughts on radicalism), 31 (1995): 40–42.

32. This is taken from a statement made by a scholar at a 1998 conference marking the hundredth anniversary of the wuxu (1898) reforms that was co-convened by *Dushu* magazine and the Tianze Institute of Economic Research. Historical research on the 1898 reforms has long focused on the study of the re-form party that had Kang and Liang as its core, paying comparatively little atten-tion to local change or the changes in the relationship between the central gov-ernment and the localities. As a consequence, from the perspective of the needs of historical research, it is essential that attention be paid to the significance changes at the local level had for late Qing dynasty social reform. The direction of related research in the 1990s, however, was not limited to concern with the 1898 reform movement itself, but rather to establishing the basis for a broader political per-spective.

33. See the 1998 essays published by Liu Junning in the *Zhongguo gaige bao* (Report on China's reform), edited by the Committee on Structural Reform of the Chinese State Council.

34. Even as the three major markets mentioned in the text were opened, the financial system was not completely freed and there was no fundamental change in the structure of rural society. For this reason, this social dislocation did not in the short run produce large-scale social disruption and conflict. This also partially explains why China was able to calmly navigate the 1997 Asian financial crisis— even as it revealed the serious crisis of the Chinese financial system. The question here continues to be not a matter of being opposed to opening markets or of ad-vocating state protection, but rather one of how to open up markets and under what conditions to open them. There is also the question of to what degree the state needs to regulate markets, in other words, the question of how to create a democratic system under market conditions. The radicalization of the process of the devolution of political and economic power runs the risk of causing the state

to completely lose its power to regulate, and consequent loss of the basic conditions underlying social guarantees. Lacking sufficient tax revenues, the state would not only lose its ability to effectively regulate markets, but also (assuming the collapse of the preexisting system of social benefits) would have no way to erect a new structure of these benefits (such as housing, medical care, and the retirement system), nor would it have a way to reestablish a system of social guarantees to provide a systemic foundation for the reform of state enterprises—since one of the predicaments in trying to reform state-owned enterprises is that the social burden of the these enterprises is already much too heavy.

35. The inauguration of the journal *Xueren* (The Scholar) in 1991 marked the beginning of this ongoing process of reflection and study. *Xueren* did not pursue any particular academic agenda, and its appearance represented the aspirations of a group of younger scholars engaged in academic work to demonstrate the necessity of serious academic endeavor no matter what the conditions. Intellectual debate accompanied various social crises in being rekindled in the late 1990s; but there remained a substantial number of scholars who, even as they expressed concern over social problems, refused to allow their own scholarly research to be reduced to a simple response to practical matters. In my view, it will require a good deal of time before the significance of this very small group of disinterested scholars is understood. I do not approve of grouping all of this research under the simplistic rubric "conservative."

36. This question, however, should not stop here. We need to pursue a number of issues like the following: one, if the student movement and the intellectuals associated with it lacked the ability to propose clear goals for reform, and had no way to come to grips with the fundamental motivations underlying this widespread and spontaneous movement, just what sort of intellectual force and ideological formation was limiting them? Two, if the student movement and its demands for democracy were unable to respond to the internal contradictions of the 1980s reforms, if it was unable to provide internal links between the broad social mobilization and its demands and the direct goals of the movement, what was the source of mobilizing power of the student movement itself? In my writings between 1993 and 1997, and especially my article "Dangdai Zhongguo de sixiang zhuangkuang yu xiandaixing wenti" (Contemporary Chinese thought and the problem of modernity), I analyzed these two questions. [This work, translated by Rebecca Karl, is included as the second essay in this book.] In the course of thinking these issues through and writing about them, I began to discover that the internal limitations of the intellectual liberation of the 1980s were directly related not just to the failure of the 1989 movement, but also explain the intellectual grounds for the inability of Chinese intellectuals in the 1990s to respond critically and creatively to the expansion of markets, their systemic monopolization, and the process of globalization.

37. Wang Shuo is an author based in Beijing who is also active in television

and film production. He takes particular delight in lampooning ideological trends, whether those launched by the government or by the intellectuals. He refers to himself as a "hooligan" *(pizi)*. Two of his more important novels have been translated by Howard Goldblatt, *Playing for Thrills* (Warde jiushi xin tiao) (New York: William Morrow, 1997), and *Please Don't Call Me Human* (Qianwan bie ba Wo dang ren) (New York: Hyperion, 2000).—*Trans.*

38. Huntington, "Wenming de chongtu?" (The clash of civilizations?), *Ershiyi shiji* 19 (1993): 5–21. In the same issue of that journal appeared Jin Guantao's "Xifang zhongxinlun de pomie: ping quanqiuhua de chongtu lun," (The destruction of Eurocentrism: a critique of the thesis of global clash), pp. 22–25; Liu Xiaofeng's, "Liyi zhongyu wenhua" (Interests outweigh culture), pp. 26–27; and Chen Fangzheng's "Lun Zhongguo minzuzhuyi yu shijie yishi" (On Chinese nationalism and cosmopolitanism), pp. 28–35.

39. The term *"datong"* or "Great Union" referred to a utopian notion of world unity devised by the late Qing reformer Kang Youwei (1858–1927) and given expression in his visionary tract *Datong shu* '(The book of the great union), completed in 1902 but not published until 1913. For more on Kang and his work, see Kung-chuan Hsiao, *A Modern China and a New World: K'ang yu-wei, Reformer and Radical, 1858–1927* (Seattle: University of Washington Press, 1975).—*Trans.*

40. These were mostly published in *Zhongguo shehui kexue jikan* (Chinese social science quarterly) and other related journals. See my essay "Contemporary Chinese Thought and the Question of Modernity" for a discussion and analysis.

41. It is difficult to imagine that without a certain amount of tacit assent and toleration on the part of the state that the smuggling activities of local governments and interest groups would have been as rampant as it was. This organized smuggling did serious damage to internal markets, and particularly the working of state-owned enterprises, thereby indirectly damaging the interests of the majority of the working class. Under conditions of monopoly markets, ordinary workers are not only in opposition to monopoly pricing and the relations of monopoly interests, but are also in opposition to the power base underlying these relationships of interest. They would demand that the state place limitations on and punish those responsible for these monopolies and their attendant corruption, and protect market competition, but over and over again the state acted as protector of these monopolies. The corruption was institutional.

42. Cui Zhiyuan published his article "'Eryuan lianbang zhuyi' de xiaowang" (The disappearance of "dual federalism") in *Dushu* 9 (1996) and also "'Hunhe xianfa' yu dui Zhongguo zhengzhi de sanceng fenxi" (An analysis of a "mixed constitution" and the three political levels in China) in *Zhanlue yu guanli* (Strategy and management) 3 (1998). In these articles he sought through political theory to conceptualize a mixed constitution and system, to establish a "top" (the

central government), a "middle" (local governments and important capitalists), and a "bottom" (the common people) that would be able to interact to the benefit of all. He put special emphasis on how to turn the demands of the common people into the will of the state, thereby foreclosing the possibility of a new "aristocracy." His political vision and the thesis of civil society were in sharp contrast to one another. I think his explorations are worthy of attention and further discussion. His thesis is hardly a radical one, but if placed in the context of the stratification of Chinese society that has taken place since 1989, I believe it to have a very positive critical significance.

43. See the related discussion in Charles Taylor's "Gongmin yu guojia zhijian de juli" (The distance between citizen and state), and in my *"Wenhua yu gongongxing* daolun" (Introduction to *Culture and the Notion of the Public*), both in *wenhua yu gongongxing* (Culture and the notion of the public) (Beijing: Sanlian shudian, 1998), pp. 199–200, 38–47.

44. Among others, see Gan Yang, "Xiangtu Zhongguo chongjian yu Zhongguo wenhua qianjing" (The reconstruction of the Chinese countryside and the prospects for Chinese culture), *Erhsiyi shiji* 16 (1993): 4; Gan Yang, "Fan minzhu de ziyouzhuyi haishi minzhu de ziyouzhuyi?" (Anti-democratic or democratic liberalism?), *Erhsiyi shiji* 39 (1997): 4–17; Cui Zhiyuan, "Zhidu chuangxin yu dierci sixiang jiefang" (Institutional innovation and the second liberation of thought), *Erhsiyi shiji* 24 (1994): 5–16; Wang Shaoguang "Xiaoshuai, gongping, minzhu" (Efficiency, fairness, democracy), *Erhsiyi shiji* 26 (1994): 21–33; Qin Hui, "Li tu bu li xiang? Ye tan xiangtu Zhongguo chongjian wenti" (Leaving the fields, but not leaving the countryside? Discussing again China's rural reconstruction), *Dongfang* (The Orient) 1 (1994); Su Wen, "Shanchong shuifu ying you lu" (There should be a way out), *Dongfang* 1 (1996). There are major theoretical differences between Cui Zhiyuan and Qin Hui, but they alike reiterate the importance of fairness and equality in contemporary Chinese social life.

45. The "state capacity" issue was first raised in 1991; see Wang Shaoguang: "Building a Strong Democratic State: On Regime Type and State Capacity," *Papers of the Center for Modern China* 4 (February 1991); see also Wang Shaoguang and Hu An'gang, "Zhongguo zhengfu jiqu nengli de xiajiang jiqi houguo" (The decline of the Chinese government's extractive capacity and its consequences), *Erhsiyi shiji* 21 (1994): 5–14; Cui Zhiyuan, "'Guojia nengli' bianzheng guan" (A Dialectical View of "State Capacity"), *Erhsiyi shiji* 21 (1994): 19–21. The discussion in the 1990s on the Chinese economy and East Asian development also touched on related points; see, for example, Zhang Shuguang's "Jingji zengzhang he guojia xingshuai" (Economic growth and the rise and decline of states), *Dushu* 9 (1996), where in his critique of Lin Yifu's foreign economic theory he addressed the matter of the relationship between the state and interest groups.

46. Wang Jin, "'Guojia' sanyi" (Three views on the "state"), *Dushu* 4 (2000). (This essay was abridged in its published form, but I am working from the full text.) A more powerful explanation of this issue is contained in Chu Wan-wen's "Quanqiuhua yu houjin guo zhi jingji fazhan" (Globalization and the economic development of the later developing countries), in which she clearly points out that "[f]or the later-developing countries to catch up to the developed countries, they must take the nation-state as their unit of organization and use tools like industrial policy to plan out a development strategy; use subsidies, rewards and penalties to foster infant industries, support local enterprises, and learn advanced technologies as rapidly as possible. In a context in which competition daily grows more fierce and the discrepancy between the advanced and the laggard constantly increases, these are the only means by which it will be possible not only to win a place in the international marketplace, but also to climb gradually up the ladder of the international division of labor, as well as to transform and raise the comparative advantage of one's own country. Only in this way will it be possible to assure continuing economic development and progress in industrial capacity." See *Taiwan shehui yanjiu jikan* (Taiwan: a radical quarterly in social studies) 37 (March 2000): pp. 91–117.

47. See Roberto Unger and Cui Zhiyuan, "Yi E wei jiankan Zhongguo" (Reflecting on China from the Russian perspective), *Ershiyi shiji* 24 (1994): 17–25. As for inquiry into the path of reform taken in Chinese society, there are a number of essays published slightly later, such as Lin Chun's "Shehui zhuyi yu xiaomie pinqiong" (Socialism and the elimination of poverty), *Dushu* 9 (1999), and "Jiaotiao tupo yu zhidu chuangxin" (Breaking through dogma and institutional innovation), *Dushu* 11 (1999).

48. See Zhang Rulun, Wang Xiaoming, Zhu Xueqin, and Chen Sihe, "Renwen jingshen xunsilu zhiyi" (Considering the spirit of humanism [1]), *Dushu* 3 (1994), and the subsequent discussions that appeared in issues 4–7 of the same journal that year. As has been the case with other discussions in contemporary China, the participants in this forum did not represent a uniform intellectual front, and there even existed among them substantial differences of theoretical perspective.

49. Han and Zhang are both important writers who emerged in the wave of new literature that began in the mid-1980s. Han, editor of *Tianya,* is based in Hainan and is close to Wang Hui. Zhang, a Chinese Moslem, is an unrepentant leftist critic of the current order, particularly concerned with interethnic issues in China.—*Trans.*

50. Zhang Yiwu and Chen Xiaoming criticized the spirit of humanism from the perspective of postmodernism, while Wang Meng criticized it from the standpoint of a secular elite or a secular idealism. See, Zhang Yiwu, "Renwen jingshen: zuihou de shenhua" (The spirit of humanism: the last myth), *Renda fuyin baokan ziliao, wenyi lilun juan* (People's University journal reprints, literary theory vol-

ume), 7 (1995), Wang Meng, "Renwen jingshen ougan" (Thoughts on the spirit of humanism), *Dongfang* 5 (1994), "Xiangqi Ridannuofu" (Reminiscent of Zhadnov), *Dushu* 4 (1995), "Juedui de jiazhi yu canku" (Brutality and absolute values), *Dushu* 1 (1999), and "Geming, shisu yu jingying qiqiu" (Revolution, secularism and elite demands), *Dushu* 4 (1999). Wang Xiaoming eventually collected a number of the relevant essays into a volume entitled *Renwen jingshen xunsilu* (Thoughts on the spirit of humanism) (Shanghai: Wenhui chubanshe, 1996).

51. Dai Jinhua and Zhang Xudong can be taken as key representatives of postmodern criticism, but their inclination differed significantly from that of Zhang Yiwu and Chen Xiaoming. They differed in their critical perspectives on globalization and the process of marketization itself.

52. Several sociologists and practitioners of a new cultural studies carried out powerful critiques of this advocacy of the market, and particularly of the ideology of consumerism. See Li Tuo, "Kaixinguo nülang" (Happy girl), *Dushu* 2 (1995), some of the work of Dai Jinhua, such as *Jingcheng tuwei* (Breaking out of the film world), and the studies of Huang Ping on consumerism. From different perspectives, these all criticize the ideology of consumerism.

53. Essays on this question include Zhang Chengzhi's "Wu Jielian de wu jing yue" (Wu Jielian's morning moon), *Dushu* 4 (1999); and Wu Yiye's "Shijie buhui da 'tong'" (There can be no great "Union" of the world), *Dushu* 6 (1999).

54. The first article in China to raise the issue of postcolonial criticism was Liu He's (Lydia Liu) "Heise de Yadian" (Black Athena), published in *Dushu* 10 (1992), but it received little attention at the time. Sheng Hong's "Dongfang shijie de xingqi" (The rise of the oriental world), published in *Dushu* 12 (1992), reexamined Eurocentrism from the perspective of economic history. These essays show that Chinese intellectuals had already begun to look into the question of Eurocentrism even before the introduction of Said's notion of orientalism began in 1993. *Dushu* 9 (1993) published a number of essays, including Zhang Kuan's "Ou-Mei ren yanzhong de feiwo zulei" (The Euro-American view of other races); Qian Jun's "Tan Saiyide tan wenhua" (Discussing Said discussing culture); and Pan Shaomei's "Yizhong xin de piping qingxiang" (A new trend in criticism), to which was appended a postscript by the managing editor entitled "Tamen wenming ma?" (Are they Civilized?). After this, Zhang Kuan published "Zaitan Saiyide" (Said revisited), *Dushu* 10 (1994); and in its second issue of 1996, *Tianya* published "Wenhua xin zhimin de keneng" (The prospect of a new cultural imperialism) and other essays that supplemented the earlier discussion. A bit later, Li Tuo published "Chayixing wenti biji" (Notes on the question of difference), *Tianya* 4 (1996); and Liu He published "Lilun yu lishi, dongfang yu xifang" (History and theory, East and West), *Dushu* 8 (1996).

55. See my "Zhixu haishi shi xu? A Ming yu ta dui quanqiuhua de kanfa" (Order or disorder?—Samir Amin and his views on globalization), *Dushu* 7 (1995);

and Chen Yangu's "Wenhua duoyuanhua yu Makesi zhuyi" (Cultural diversity and Marxism), *Yuandao* (Origins of the Dao), vol. 3 (Beijing: Zhongguo guangbo dianshi chubanshe, 1996).

56. For related discussion, see Li Shen's "(Shuliang youshi xia de kongju" (The fear of being in the majority) and Zhang Xudong's "Nationalism and Contemporary China" (Minzu zhuyi yu dangdai Zhongguo), both in *Dushu* 6 (1997); in the *Beijing qingnian bao* (Beijing Youth News) and other papers, Sheng Hong published a number of essays critical of Social Darwinism and Eurocentrism. In none of the essays on nationalism from this period, however, did I discover any note of isolationism *(biguan suoguo)*, any words expressing a wish to return to the Cultural Revolution, or any antiforeignism of the so-called Boxer Rebels sort.

57. See books like my *Wang Hui zixuanji* (Self-selected works of Wang Hui) (Guilin: Guangxi shifan daxue chubanshe, 1997), Zhu Suli's *Falü de bentu ziyuan* (Indigenous sources of law) (Beijing: Zhongguo zhengfa daxue chubanshe, 1996), and Liang Zhiping's *Qingdai xiguanfa* (Customary law in the Qing dynasty) (Beijing: Zhongguo zhengfa daxue chubanshe, 1996). This research is focused on China's own historical resources and their contemporary significance, intending to embark on an explanation of the changes in modern China from the perspective of the interaction of internal and external perspectives. It seeks in the course of the modern transformation to take seriously historical and popular resources. Not all of this research was itself directed toward contemporary problems, but in the context of market expansion, this concentration on indigenous historical resources and the popular tradition differed quite plainly from mainstream research.

58. See my "Contemporary Chinese Thought and the Question of Modernity" [in this volume]; Perry Anderson, "Wenming jiqi neihan" (Civilization and its connotations), *Dushu* 11–12 (1997); Chen Yangu, "Lishi zhongjie haishi quanmian minzhu?" (The end of history or complete democracy?), *Dushu* 12 (1998).

59. He Qinglian's *Xiandaihua de xianjing* (The pitfall of modernization) (Beijing: Jinri Zhongguo chubanshe, 1998) and a number of Qin Hui's articles are examples. Also see, among others, He Qinglian, "Jingjixue lilun yu 'tu long shu'" (Economic theory and "killing the dragon"), *Dushu* 3 (1997), "Jinrong weiji tiaozhan jingji qiji" (The financial crisis challenges the economic miracle), *Dushu* 12 (1997), and "'Shizhe shengcun' yu 'youxian jieji' ("The survival of the fittest" and "the leisure class"), *Dushu* 10 (1998); Bian Wu (Qin Hui), "Jujue yuanshi jilei" (Repudiate primitive accumulation), *Dushu* 1 (1998), and "Youle zhen wenti cai you zhen xuewen" (There can only be real learning in addressing real problems), *Dushu* 6 (1998).

60. For conservative discussions of liberalism, see, among others, Liu Junning's "Dang minzhu fang'ai ziyou de shihou" (When democracy obstructs

freedom), *Dushu* 11 (1993), "Baoshou de Baike ziyou de Baike" (The conservative Burke and the liberal Burke), *Dushu* 3 (1995), "Wuwang wo" (Don't forget me), *Dushu* 11 (1995), and "Shan'e: liangzhong zhengzhi guan yu guojia nengli" (Good and evil: two political views and the capacity of the state), *Dushu* 5 (1994). In the latter part of the 1990s, one of the principal expositors of neo-authoritarianism, Xiao Gongqin, publicly expressed his affinity with contemporary China's neoliberalism, along with his view that the greatest danger to the country was the "New Left." During the course of the commodification of power and in light of China's particular political circumstances, it must truly be accounted a great discovery that democracy "obstructs" freedom. The authors of this thesis never inquire, of course, as to whose freedom this might be and the location of this democracy.

61. See such essays as Gan Yang's "Fan minzhu de ziyouzhuyi haishi minzhu de ziyouzhuyi?" (Antidemocratic liberalism or democratic liberalism?), *Ershiyi shiji* 39 (1997): 4–17, "Bailin yu houziyouzhuyi" (Berlin and postliberalism), *Dushu* 4 (1998), and "Ziyouzhuyi: guizude haishi pingminde?" (Liberalism: aristocratic or popular?), *Dushu* 1 (1999); my "*Wenhua yu gonggongxing* daolun"; Qian Yongxiang, "Wo zongshi huo zai biaoceng shang" (I always live on the surface), *Dushu* 4 (1999); Zhao Gang, "Duwei dui ziyouzhuyi de pipan yu chongjian" (Dewey's critique and reconstruction of liberalism), *Xueshu sixiang pinglun* (Review of Academic Thought), vol. 3 (Shenyang: Liaoning daxue chubanshe, 1998); Luo Yongsheng, "Jingjixue haishi ziyouzhuyi" (Economics or liberalism) *Dushu* 9 (1998); Wan Junren, "Quanqiuhua de ling yimian" (Another aspect of globalization), *Dushu* 1 (2000).

Hayek became a hot topic in the 1990s, but the neoliberals seem to have given no thought to the internal contradictions between their radical advocacy of markets and Hayek's attitude toward historicity, nor did they give any consideration to the internal contradiction between their political conservatism and their radical plans for free markets with Hayek's critique of planning. In this context, the criticism of neoliberalism not only did not imply any simple rejection of inquiry into the theory of liberalism, but just the opposite: I think that the deeper and more systematic the inquiry into this sort of theory, the weaker the theory of neoliberalism began to appear.

62. See Fan Gang, "'Budaode' de jingjixue" ("Immoral" economics), *Dushu* 6 (1998); Zhang Shuguang, "Piping guize, jiaowang lixing he ziyou jingshen zhiyi, zhier" (A standard for criticism, communicative rationality and the spirit of liberalism, #1 and 2), *Dushu* 10 (1999), 3 (2000).

63. Immanuel Wallerstein, "Jintui liangnan de shehui kexue" (The dilemma of social science), *Dushu* 2–3 (1998); Xu Baoqiang, "Weizhong zhi ji" (The opportunity in the crisis), *Dushu* 4 (1998); Perry Anderson, "'Qiji' beihou de youling" (The specter behind the "miracle"), *Dushu* 8–9 (1998); my "Kexue zhuyi yu shehui lilun de jige wenti" (Several problems of scientism and social the-

ory), *Tianya* 6 (1998); Lu Di "Dongya jingyan yu lishi zibenzhuyi" (Historical capitalism and the East Asian experience), *Dushu* 9 (1998); Han Yuhai, "Zai 'ziyouzhuyi' zitai beihou" (Behind the pose of "liberalism"), *Tianya* 5 (1998); Lu Di, "Chongdu Sun Yefang de diguozhuyi lun" (Rereading Sun Yefang on imperialism), *Dushu* 6 (1999).

64. On November 16, 1999, China and the United States reached an agreement on China's entry into the WTO; the same day *Duowei xinwen* (Multidimension news) published a special article by Liu Junning entitled "Zhongguo jiaru WTO de zhengzhi yiyi" (The political significance of China's joining the WTO), which expressed support for the agreement. The *Financial Times* published a report by James Kynge and Mark Suzman entitled "China to Enter WTO after Signing US Deal" that quoted Chinese scholars as saying this was the second stage of the policy of openness that had begun in 1978. The next day, the *Washington Post* published a report by John Pomfret and Michael Laris entitled "WTO Deal Welcomed by China's Reformers" that quoted Wang Shan, Li Ke, Mao Yushi, and Xu Youyu as welcoming the WTO, the content of which mainly focused on how the WTO would assist democracy and the rule of law. This sort of opinion did not differ from the voice of the state and its media, and was welcomed by the American media as well. In 2000–2001, following the deepening of the discussion of neoliberalism among the intelligentsia, a number of liberals attempted to differentiate between "economic liberalism" and "humanistic liberalism." As the examples cited above should demonstrate, however, this sort of distinction is difficult to maintain, as we cannot find any divergence between the two on matters like the WTO.

65. Cui Zhiyuan, "Zhongguo jiaru shijie maoyi zuzhi zhi wojian" (My view on China's entry into the World Trade Organization), *Lianhe zaobao* (United morning news), 4 July 1999; Wen Tiejun, "'Sannong wenti': shijimo de fansi" (The 'three rurals' [i.e., rural society, the rural population and agriculture itself] question: reflections on the fin-de-siècle), *Dushu* 12 (1999); the July-August edition of *Guoji jingji pinglun* (International economic review) 4 (1999), published a special issue on "the WTO and China," which carried out a discussion of the details of China's entry into the WTO. The individual articles were: Song Hong's "Gongye youshi, bijiao youshi he jingzheng youshi—Zhongguo jiaru shijie maoyi zuzhi de shouyi yu daijia" (Industrial advantage, comparative advantage and competitive advantage—the costs and benefits of China's entry into the World Trade Organization); Sun Zhengyuan's "Jiaru shijie maoyi zuzhi de Zhongguo nongye ji duice sikao" (Reflections on Chinese agricultural and countermeasures in China's entry into the World Trade Organization); Wang Songqi's "Jiaru shijie maoyi zuzhi hui yingxiang Zhongguo de jinrong anquan ma?" (Will entry into the World Trade Organization influence China's financial security?); Zhang Yansheng's "Zhongguo ying ruhe zoujin shijie maoyi zuzhi?" (How should China join the World Trade Organization?); and Wang Xiaoya's and Xu Guoping's

"Jinru shijie maoyi zuzhi dui Zhongguo yinhangye de yingxiang" (The impact of China's entry into the World Trade Organization on China's banking industry).

66. See my "Xiandaixing wenti dawen" (Responses to the question of modernity), *Tianya* 1 (1999); Xu Baoqiang, "Zhishi, quanli yu 'xiandaihua' fazhan lunshu" (The discourse on knowledge, power, and "modern" development), *Dushu* 2 (1999), and "Fazhan zhuyi de misi" (The mystified thinking of developmentalism), *Dushu* 7 (1999); Huang Ping, "Guanyu 'fazhan zhuyi de biji" (Notes on "developmentalism"), *Tianya* 1 (2000). At the end of October 1999, the Hainan Province Writers Association and the Hainan branch of China Southern Airlines held an international conference on "Literature and the Environment" in Hainan, during which a number of the participants held a panel discussion on such issues as ecology, the environment, and development. In its first issue of 2000, *Tianya* published an edited summary of this panel as "Nanshan jiyao" (Minutes from Nanshan), which systematically criticized development from an ecological standpoint. Participants included Huang Ping, Li Tuo, Chen Yangu, Dai Jinhua, Wang Xiaoming, Chen Sihe, Nan Fan, Wang Hongsheng, Geng Zhanchun, and Han Shaogong.

67. The opening up of the public arena was not necessarily directly expressed as an appeal for freedom of speech, but more frequently articulated through energetic discussion within each important domain of activity, by which it touches on every sort of social problem. In this sense, even though there are many limitations, after years of effort the conversation among the intelligentsia has been able to encompass all facets of social problems, thus securing for itself a definite discursive space in complicated circumstances. There has been in the discussion of the intellectuals, however, a tendency to blame intellectual deficiency on external factors—not that I would at all deny the importance of external factors. I think, however, this represents a shifting of responsibility. For direct discussion of freedom of speech and the problems of the press, see such essays as Lü Xinyu's "Dangdai Zhongguo de dianshi jilupian yundong" (The contemporary Chinese movement for television documentaries), *Dushu* 5 (1999); Lin Xudong and Chen Meng, "'Shenghuo kongjian': yizhong jilu/meiti shijian" ("Living space": a documentary/media practice"), *Dushu* 5 (1999); Bu Wei, "V-chip yu Meiguo yanlun ziyou" (The V-chip and America's freedom of speech), *Dushu* 5 (1999); and Wang Huazhi "Meiti yu jinri zhi xianshi" (The media and today's reality), *Dushu* 8 (1999).

68. See such essays as Chen Yangu, "Chao diguo zhuyi shidai de shengzhan" (Holy war in the era of hyper-imperialism), *Tianya* 4 (1999); Yue Gang, "Jiegou Kesuowa" (Deconstructing Kosovo), *Dushu* 11 (1999); Zhang Rulun, "Habeimasi he diguo zhuyi" (Habermas and imperialism), *Dushu* 9 (1999); Wang Xi "Minzhu de feiminzhuhua" (Democratic antidemocratization), *Dushu* 10 (1999).

69. See Cui Zhiyuan, "Minzu zijuequan, renquan yu zhuquan" (National self-determination, human rights, and sovereignty), *Dushu* 8 (1999).

70. See Han Shaogong, "Guojing de zhebian he nabian" (Inside and outside national borders), *Tianya* 6 (1999); and my preface to *Sihuo chongwen* (Rekindling dead ashes) (Beijing: Renmin wenxue chubanshe, 2000).

71. In their deconstruction of the revolution and their repudiation of heterodoxy, intellectuals frequently let slip their "political unconscious" toward gender issues. The rhetoric that follows is not an isolated phenomenon: "women always accompany . . . pathological fanaticism," this is the era of "toadying to women, an era in which everything is dictated by female taste, from men's hairstyles to the design of automobiles; even revolutionary history contains fatuous adulation of women." This sort of essay does not set out to intentionally defame women, but the problem revealed by the rhetoric itself is perhaps even more insidious. See Zhu Xueqin, "Pingjing de huai xinqing" (A tranquil foul mood), *Tianya* 3 (1996).

72. *Dushu* 3 (1999) published a special discussion on "feminism and nationalism," which included Liu Jianzhi's "Kongju, baoli, guojia, nüren" (Fear, violence, the state, women); Dai Jinhua's "Jianzheng yu jianzheng ren" (Witnessing and witnesses); Chen Shunxin's "Qiangbao, zhanzheng yu minzu zhuyi" (Brutality, war, and nationalism). Related essays included Xia Xiaohong's "Cong fumu zhuanhun dao fumu zhuhun" (From parents controlling marriage to parents merely presiding) in *Dushu* 1 (1999).

73. The discussion about Asia began in 1996 with Sun Ge's contribution of several essays commenting on *Zai Yazhou sikao* (Thinking in Asia), a scholarly series of essays by Japanese scholars. For a more extended discussion, see Sun Ge, "Yazhou yiweizhe shenma?" (What is the significance of Asia?), in *Xueshu sixiang pinglun, di wu ji* (Review of academic thinking), vol. 5 (Shenyang: Liaoning daxue chubanshe, 1999). See also Paek Yung-suh (Korea), "Shiji zhi jiao zaisi Dongya" (Rethinking East Asia at the turn of the century), *Dushu* 8 (1999); Kojima Kiyoshi (Japan), "Sikao de qianti" (Premises of reconsideration), *Dushu* 3 (2000); Mizoguchi Yuzo (Japan), "'Zhanzheng yu geming' zhiyu Riben ren" ("War and revolution" for the Japanese), *Dushu* 3 (2000); Choi Won-sik (Korea), "Disanzhong daan" (A third type of answer), *Tianya* 3 (1999); Kuang Xinnian, "Zai Yazhou de tiankong xia sikao" (Thinking under the Asian sky), *Tianya* 3 (1999).

74. The "three great differences" refer to those between workers and farmers, country and city, and mental and physical labor. Wang's point here is that even Mao, for all he is thought to be the great leveler, assumed these differences to be fundamental.—*Trans.*

75. That is, the notion that social virtue is a function of, in this case, low birth. Yu, an urban youth rusticated during the Cultural Revolution, dared to criticize this policy, and was executed for his pains. He was posthumously rehabilitated in 1980.—*Trans.*

76. The social crisis and the contradictions involved have obliged people to focus attention on real social problems, and also forced theoreticians to more di-

rectly participate in social and intellectual struggles. This process is directly related to the tendency toward commercialization in the media age, and easily leads to the rejection of theoretical work itself. The more urgent the social issues become, however, the more we need to undertake wide-ranging theoretical inquiry and to reestablish our perspective on history and actual events. Without conscientious dialogue and study on the theoretical level, there will be no way to gain a grasp on the present. In respect of scholars, the task of the freedom of thought must be fulfilled through the rigor of the theoretical work itself. Thus, we must reject superficially plausible blame directed at theoretical work, and reject the attitude that repudiates theoretical innovation on the grounds of the practical nature of the problems we face.

77. Chu Wan-wen, "Ziyou kaifang youliyu jingji fazhan?" (Is free opening beneficial to economic development?), *Dushu* 3 (2002): 36–44.

78. David Coates, *Models of Capitalism: Growth and Stagnation in the Modern Era* (London: Polity Press, 2000), p. 19.

79. Thomas W. Pogge, "Yiguo jingji zhengyi yu quanqiu jingji zhengyi" (Economic justice, national and global), *Dushu* 1 (2002): 3–9.

80. For example, in order to preserve China's relatively small expanse (at 3.414 billion *mou* [one-sixth acre]) of forests, the Chinese State Council asked that the majority of these forest regions be closed off to promote regeneration, as a result of which the lumber industry faced unemployment and the country a lumber shortage. The Lumber Bureau thus went to the Molungbala Forest in the southern African nation of Mozambique to cut wood. In order to restore its national economy, the Mozambique government has opened its forests to exploitation on a large scale. This trade in lumber is entirely legal under the laws of both nations, but it does illustrate how the logic of development itself brings about economic expansion, transformation of the employment situation, and ecological crisis. See the reports of the Johannesburg correspondent Xu Yuanchao in *Jingji ribao* (Economic daily), 4 February 2002, p. 7.

Contemporary Chinese Thought

The translator consulted a translation by Sylvia Chan of a shorter version of this essay. The present translation has been edited to bring it into conformity with the emended version of the article published in Wang Hui's *Sihuo chongwen* (Rekindling dead ashes) (Beijing: Renmin wenxue chubanshe, 2000), pp. 42–94.—*Ed.*

1. It would be better to call this essay a set of notes on my thought process rather than an academic article. I wrote a first draft in 1994 and have revised it several times since, but because of the limitations of the original version, and the fact that most of my efforts of late have been devoted to research on the intellectual history of the late Qing to the modern period, I have not been able to in-

clude any analysis of any of the discussions that have taken place since 1994. I am well aware that the essay's framework and content need further revision and augmentation. But my friends have urged me repeatedly to publish it, and I do so now mainly in the hope of eliciting further discussion.

2. So-called market society is equivalent neither to the market itself nor to market economics, but refers instead to a situation in which the basic structures and functions of society are market structures and functions. As Karl Polanyi explains, market society means modern capitalist society. See Polanyi, *The Great Transformation: the Political and Economic Origins of Our Time* (Boston: Beacon Press, 1957).

3. For example, see Gilbert Rozman, ed., *The Modernization of China* (in Chinese) (Nanjing: Jiangsu renmin chubanshe, 1988).

4. The problem of the urban–rural relationship and its position in China's modernization process through the 1950s is also related to the decision by the Chinese Communist Party (CCP) to abandon New Democracy and move directly into socialism. On this question, see Jin Guantao and Liu Qingfeng, *Kaifangzhong de bianqian: Zailun Zhongguo shehui chaowending jiegou* (Changes in the course of opening: a further discussion of the superstable structure of Chinese society) (Hong Kong: Chinese University of Hong Kong Press, 1993), 411–460.

5. See Mao Zedong, "The Chinese Revolution and the Chinese Communist Party," in *Mao Zedong's Selected Works* (Beijing: renmin chubanshe, 1996), 610–650.

6. The significance of the post-1979 rural reforms must be understood in the post-1950s historical context, when it seemed that the collective model could avoid the motivational problems of capitalism at the same time as it transformed a small-scale peasant economy into a modern one. Yet, without the encouragement of incentives, once collectivization reached a certain point, it led to a decrease in efficiency. See Lin Yifu, *Zhidu, jishu yu Zhongguo nongye fazhan* (Systems and technology in China's rural development) (Shanghai: Sanlian shudian, 1992), pp. 16–43. More important still, according to Gao Shouxian, "[this situation] obstructed the expansion of employment opportunities outside the agricultural sector. Although the government made industrialization a primary goal, in the villages, they strenuously limited the opportunities for employment outside agriculture. Because the government . . . exerted unprecedented control over the countryside, these restrictions were particularly effective. In contrast to what had gone on previously, during collectivization the degree of individual freedom of choice not only did not increase, it contracted severely. This radically restricted the development of the rural economy." In Gao's opinion, the post-1979 rural reforms "offered a relatively free 'structure of opportunity' and gave local collectivities and individual peasants both autonomy and the freedom to experiment. In this way, they could more flexibly search for and find different paths to economic

development and other employment opportunities." Gao Shouxian, "Zhidu chuangxin yu Ming Qing yilai de nongcun jingji fazhan" (Institutional innovation and rural development since the Ming and Qing dynasties), *Dushu* 194 (May 1995): 123–129.

Philip Huang points out that the changes since the reforms came not from the "private crop production and petty commerce that were given so much press, but rather from rural industry and new sidelines." He adds that "in the reformist China of the 1980s . . . the rural change of the greatest long-term import was the de-involution in crop production that came with the diversification of the rural economy, and not the turn to marketized farming in crop production as is commonly assumed. . . . [C]rop yields failed to advance with the introduction of the household responsibility system in farming in the 1980s, and few peasants grew rich along the lines predicted by the classical model and official propaganda. To put it bluntly, marketized farming in the 1980s did no better in crop production than it did in the six centuries between 1350 and 1950, or than collective agriculture did in the preceding three decades." Huang continues: "The really important issue for the Yangzi delta countryside, in other words, was not—and is not—between marketized family farming and planned collectivist agriculture, or capitalism and socialism, but rather between involution and development." (Philip Huang, *The Peasant Family and Rural Development in the Yangzi Delta, 1350–1988* (Stanford: Stanford University Press, 1990), pp. 17, 18.

7. Luo Yuping, "Shizhong buneng wangji nongcun de fazhan—fang guowuyuan yuanjiu zhongxin nongye wenti zhuanjia Lu Mai" (Never forget rural development—an interview with the agricultural expert Lu Mai of the Research Institute of the State Council), in *Sanlian shenghuo zhoukan* (Sanlian life weekly) 14 (1998): 26.

8. See Su Wen, "Shanchongshuifu ying you lu: Qian Su Dong guojia zhuangui guocheng zai pinglun" (There should be a way out: a further discussion of perestroika in the former Soviet Union and Eastern Europe), *Dongfang* 1 (January 1996): 37–41. This article discusses economic reform in the former Soviet Union and Eastern Europe. It focuses on the experience of the Czech Republic.

9. Although the debates on Marxist humanism were not started by Zhou Yang, the report he gave at the conference in commemoration of the centennial of Marx's death attracted much criticism. The revised and edited version of his report was published in *People's Daily*, (16 March 1983) but the original text, distributed to the conference delegates, was confiscated. The report's original title was "An Exploration of Several Theoretical Problems in Marxism." The most trenchant criticism came from then party theorist Hu Qiaomu, who, in a speech to the Central Party School on January 3, 1984, took Zhou Yang's and others' perspectives on Marxism to task without naming them. His speech was first pub-

lished in the Central Party School's *Lilun yuekan (Theory monthly)*, and it was followed by a pamphlet published under the title *Guanyu rendao zhuyi he yihua wenti* (On humanism and alienation) (Beijing: Renmin chubanshe, 1984). Actually, this issue had already attracted the attention of several theorists after 1978, and the People's Publishing House had already put out an anthology in 1981 titled *Ren shi Makesizhuyi da chufadian: renxing, rendaozhuyi wenti lunji* (Man is the starting point of Marxism: a collection of articles on human nature and humanism), which included essays by Wang Ruoshui, Li Pengcheng, and Gao Ertai, among others. It is worth noting that in those discussions, an abstract conception of man and human nature were the bases of the debates on humanism.

"Theism" and "bestialism (shoudao zhuyi)" are the two terms most often used as opposites of *"humanism."* The former indicates the tyranny of religion, and in Chinese discourse it is a metaphor for the Cultural Revolution's "contemporary superstition"; the latter indicates feudal dictatorship or fascism, and in Chinese discourse it is a metaphor for the "complete dictatorship" of the Cultural Revolution. Perhaps because of the influence of related discussion in the Soviet Union and Eastern Europe, Chinese Marxist humanism considers the rethinking of man to be the primary problem of Marxism; it points out that Stalin's *Dialectical Materialism and Historical Materialism* paid insufficient attention to this problem. In addition, Chinese Marxist humanists point out that Lenin was not familiar with Marx's *Economic and Philosophical Manuscripts of 1844* (which was published only in 1932). Wang Ruoshui's essay "Man Is the Starting Point of Marxism" mentions that Mao in 1964 supported the concept of alienation and thought it an omnipresent phenomenon. This all makes it clear that China's Marxist humanism was launched as a critique of China's socialist historical experience, using, on the one hand, an allegorical strategy to subsume China's socialism under feudalism and, on the other hand, taking advantage of the universality of the concepts of humanism and alienation. Both these features of the argument suggest an affirmation of the values of modernity and particularly of the values of the New Enlightenment movement. In this explanatory model, socialism was never a noncapitalist critique of modernization; on the contrary, the critique of the socialist historical experience was a complete affirmation of the values of European modernity.

10. The history of the formation of the 1980s New Enlightenment movement is exceedingly complex. One can probably point to a 1979 conference on theory, attended mostly by CCP theorists, as an origin. Previously, Nanjing University professor Hu Fuming had circulated a draft of the article "Practice Is the Sole Criterion of Truth," which was revised by Sun Changjiang, Wang Qianghua, and Ma Peiwen and published in the *Guangming Daily* (11 May 1978). This article provided the theoretical justification for the Thought Liberalization movement. Even though there are different accounts of the creation of this article from those

who wrote it (Hu Fuming considers it to be a revision based on his earlier essay, while Sun Changjiang believes it be a hybrid of Hu's work and the revisions), they all allow that it was the product of the particular political circumstances of the time and an expression of the national will. Sun Changjiang said quite clearly: "This discussion was not the product the brainstorming or deep thoughts of any particular whiz kid or group of whiz kids. The discussion was a product of history, and 'Practice is the Sole Criterion of Truth' was the product of history." "The direct participants in the discussion included politicians as well as theorists." It is worth pointing out that what we refer to as "the national will" cannot be understood as a united national will, because there were significant fractures at both the state level and in the party, and this essay was precisely the expression of those fractures. The "state" or the "party" thus cannot be seen as monoliths. For an account, see Hu Fuming's reminiscence, "Zhenli biaozhun da taolun de xuqu: Tan shijian biaozhun yiwen de xiezuo, xiugai he fabiao guocheng" (Prelude to the great debate on the criterion of truth: a discussion of the writing, revising, and publication of the practice criterion essay), *Kaifang shidai* (Guangzhou) 1–2 (1996): 1–25. From the memoirs of Li Chunguang and other protagonists in the event, it is clear that the Thought Liberalization movement was closely tied to top-level leaders. The Zouxiang weilai (Toward the Future) Group of young intellectuals is representative of this: although a good number of them have gone abroad since 1989, there are still some in China who are in important posts. Beijing University professor Li Yining, who, in the 1980s, was for a time quite famous for introducing Western economic thought, is now a vice director on the legal committee of the Chinese People's Consultative Congress. In contrast to that group, there are also the literary and humanist groups, such as the early 1980s *Jintian* (Today) faction and the mid-1980s *Culture: China and the World* editorial board. These groups were basically apolitical, committed as they were to literature and knowledge. It is worth noting that even though *Jintian's* representative voice, Bei Dao, was implicated in the then political Misty Poetry movement, he is a strong supporter of literary autonomy. The *Culture: China and the World* group took "culture" as its mission and also did not get directly involved in political questions. Both groups' relatively apolitical stances of course had political consequences, yet they also helped forge social space for autonomous intellectual activity and values.

11. Initial discussions of the law of value and of a commodity economy were conducted within the framework of a Marxist political economy. The most influential contributions were those of Sun Yefang. But recent scholarship has revealed that Gu Zhun first raised the issue and discussed it with Sun. These discussions of the law of value are representative of the major developments in Chinese thought in the 1980s. It was these rethinkings of basic categories of Marxism that served as the theoretical foundation for the implementation of the market reforms.

12. The calls for legal reform were connected to the reevaluations of wrongly adjudicated cases of the Cultural Revolution and were initially undertaken under the aegis of the popular post-Cultural Revolution proposition that "everyone is equal before the law," put forward by Peng Zhen, the former chairman of the Standing Committee of the National People's Congress. But the theoretical foundations for these ideas derived from scholars like Yu Haocheng and Yan Jiaqi.

13. In its systematic study of Chinese history, Jin Guantao and Liu Qingfeng's *Xingsheng yu weiji* (Booms and crises) (Changsha: Hunan renmin chubanshe, 1984) was the first book to argue that the structure of China's feudal society was "superstable." Underlying this thesis is the question of why China did not succeed in achieving Western-style modernization. This thesis continues to inform their most recent book, *Kaifangzhong de bianqian* (Change in the course of opening up) (Hong Kong: Chinese University of Hong Kong Press, 1993).

14. The problem of subjectivity was first put forward by Li Zehou in his work on Kantian philosophy; he later published several essays on the question. See Li Zehou, *Pipan zhexue de pipan* (A critique of critical philosophy), rev. ed. (Beijing: Renmin chubanshe, 1984). This theory was made known to a wider audience through its substantial influence on Liu Zaifu. In "Lun wenxue de zhutixing" (On subjectivity in literature) and other essays, Liu turned a metaphysical problem into the banner for a literary and thought movement. See Liu Zaifu, "Lun wenxue de zhutixing," part 1, *Wenxue pinglun* 6 (1985): 11–26; part 2, *Wenxue pinglun* 1 (1986): 3–15.

15. Contemporary Chinese intellectuals' understanding of Nietzsche is not nearly so profound as that of the early-twentieth-century Lu Xun. While today's intellectuals take both Nietzsche and Sartre as representatives of the Western notion of individual autonomy, Lu Xun as early as 1907 noted the antimodern strain in Nietzsche and other thinkers of his time.

16. Liu Xiaofeng, *Chengjiu yu xiaoyao* (Salvation and leisure] (Shanghai: Shanghai renmin chubanshe, 1988), was the first book to raise this issue, around which there was much subsequent debate in the intellectual world. Liu himself has gradually moved from the study of German philosophy to the study of Christianity theology.

17. Gan Yang, "Xiangtu Zhongguo chongjian yu Zhongguo wenhua qianjing" (The reconstruction of rural China and the prospects for Chinese culture), *Ershiyi shiji* 16 (April 1993): 4–7. For a critical view of Gan Yang, see Qin Hui, "Litu bu lixiang: Zhongguo xiandaihua de dute moshi?" (Leaving the land without leaving the village: is this a unique Chinese model of modernization?), *Dongfang* 1 (1994): 6–10. On rural industries, see Yang Mu, "Zhongguo xiangzhen qiye de qiji: Sanshige xiangzhen qiye diaocha de zonghe fenxi" (The miracle of China's rural industries: a general analysis of investigations into thirty

rural industries); Wang Hansheng, "Gaige yilai Zhongguo nongcun de gongyehua yu nongcun jingying goucheng de bianhua" (Transformations enabled by rural industrialization and village elites since the reforms in China); and Sun Bingyao, "Xiangzhen shetuan yu Zhongguo jiceng shehui" (Village-level collectives and Chinese grassroots society), *Zhongguo shehui kexue jikan* 9 (Fall 1996): 5–17, 18–24, 25–36.

18. See Wang Ying, *Xin jitizhuyi: Xiangcun shehui de zaizuzhi* (New collectivism: the reorganization of rural society) (Beijing: Jingji guanli chubanshe, 1996); and Wang Ying, She Xiaoye, and Sun Bingyao, *Shehui zhongjianceng: Gaige yu Zhongguo de shetuan zuzhi* (The middle stratas of society: reform and China's social organization) (Beijing: Zhongguo fazhan chubanshe, 1993). These books analyze Chinese society in detail after the reforms, particularly with reference to rural organization and industrialization. They are both extremely valuable for the study of contemporary Chinese development.

19. Wang, *Xin jitizhuyi*, p. 204.

20. In regions like Jiangsu, Zhejiang, and Guangdong, village and township enterprises have developed extremely successfully; however, according to research done by Huang Ping and others under the aegis of the Institute of Sociology of the Chinese Academy of Social Sciences, the form of these enterprises has been undergoing great transformation since 1992. One particularly telling change is that many rural industries, including many successful ones, are beginning to link up with foreign investors and are being transformed into jointly owned enterprises. On the other hand, because of regional differences within China, village and township industries differ widely by region. More important, those regions where rural industries are the most successful have not put in place any measures for the protection of the environment. The result has been severe environmental degradation. In 1992, I had the opportunity to go on a research trip to Daqiuzhuang, Hebei Province, where rural industries and collectivized development are nationally famous. But obscured by the productivity and the prosperous lifestyle were serious instances of environmental pollution, the degradation of the environment around production sites, and serious illegalities. This all makes it clear that concrete analysis needs to be done regarding rural industries. On changes in contemporary Chinese villages, see Guo Yuhua, Shi Ran, Wang Ying, and Huang Ping "Xiangtu Zhongguo de dangdai tujing" (Perspectives on the contemporary Chinese countryside), *Dushu* 10 (October 1996): 48–70.

21. Discussions on "the spirit of humanism" began in the magazine *Dushu* and later spread to many other journals. For the first mention of the subject, see Zhang Rulun, Wang Xiaoming, Zhu Xueqin, and Chen Sihe, "Renwen jingshen xunsilu zhiyi" (Meditations on the spirit of humanism, part 1), *Dushu* 3 (March 1994): 3–13. In later issues that same year, (nos. 4–7), *Dushu* published a series of responses sent by young scholars in Shanghai.

22. See Zhang Fa, Zhang Guwu, Wang Yiquan, "Cong 'xiandaixing' dao 'Zhonghuaxing'" (From "modernism" to "Chineseness"), *Wenyi zhengming* 2 (1994): 10–20.

23. The new mode is seen by some contemporary literary critics as a major feature of contemporary Chinese literature. It indicates an ideology-free, "pristine" condition.

24. Zhang, Zhang, and Wang, "Cong 'xiandaixing' dao 'Zhonghuaxing,'" p. 15.

25. See Cui Zhiyuan, "Zhidu chuangxin yu dierci sixiang jiefang" (Institutional innovation and the second liberation of thought), *Ershiyi shiji* 24 (August 1994): 5–16. For a critical view, see Ji Weidong, "Dierci sixiang jiefang haishi wutuobang?" (A second liberation of thought or utopia?), *Ershiyi shiji* 25 (October 1994): 4–10.

26. Cui Zhiyuan's treatment of contemporary China's economic reforms has precipitated a debate. For example, the major theoretical target of Su Wen's, "Shanchongshuifu" (see note 8 above) is Cui Zhiyuan's perspective on China's privatization process. This is because Cui's analysis is based on a comparison of the Chinese reforms with those of the former Soviet Union and Eastern Europe. Apparently, these debates about the Chinese reform path are premised not only on the Chinese reforms but also on the reforms in the former Soviet Union and Eastern Europe. For the foreseeable future, the success or failure of the Soviet and Eastern European reforms will undoubtedly continue to influence the thinking of Chinese scholars about reform.

27. Zhang Shuguang, "Geren quanli he guojia quanli" (Individual rights and state power), *Gonggong luncong* 1 (1995).

28. See Fernand Braudel, *Ziben zhuyi de dongli* (The wheels of commerce) (Beijing: Sanlian shudian, 1997), p. 85.

29. Philip Huang, in his discussion of the mobilization of civil society/public sphere discourse among American China scholars, has pointed out that "in using the twin concepts of 'the bourgeois public sphere' and 'civil society' in China, often there is an opposition set up between the state and society. . . . I believe that this state/society dichotomy has been abstracted from modern Western history, and is not necessarily applicable to China." Philip C. C. Huang, "Public Sphere/ Civil Society in China? The Third Realm between State and Society," *Modern China* 2 (April 1993): 216–240. Although Huang's discussion is specifically aimed at the situation in early modern China, I believe that it is also appropriate for a discussion of contemporary China.

30. *Xueren* is edited by Chen Pingyuan, Wang Shouchang, and Wang Hui. It is funded by the Japan International Academic Friendship Foundation and published by Jiangsu wenyi chubanshe. *Zhongguo shehui kexue jikan* is edited by Deng Zhenlai and registered in Hong Kong. *Yuandao* is edited by Chen Ming and was

initially funded by the Chinese Academy of Social Sciences Press. When the latter organization encountered financial difficulty, the journal was picked up by Tuanjie chubanshe. *Gonggong luncong* is edited by Liu Junning, Wang Yan, and He Weifang. It receives financial assistance from the Ford Foundation and is published by Sanlian shudian.

31. *Zhanlue yu guanli* is edited by Qin Chaoying, with Yang Ping and Li Shulei as managing editors. It is run by the official Chinese Association for the Study of Strategy and Management. *Dongfang* is edited by Zhong Peizhang, with Zhu Zhengling as vice editor. It is run by the Chinese Association for the Study of Oriental Culture.

32. Under the influence of Eastern European and Euro-American scholars, Chinese scholars began discussing civil society in 1990. Invoking the society/state dichotomy, Western scholars have ascribed the rise of Poland's Solidarity movement to the collapse of central state power in Eastern Europe as a consequence of the maturation of civil society. Scholars of modern Chinese history in the United States have been deeply influenced by Habermas's *Structural Transformation of the Public Sphere* and have used the concept of the public sphere to reexamine modern Chinese historical change, thereby producing a large number of valuable studies. However, in their discussions of civil society in contemporary China, there clearly persist idealistic dreams about the natural connection between marketization and democratization.

While China's market reforms have clearly produced new social strata, it is unclear whether these new social strata can provide the motivating force for political democratization. I have already mentioned that in the course of the Chinese reforms, there has been a joining of political and economic elites. Together with the complex relationship between political corruption and marketization, this demonstrates that neither marketization nor new social strata can possibly guarantee the emergence of political democracy. More important, under the present conditions in China, it is impossible to separate the problem of democracy from the economy, and it is particularly inseparable from the question of social distribution. With respect to the discussions on civil society, many Chinese intellectuals believe that "opening" in and of itself will result in China's drawing closer to the West, thereby resolving the problem of democracy. The problem is that one of the biggest motive forces for political corruption in China today is linked to the integration of Chinese economic activity with international capital. This demonstrates that the simplistic idea that opening up will lead to democracy has no basis in reality. I bring this up not simply to reject a discussion of civil society and even less to suggest that China should move back into isolation; my intention is merely to point out that we must develop more complex paradigms for the study of contemporary Chinese social questions.

See Deng Zhenglai and Jing Yuejin, "Jian'gou Zhongguo de shimin shehui" (Constructing Chinese civil society), *Zhongguo shehui kexue jikan* 1 (1992): 58–

68; Xia Weizhong, "Shimin shehui: Zhongguo jinqi nanyuan de meng" (Civil society: a dream not to be realized in the near future), ibid. 5 (1995): 176–182; Arif Dirlik, "Xiandai Zhongguo de shimin shehui yu gonggong lingyu" (Civil society and public sphere in modern China), ibid. 4 (1994): 10–22; Xiao Gongqin, "Shimin shehui yu Zhongguo xiandaihua de sanzhong zhang'ai" (Civil society and three barriers to China's modernization), ibid., 183–188; Zhu Ying, "Guanyu Zhongguo shimin shehui de jidian shangque yijian" (Several points of discussion concerning civil society in China), ibid. 7 (1996): 108–114; Shi Xuehua, "Xiandaihua yu Zhongguo shimin shehui" (Modernization and Chinese civil society), ibid., 115–120; and Lu Pinyue, "Zhongguo lishi jincheng yu shimin shehui zhi jian'gou" (China's historical process and the construction of civil society), ibid. 8 (1996): 175–178.

33. On the problem of globalization, see Wang Hui, "Zhixu haishi shixu?—A Ming yu ta dui quanqiuhua de kanfa" (Order or disorder?—Samir Amin and his views on globalization), *Dushu* 7 (July 1985): 106–112.

INDEX

Africa, 185
Agricultural policies, 13, 14, 20–21, 56, 82, 213nn4,6; People's Communes, 17, 48, 149, 150–151, 163, 164; between 1978 and 1984, 20, 48–51, 55, 194n5, 195n7; household responsibility system, 48–49, 51, 55, 70, 71, 151, 152, 194n5, 214n6; prices for agricultural products, 49, 55, 152–153, 194nn4,5; and World Trade Organization (WTO), 121. *See also* China, rural
Alienation, 154, 215n9
Arac, Jonathan, 190n10
Arendt, Hannah, 100
Argentina, 4, 124
ASEAN (Association of South-East Asian Nations), 131
Asia, 90, 181, 185, 211n73; financial/economic crisis of 1997 in, 24, 29–30, 70, 85, 91, 96, 97, 109, 125, 200n30, 201n34; and globalization, 109–110, 131–133, 185
Association of South-East Asian Nations (ASEAN), 131

Authoritarianism: repression and coercion by the state, 9, 16, 20, 21–22, 26, 27, 28, 62, 66–67, 82, 83, 86, 89, 91, 92, 98, 116–117, 119, 120, 154, 182; neo-authoritarianism, 28, 44, 59–60, 81, 208n60

Background to the Demonization of China, The (Yaomohua Zhongguo de beijing), 95
Bandung conference, 34, 74
Barmé, Geremie, 24, 192n32
Bei Dao, 216n10
Beijing, 13, 63; Tiananmen Square demonstrations in, 8, 21–22, 26, 43, 62–63, 86, 117, 141–142; groupings *(quanzi)* of intellectuals in, 46, 193n1; bid to host Olympic Games, 85–86
Berlin, Sir Isaiah, 100
Bernstein, Richard, 189n1
Bertens, Hans, 190n10
Binary paradigms: tradition/modernity, 31, 133, 144, 157, 186; China/West, 31, 134, 144, 146, 170, 172, 186; free market/state intervention, 116, 117, 146, 176; capitalism/socialism, 116, 118,

223